PERENNIALS

Toward Continuous Bloom

PERENNIALS
Toward Continuous Bloom

Edited by Ann Lovejoy

New Voices in American Garden Writing

Capability's Books

Deer Park, WI
54007

Acknowledgements

A slightly different version of "Developing a Perennial Border: North Carolina State University Arboretum 1982–1988" appeared in the *1988 Perennial Plant Symposium*, The Perennial Plant Association, 3383 Schirtzinger Road Columbus, OH 43026. Copyright © 1988 by Edith R. Eddleman, Reprinted by permission of the author and The Perennial Plant Association.

"Gardening: Countering the Crack Attack," by Patti Hagan, Copyright © 1989 by *The Wall Street Journal*, Reprinted by permission of the author.

A modified version of "Perennial Borders for the Best of Both Worlds" appeared in the Summer 1988 issue of the *Santa Barbara Botanic Garden Newsletter*, Copyright © 1988 by Laura Baldwin, Reprinted by permission of the author.

A modified version of "The Stately Iris: Perennial Elegance in the Garden" appeared in the July-August 1986 issue of *Southern Accents*, 1760 Peachtree Road, Atlanta, GA 30357, Copyright © 1986 by Tom Woodham, Reprinted by permission of the author.

An altered version of "New Perennials" first appeared as "Offbeat Perennials" in the April 1989 issue of *Horticulture, The Magazine of American Gardening*, 20 Park Plaza, Suite 1220, Boston MA 02116, Copyright © 1989, Horticulture Partners, Reprinted courtesy of *Horticulture* and by permission of the author.

A slightly different version of "A Plea for Real Gardens and Real Gardening" appeared in the October 1, 1987 issue of *The American Nurseryman*, 111 North Canal Street, Chicago IL 60606, Copyright © 1987 by Henry A. Ross, Reprinted by permission of the author.

Design and production by Stanton Publication Services, Inc.
Jacket art by Lou Gordon
Botanical illustrations by Gemma Nesbitt and Denae Johnson

Published by
Capability's Books
2379 Highway 46
Deer Park, WI 54007 U.S.A.
(715) 269-5346

CAPABILITY'S BOOKS and colophon are
trademarks of Capability's Books

CONTENTS

CONTENTS

CONTENTS

CONTENTS

INTRODUCTION

New Voices in American Garden Writing was conceived as a forum for contemporary American gardeners. Although it is the first of its kind, we who have instigated this anthology very much hope it will be but the vanguard of a long series. Written by its readers, such a series would echo the concerns dearest to the hearts of American gardeners. As we see in this volume, such a series would also create a patchwork portrait of its contributors, reflecting the state of the nation as a whole. This first volume, on perennials, combines voices and experiences from all across the country. Successive volumes suggest themselves almost immediately: why not devote a volume to shade gardening, water gardening, dry gardening, or gardening with native plants? Why not, indeed?

This book has a special significance in a day dominated by garden writers from other shores. Until very recently, American gardeners had largely forgotten the gardens and gardeners of our past. After years of avid urbanization with our lives increasingly distant from the natural world, we are relearning the affection for plants that characterized the gardens of our grandparents. Like artists in training, novice gardeners need time and information before they can develop an individual garden identity and style. It is natural that much of our garden guidance should come from beyond our shores, often England, or perhaps Japan, for both countries assiduously preserve a cultural heritage of traditional gardening lore. In America, only a few lone voices were to be heard, championing interactive gardening in a hands-off age. For us, the thrills and skills of ornamental garden making had been largely obscured for some fifty years, partly by the economic aftermath of war and partly by the misguided craze for low maintenance gardens. This is not to say the only good garden is a complex one, but rather to underline the loss of delight that comes from viewing gardening as work or chores rather than as part of an ongoing, life-giving process.

PERENNIALS

Perhaps it is largely a public relations problem. Refer to gardening as "yard work" and it is instantly made dull. Call it "maintenance" and we suggest that the garden is finished, with no further development contemplated. We do not learn new and fascinating things about our clothing or dishes when we wash them, yet each time we weed our gardens, water thirsty plants, or separate intractable floral neighbors, we gain knowledge from the act. Tending plants gives us a clearer understanding of the current state of our ever-changing garden community, and directs our plans for its future. Garden making might better be compared to parenting than to chores, for plants, like children, are alive and always in flux. Naturally there is work involved, but as with parenting, when we do it grudgingly, we get exactly what we earn; but give it our intelligent, whole-hearted attention and the results are often pure synergy. "Plant parenting" sounds silly, but "garden making" nicely implies the open-ended, creative aspect of the process.

When we first awaken to gardening, we want all the direction and support we can get. Like nervous new parents, we take advice from anybody who will offer it, conflicting or inappropriate though it may be. Fortunately, the courage to fail comes more easily to advancing gardeners than to parents, for plants are forgiving, our gardens ever flexible, and very little is irreplaceable. As we gain experience, the advice of others becomes excitingly open to question; now we can evaluate and second-guess with the best of them. As we gain confidence, we discover with delight that in our own gardens, we are the experts; ours are the plans, ours the guiding hands. We dare to make our own mistakes, recognizing that there is often more to be learned from failure than from success.

At this point, we are really at the beginning of everything. When we consciously own our gardens, they soon become personal, distinctive, unique. When we know in our bones that gardening is an art rather than a hard science, we can begin to forge a lasting tradition of our own. Now, we are on the brink. Even now, such new traditions are developing. As we experiment and analyze, fail and succeed, American garden making will blossom. In our gardens, a series of distinct regional styles will be born or reawakened. In our lifetimes, they will be questioned, probed, modified, and confirmed as American Gardens. If they are to live, they must truly belong to us.

We hope that in the *New Voices* series, we may discover in ourselves the answers to our boundless questions. Within the chapters of this first volume, again and again a query posed by one writer is answered by another, a puzzle pondered by this one is solved by that one, a difficulty raised here is resolved there. We travel from Vermont to Texas, from Florida to Washington, noticing that though conditions vary remarkably, the gardeners themselves all speak a common language and celebrate common themes. We hear in the varied voices the same joy of plant love, the refreshment and challenge that comes from developing regionally appropriate gardens. All are making gardens that, whether ambitious or grand, reflect the pleasures and tastes of the gardener as well as the realities of the region.

From the time it was conceived, I thought of *New Voices* as a pieced quilt combining gardens from all across the country with plants antique and modern, from old world and new world alike. Scott Kunst speaks of heritage plants preserved by a faithful few. The old country garden that awoke the gardener in Daphne Stewart held plants lovingly placed by Margaret Ward many years earlier. We watch the garden's renewal with interest, noting how old and new coexist, sometimes melding smoothly, sometimes locked in bitter combat. Kevin Nicolay's tiny urban garden was filled and refilled with antique florist's flowers, connoisseur's plants, rare hybrids, and newly discovered species, plants he passed on to make part of thousands of gardens across the country. Our gardens, like our grandmothers' quilts, combine bits and pieces from past and present, predicting but not restricting the future.

It was fascinating to see, as stories came in from all over the country, how many of us are growing and enjoying the same plants in wildly different climates, and how variably these plants can behave. Perhaps not surprisingly, more than a few are American natives; *Coreopsis* 'Moonbeam' blooms in gardens from North Carolina to Washington as well as in New England. New England asters travel to the Northwest via England, while 'Palace Purple', a form of the North American native heuchera, seemingly travels everywhere. If our favorite plants get around, so do we; Allan Armitage transports plants and family from cold Canada to the hot American South. Stephanie Spencer relocates from the Midwest to North Carolina, Betty Mackey from New Jersey to Florida. Our travels affect our gardens and our gardening style as much as do the altering factors of climate and soil.

Many of the writers speak of themselves and their gardens in terms of evolution, with garden and gardener alike growing ever more sophisticated. For many, the endless path began in long-ago-gardens, those known in earliest youth. Those gardens of memory provided the spark that sooner or later caught fire, bringing a new gardener to life. Once ignited, the garden flame is irrepressible, often continuing as long as life itself. Perhaps the seeds of floral love—like most others—thrive best when sown in childhood. So often the first plants we put in our first gardens are the friendly, familiar flowers recalled from our youth. With hollyhocks and lilies, sweet peas and lilacs, we may unconsciously recreate the long-ago gardens we knew best. The first garden I knew was my mother's, who replaced a Victorian clutter of cut-out lawn beds with a curving sweep of gray stone, making a wall low enough to sit on. Behind it, her raised beds were filled with perennials, mostly old-fashioned ones rescued from the previous garden, though I remember my mother being quite proud of her funkias (what we now call hostas), which were considered progressive plants in those days. Tawny daylilies (*Hemerocallis fulva*) and globe thistles (*Echinops*), oriental poppies (*Papaver orientale*) and New England asters (*Aster novae-angliae*), black-eyed Susans (*Rudbeckia hirta*) and spiky blue veronica (*Veronica spicata*) filled the garden proper. A little wild garden held Jack-in-the-pulpit (*Arisaema triphyllum*) and bloodroot (*Sanguinaria canadensis*), a sunny patch of winter aconites (*Eranthis*) and a spicebush (*Calycanthus floridus*) with its odd, wooden flowers the color of faded strawberries.

An amazing number of these plants have found their way into my own garden, put there, I realize belatedly, for my own children to discover. I was fascinated by Dutchman's pipe (*Aristolochia durior*), an oddball perennial vine from the East Coast woods with giant, heart-shaped leaves and curious speckled green and purple flowers shaped like deep-bowled pipes. A huge plant covered the trellised walls of our shady side porch, where a creaking old summer couch swung on rusted chains. Nowadays, this lusty vine is making its way over trellis panels on my shady front porch. A great deal of time and distance lie between that Massachusetts garden in which I grew up and this aging island farmhouse on Washington's

Puget Sound, but my children play in my garden just as my brothers and I played in my mother's. The garden then was not a showcase, but the place where my mother lived in summer, and in all seasons it formed the background of our days.

Now that I have children of my own, I want this same, uncomplicated appreciation for them. Was it for my boys or myself that I planted the heady, fragrant phlox and the single peonies, the May apples (*Podophyllum peltatum*) and the Siberian squills (*Scilla siberica*)? My children have a fort behind the swinging curtains of a huge forsythia, golden in spring, green in summer, and full of tangled tunnels. So did we—yet I never told my boys about that long-ago play place. We played in caverns tall as a cathedral, dim and cool in the worst summer heat, caverns hidden under the huge rhododendrons that reached the second story windows. This was the most magical of our hideaways, both when winter snow filled the dry cave with pale reflected light, and when pleated, sticky buds opened into bubbling bouquets of bloom, each truss a good foot across, each pale pink blossom fading to cream at the heart, which was freckled faintly with gold. My children, too, have a secret garden tucked behind a wall of species rhododendrons that flank the skirts of a silvery blue spruce. They, too, bring the tumbled flowers into the house when they fall, stamenless, to the ground. Gingerly, aware they hold something of great import, they bring them to me, and bring me my childhood as well.

It is a wonderful lesson, and the most important one in garden making; a proper garden is not only full of flowers, but of magic and secret places. It is not so much a showplace as a retreat, a place for renewal, for sensory enjoyment, for escape from self. Adults lead such overly busy lives, full of pressures and performance anxieties. Our inner ears and eyes are more often tuned to critical nagging than to the ecstatic wonder that belongs to childhood. Too often when I go to the garden to admire plants and plantings, I end up focused on undone duty. This is the Rorschach test of the garden: Do you see the positive or the negative? Are you looking at what is here, or what is not here? Do you dwell on what is right, or what is wrong? When I can refocus, looking past my part of the garden to that community made by the plants themselves, the experience is completely altered.

This refocusing is greatly aided by two things, one mental, one physical. Getting rid of the burden of expectation — our own and that of others — helps enormously. When expectation is part of delight, cherish it. When it blinds you to pleasure, set it firmly aside. A wonderful woman who came late to gardening told me Abraham Lincoln's favorite saying: "The key to happiness is the ability to overlook." Garden makers need to remember this, especially when their gardens are young and mostly incipient. The physical trick is one any child could tell us; make small, private viewing places, from which the garden is revealed in a whole new way. Set up secret seats for one in unexpected corners. Weave tiny access paths through deep borders, partly for weed control but mostly for your feet alone, so you can be intimately inside the garden.

Whether we landscape on the grandest scale or make a cosy home garden, the principle applies. Both sorts of gardens can hold our secret spots quite comfortably. Snug in our small places, we slow down. In quiet privacy, we may watch a rose unfurl or observe a peony slitting its tight bud sheath, sights as magical as anything life offers. Small places encourage us to truly look, to see with all the clarity of childhood the shapes of the flowers, the details of coloration, the stipples and stripes, speckles and spots. When we see these things, we are really learning our plants. When we see our plants in community, we are recognizing the garden. When we share all this with others, children or adults, in the garden or on paper, we are sowing garden seed. The impressions we nurture may lie fallow for years, but they persist, for these garden seeds are patient. When the proper conditions arise, the steady growth is marvelous to watch, but the bloom is best of all, for it provides the gardeners of tomorrow.

IN THE BEGINNING

P oised between two worlds, Linda Hillegass represents the majority of American gardeners today. While her early gardening efforts were devoted to foodstuffs, the persuasive beauty of herbs gradually won a subtle victory. Slowly she comes to realize that she is no longer dealing with pragmatic plantings but a garden full of whole, living plants with singular attractions. Hoping to extend the seasons of pleasure her garden offers, she adds bulbs in variety and profusion. This experimental state has its problems, but they are resolved in time, thanks to her flexibility and willingness to explore the possibilities. She learns the ways of her plants through trial and error, settling on techniques that maximize their strengths and minimize their weaknesses. Periodic and unavoidable lapses in loveliness are taken in stride. Now, a few years down the road, it has become a living garden of delight through several seasons, and Hillegass has become a gardener.

Yet she is hesitant to acknowledge herself as an accomplished ornamental gardener. This is true of thousands of fine gardeners across the country, who view their efforts with needless humility. Is this a leftover from our Puritan ancestry? Whatever the source, the feeling is usually unfounded. The fact is, a lot of us are standing where Linda stands now, teetering on the brink of full-bore avant-gardening. Already she is weaving bulbs and herbs in mutually supportive community—no small feat, as anybody who knows both families will realize. Already her garden holds its own from early spring through summer. Already, one senses, she is looking ahead, wondering where this engrossing activity will lead her.

Like so many American gardeners, Hillegass is newly savvy; she has figured out that those stunning photographs in the glossy books improve rather than reflect reality, and she politely refuses to compete with illusions. She accepts the "trashy" look of the garden in transition as inevitable, part of the process. Don't we all have days when our hair won't cooperate, when our clothes refuse to fit? The Sisyphean burden of perfection is declined with equal politeness: "No, thank you, I'd rather not labor in vain. I want to have a real garden." Best of all, she finds the effects she has achieved satisfying; she loves what happens. Through this success, one senses a long and happy garden future. What will come next? Will there be an autumn garden, a winter garden, a mixed border? We are sure there will be more, for we know with certainty that the writer is hooked. This accomplishment will lead irresistibly to others, which will in turn stimulate further growth and experimentation. What lies ahead for Hillegass is available to us all, for the garden path is endless, and there is always something wonderful just a little bit further along.

LINDA HILLEGASS was born and raised in Nebraska, and is now the co-owner of two bookstores in Lincoln, where garden books are a not-too surprising specialty. Her herb-and-bulb garden (USDA zone 5) is on heavy clay soil, the site exposed to fierce winds and punishing extremes of heat and cold, which makes its success all the more admirable. Her published writings include articles on and beyond the garden.

Double Vision
Linda Hillegass

I'm not sure why I have an herb garden. It isn't that I really use the herbs all that much. Oh, the parsley, of course, and the chives, and the occasional snippet of black peppermint in iced tea. I did season the stuffing for one memorable Thanksgiving turkey with frosty sage plucked from a half-frozen garden. But I've grown thyme and oregano for a decade without tossing them into a sauce. My garlic chives are glorious, lush in summer and enchanting in fall with their starry blooms, but I've yet to try their leaves among salad greens. I go right on buying those bottled herbs at the grocery store just as if I had no herb garden at all.

The truth is that my herb garden is a sensuous experience that has far more to do with scent, sight, and texture than with taste. I love the silvery green of sage as a background for darker colors like the deep green of chives that produce a shower of lilac clover-like bloom in spring. My black peppermint mats the ground in a thick, rich, and completely satisfying way. When it strays beyond its bounds I enjoy pulling up its pungently-scented runners. The drift of aroma from a thyme plant brushed against while weeding is earthy and exotic, like a fresh wind from Greece.

I can't think of a part of my garden I enjoy more than my patch of herbs and lately it's become one of my true successes, too. My great love is flower gardening. I spend hours and dollars and sweat on that, but I'm sorry to say the flower garden in midsummer seldom lives up to my hopes for it in January. My failures are all too frequent. I've developed a philosophical outlook on these disappointments since taking up garden photography. I begin to see just how the illustrations in garden books can look so lovely; it's all a

4

question of angle, foreshortening, and focus. Those seemingly perfect gardens no doubt have their share of gaping holes.

But success is mine in the herb garden, at least since I hit upon the idea of interplanting bulbs and spring flowers among the perennial herbs. Early in my career as an amateur herbalist, I made the usual mistake of planting too closely. It was a natural error. In spring the early gaps around a tiny oregano plant and a pruned thyme loomed large. Closer planting gave the herb bed an established look in May, but later in the season this approach created havoc. Reveling in the sunny site and the heat of a Nebraska summer, the herbs ran riot.

> **The drugstore bargains were to be disposables . . . Ironically, they have lived on and bloomed lustily for years.**

Now among more widely and properly spaced herbs I insert bulbs and other spring flowers to fill the gaps. Their foliage dies away to make room for the vigorous summer growth of sage, oregano, and parsley. I've planted daffodils, for instance, between a well-established sage and a big clump of chives. In early spring, when the daffodils rise along with the temperatures, I prune the sage sharply back to give space to the bulbs. By the time the daffodils have finished blooming, the sage has put on new growth and begun to fill in around and over them, hiding their withering leaves.

The plantings, designed to create a spring wave of bloom, give heavy emphasis to daffodils—lovely orchid-like white 'Thalia' and gloriously sunny 'King Alfred', as well as a few whose names have been forgotten. Since daffodils return reliably year after year and even increase, they provide a reliable backbone for the garden's early season. The remaining springtime spaces are filled with a sprinkling of tulips, a pair of bleeding hearts (*Dicentra spectabilis*), yellow columbines (*Aquilegia*), perennial gold alyssum (*Aurinia saxatilis* 'Gold Dust') and white candytuft (*Iberis sempervirens*).

The tulips were bought cheap at the drugstore after years of hard luck with expensive tulips that bloomed splendidly one season only to languish a second year and fizzle out completely by a third. The drugstore bargains were to be disposables, bought with the idea of discarding them after a season or two of bloom. Ironically, they have lived on and bloomed lustily for years. They were labeled "mixed" which I took to mean red, purple, yellow, pink, and so on, but one batch of them came up all white. Planted near white 'Thalia' they created what I at first regarded as an unfortunate color association. I have come to admire this white on white look and enjoy the lovely bride-like bouquets I can cull from this garden in spring, sometimes with the addition of a few branches from the nearby apple tree.

The overall springtime effect of delicate white and yellow blooms with a dash of pink from the bleeding hearts and an accent of red from a few of the tulips is quite breathtaking. Sometime between late March and mid-April this combination bursts into bloom in unison and lasts a few days to a few weeks depending upon how quickly the hot winds come. The garden appears almost solid with daffodils and their compatriots at this point, while the herbs are hardly noticeable.

Tucked up against the stone wall of the garage, with a fence on its southern side, my herb garden has a western exposure that gives it a sunny site while still protecting it from the full blaze of the sun that scorches plants all too easily in a Nebraska July and August. The bed is large—an elongated triangle about 32 by 30 by 12 feet—with plenty of space for a liberal use of bulbs and spring plants that return year after year. Such interplanting seems just as suited to a tiny plot outside the kitchen door where, among half a dozen plants of parsley, thyme, and chives, one might tuck a few crocus or species tulips.

After the glory, of course, comes the inglorious moment when the lovely spring bloom dies away, leaving the trashy fading foliage of daffodils, the flopping tulip leaves, the withered bleeding hearts. But this period soon passes. A second wave of bloom in late May and well into June helps to hide the leafy remnants. Yellow columbines and orange poppies set off the blue of Siberian iris and the blue to purple range of herbal blossom just coming on: lavender chives, blue sage, and purple-blue catmint.

The trash of early spring withers away, the herbs expand into the holes left behind, and by midsummer I can smugly survey the thriving, sweet-smelling, bee-busy herb garden which has magically replaced my springtime fairyland.

Part 1. BORDER BUILDERS

F or many years, perennials were out of favor with most American gardeners, who by and large preferred the popular combination of evergreens and spring-flowering shrubs, bulbs and annual bedding plants. A handful of dedicated gardeners kept the traditional perennial border concept alive through those difficult years, growing plants from seed and bringing them from vacations abroad. Now, the faithful few have been joined by thousands of enthusiasts who have come to appreciate these giving, forgiving plants that so enrich our gardens. Perennials are to be found in every nursery and garden center from coast to coast, in ever-increasing variety. Fancy catalogs tempt us with astonishing pictures and garden magazines suggest elegant combinations. Thanks to this exposure, perennials are winning their way back into the gardener's good graces, finding, one hopes, a permanent place in our gardens.

Not all of the gardeners who contributed to this chapter have made traditional borders, yet all rely on perennials for leaf texture and structural form as well as colorful blossoms. They have learned that perennials can contribute to the garden not just in summer, but all through the year. In earliest spring, *Adonis amurensis* and *Hacquetia epipactis* melt away the snow with their sunny blossoms. Doronicums and primroses mingle with daffodils, euphorbias and arabis encircle tulips. These gradually give way to the thousands of summer-blooming perennials that brighten sunny beds and shady borders alike during the warmest months. Autumn brings waves of asters and salvias, boltonias and Kaffir lilies (*Schizostylis*) as well as the usual chrysanthemums. Perennials contribute even into the depths of winter, when the stalwart Christmas roses (*Helleborus niger*) bloom.

Although our contributors focus on perennials, their individual approaches differ. All, however, are working to extend the period in which their gardens are in full flower, for none wants the garden season to end. We hear from gardeners who use perennials to bridge the gap between spring bulbs and roses, and to hide the fading foliage of those same bulbs in decay. Some chronicle the progression of related colors through their borders, while others follow the passing seasons, characterizing each in terms of their associated perennials. A few are deeply concerned with garden design, while others simply love plants, combining them more for cultural reasons than visual or artistic ones. Some are interested primarily in arranging sequential bursts of color, others in creating textured tapestries that both in and out of bloom time satisfy the eye.

This harmonic interaction of plants and people over an extended period is what contributor Kevin Nicolay called "painting through time with plants." Though we often seem united in a common impatience, gardeners come to realize that time can be the garden's best friend. In time, gardens grow up, plants mature, pictures form and reform before our eyes. The complex gardening that some of these contributors are describing takes time to master, and richly interwoven borders require time to come together. These gardeners are well aware of the fact, and though some express a momentary desire to speed up the process, every one of them also rejoices in nature's schedule. Though many write of failure as well as success, the tone throughout is unfailingly cheerful. The depredations of dogs and cats, inclement weather, pest and disease may lay waste to the garden, but the true gardener, though disgusted and definitely irate, elects to go on. Oh well, try again. For border builders, the point is rarely just "getting it right," for they all find the changing garden endlessly fascinating in and of itself. Their accounts demonstrate that they find the process of gardening as rewarding as the most spectacular of results.

SUSAN BUCKLES, born in England, now lives and gardens in the gentle maritime climate of Seattle, Washington (USDA zone 8). She is a professional gardener who has developed extensive ornamental borders at Children's Orthopedic Hospital, where the garden (on heavy Seattle clay) provides a soothing retreat for the children and their families. At home, her mixed borders thrive despite the light, sandy soil. She contributes occasional garden pieces to the bulletins of the Hardy Plant Society and the Washington Park Arboretum Foundation.

In Succession
Susan Buckles

If we could watch the succession of plants throughout the year in a good perennial border as we watch the progress of clouds across the sky on accelerated film, we would have the perfect visual aid for gardeners. We would be able to see how each plant holds its place and for how long, how one plant's fading form affects the look of an oncoming one, and where and when the awkward gaps occur.

We do have books on the subject of succession, and how easy the garden writers make it sound. It is possible to have perennials growing together, producing their blooms, maximum heights and widths, and variously colored or textured foliage at different times. Each plant can be placed so that the space they fill collectively shows a constantly changing succession of delightful harmonies or contrasts, one taking over from another throughout the year.

It is possible, but don't let the garden writer or designer fool you. Most haven't actually tried it out in the dirt—on their knees—in the unseasonably cold spring after a hard winter, wondering what to substitute for the vital plants they could not buy, with the poppy seedlings that were to tie the whole scheme together having been scratched up in a heap by the cat next door. You can have great fun trying, however. If you are like me, sometimes it works and sometimes the chance combination even takes your breath away. With each year, as you acquire more experience, the succession of colors, forms, and textures becomes increasingly exciting and innovative.

To be successful, I suggest you find an efficient system for recording the whole process and noting down what needs doing — and when. Lack of system efficiency spells my doom. Two Junes ago, I made notes to replace the *Stachys byzantina* (lamb's-ears) in front of the *Salvia* x *superba* 'Viola Klose', with a non-flowering form; but, last June, I took my vacation — with some garden visiting included, of course — and saw a good combination of pale blue *Amsonia tabernaemontana* (blue star flower) with 'Viola Klose'. In the fall, I moved the salvia next to the amsonia, forgetting to check my notes. The notes would have told me that the salvia was there to hide the dying foliage of an early iris, moved there the year before to make room for a dictamnus, which died. In the course of all this, I discovered a planting of golden Marguerite, *Anthemis tinctoria*

> **I think it's the hurried weeding session in the dusk before dinner that does them in.**

'Pale Moon', previously hidden by the now deceased gas plant. And so it goes. I take careful notes but I need notes to tell me to look at my notes at the right times. What I need is a time sequence camera! I could project the film, stop it at every week of the progress, and make some more notes.

Let us create an imaginary border — in sun, facing southeast — and compress its year's growth into 15 minutes on an imaginary time-lapse film. (In another film or another garden, the subject of succession could be approached just as well from the perspective of color, but my viewpoint is structure and form first, then color.) There should be some sort of wall, fence, trellis, or hedge to provide a permanent background, and there should be flowering shrubs and evergreens to give internal structure to the planting's design. I have found the low-growing *Deutzia* x *kalmiiflora*, spiraeas of all kinds, daphnes, viburnums, and old roses to be good border shrubs. Small, slow-growing conifers like *Abies koreana* (Korean fir) can be used; but many conifers are too solid, rather rigid and therefore liable to stand out from rather than blend into a border. Transitional plants are needed. Hardy geraniums are invaluable for this, as are violas like *Viola cornuta* (horned violet) which will hoist itself into the branches of a fir. Ferns could give a structural effect but our border is in full sun, which is not so good for ferns. Instead, we can use grasses. The large spikey mound of *Helictotrichon sempervirens* (blue oat grass) is just as good as a small conifer; *Stipa arundinacea*, the feather grass from Australia and New Zealand, grows to the same size, or a little larger than the *Helictotrichon*, and has leaf colors that subtly change from light green to gold and bronze with violet undertones.

Having selected and carefully placed the structural plants, we can start. Begin the film in early spring, of course. This is the easiest part, for after winter anything looks good. After blossoming, most spring bulbs die down by April or May. The choice of plants to fill in the resulting gaps is large. Be careful of early flowering plants like *Helleborus orientalis* (lenten rose), *Pulmonaria* species (lungworts), or *Brunnera macrophylla* (heartleaf brunnera). Their leaves grow larger after flowering and can go on getting larger for quite some time. Suddenly you have a very large green clump adding nothing to the border's progression while swamping emerging delicacies. There are other plants with manageable and interesting post-flowering leaves that work well in the border. *Sanguinaria canadensis* 'Flore Pleno' (also listed in catalogs as 'Multiplex', *S. c. plena*) is one of them. This bloodroot has rich white flowers with matt-textured mid-green leaves. The outwardly facing leaves are scalloped and reach a foot in width. All aspects of its foliage make it easy to combine sanguinaria with other plants. A successful combination to try is a white *Primula sieboldii*, delicate and flimsy, placed in front of the bold sanguinaria leaves. This primrose disappears completely by June, and its place can be taken by other small plants, *Corydalis lutea* (yellow corydalis) or *Coreopsis verticillata* (thread leaf coreopsis), for example. All of these plants like partial shade, so in our time-lapse film, these plants could be placed on the shady side of one of the structural plants.

On the sunny side, *Heuchera* 'Palace Purple' could be a strong statement with its bold evergreen red-brown leaves. At its feet, an early violet like *Viola* 'Beshlie' would provide a long season of soft yellow color. *Coreopsis verticillata* 'Moonbeam', with the same soft yellow flowers but quite different foliage could surround it, and the medium yellow hybrid globeflower, *Trollius* x *cultorum* 'Prichard's Giant', could appear behind the heuchera. Add a group of Siberian irises, perhaps the dark blue *I. sibirica* 'Caesar's Brother', to offer a contrast in leaf shape. As a finishing touch, hardy geraniums — perhaps *Geranium clarkei* 'Kashmir White' or *Geranium endressii* — will weave their way around the other plants and fill any spaces open to them. Many hardy geraniums are low- to medium-growing and are invaluable for a mixed border.

I'm not sure about *allowing* annuals to seed here and there. It sounds ideal but, in reality, I find it more a matter of *persuading* them to grow in the right places. In my own garden, I haven't managed to attract either the poppy, *Papaver rhoeas*, or the annual flax, *Linum grandiflorum* 'Rubrum', to settle in selected gaps. I think it's the hurried weeding session in the dusk before dinner that does them in. Perennial in warmer zones, but a freely self-seeding annual in zones 4 and 5, *Oenothera berlandieri*, or Mexican evening primrose (listed sometimes as *O. speciosa* var. *childsii*), works for me because I like to grow lots of purples and magentas and the pink of this plant's blossoms mingles well with these colors. It seeds itself freely, but care is needed not to weed it out by mistake.

In our imaginary garden, by the time early summer rolls into view, the taller plants are becoming noticeable. Some, like phlox and aster, are invaluable fall perennials and we must plan space for them. Vines and climbers are filling in on the wall and we already have the wispy seed heads of *Clematis macropetala* showing. The mid-level plants are the main eye-catchers with *Thalictrum aquilegifolium* (columbine meadow-rue), *Astrantia major* (great masterwort) and a hybrid *Kniphofia* 'Primrose Beauty' or cultivars of *Iris sibirica* for contrast. *Campanula persicifolia* 'Hidcote Amethyst' (once known as *C. latiloba*) looks good with the foliage and emerging buds of eryngiums. Some late-flowering plants have interesting mid-summer foliage — like *Aconitum* (monkshood), for instance — and other plants, with variegated leaves or large, felty, silvery leaves, look handsome now.

None of the plants mentioned so far are invasive. We should always keep in mind the ultimate space a plant will need when fully grown. It should not invade the space of others. The monardas, some artemisias and campanulas, *Campanula takesimana* or *C. punctata*, for example, can wreck the succession. Beware of outright invaders, such as *Meconopsis cambrica* (Welsh poppy). Do not be tempted to include them.

There are some perennials that fit naturally into assorted groups and should always be considered for inclusion. I would not be without columbines which are well-behaved, tolerant, and substantial, yet light and airy in flower. Columbines fit well in a wildflower scene, or at the edge of woodlands where they do not need companion plants. This applies also to snakeroots. *Cimicifuga racemosa*, with its tall wavy spikes, is effective at the back of a border. The cool white flowers are welcome in September, while the handsome foliage has been looking good all summer.

At the close of our imaginary film, we should see autumn colors in the shrubs and mauves, reds, and purples in the tall asters; golds, bronzes, and yellows in heleniums; and soft yellow in the bells of *Kirengeshoma palmata*. Some recurrent old roses might show in the back, and a *Clematis orientalis* might weave along the fence, while the foreground flourishes with *Crocosmia* x *crocosmiiflora* 'Emily McKenzie' and a late sedum.

The year ends with as great a show as at the beginning. We are ready to go over our notes during the winter in hopes of getting it all right again the next year. The wider one's knowledge of plants, the easier are the choices and decisions. One thing is certain, though: To create a good perennial border, those choices and decisions must be consciously made and constantly improved. The succession is then assured.

The season is dead; long live the season — and may it linger in all its glory, not rush across our field of vision like all those hurried clouds.

RESOURCES
(See "Sources & Resources" appendix for complete addresses.)

Northwest Perennial Alliance
Oregon Hardy Plant Society

CHARLES APPLEGATE is the senior gardener at a large estate garden in north central Ohio (USDA zone 5). Kingwood Center is open daily, and for the gardeners who tend the extensive grounds, the challenge is to minimize effort and maximize effect. Applegate relies on long-blooming perennials that retain their good looks through several seasons, and identifies here a surprising number that rebloom in late summer or autumn. Though the scale of gardening at Kingwood Center is grand, the lessons Applegate offers hold true anywhere.

Getting the Maximum
Charles Applegate

Gardeners all over the country like to get the best possible return for all the effort, time, and money we put into our gardens. As senior gardener at the Kingwood Center in Mansfield, Ohio (between Cleveland and Columbia, USDA zone 5), I am always looking for perennials that are colorful over a long season, yet remain attracive even when out of flower. Once a private residence, the Kingwood estate is now open to the public daily. During the colder months, most of the floral interest is found in the greenhouse, but when spring arrives, the many gardens come alive. Specialty gardens hold collections of irises and daylilies, roses and peonies. Formal gardens spread behind the house, while the front lawns are filled with free-form beds. The perennial garden was designed after the pattern of an English border, with wide brick paths winding through the beds. Evergreen hedging makes a solid framework for a wide variety of bright perennials, which show color from early summer until frost stops the show in the fall.

Over the years, I have developed a considerable list of good performers here in north central Ohio, plants that give the greatest quantity of bloom for the longest possible time. Most of my favorites are also popular with the public, who frequently ask for such a list to take home. Among the very best are ever-blooming or repeat bloomers, a prime example of which is the hybrid dwarf daylily, *Hemerocallis* 'Stella de Oro'. This one is appearing in almost every flower catalog, and is being used by landscapers in great quantities. 'Stella de Oro' is low-growing, with grassy foliage, and it begins to open its small gold flowers in early summer. It continues blooming throughout the summer and can still be making a nice show in October or until stopped by the first freeze of fall.

BORDER BUILDERS

Plant breeders are trying to develop daylilies in other colors and sizes that share this ever-blooming habit. Gardeners who delight in the performance of 'Stella de Oro' might also try the following hemerocallis hybrids. 'Daily Bread' also has small, golden flowers, though on taller scapes. 'Bitsy', taller than 'Stella de Oro', has lemon yellow flowers. A couple of long bloomers with unusual form are 'Jersey Spider', with spidery, narrow petals of dark orange, and 'Fuzz Bunny', with ruffled, doubled flowers of clear yellow. We will see many more continuous bloomers in the next few years, but only time will tell whether they will rebloom in Ohio as they do in milder climates.

A surprising perennial that offers some reblooming varieties is the iris. Not many people know that certain varieties of tall bearded iris and of Siberian iris (*I. sibirica*) bloom twice. The old Siberian iris, 'My Love', is a reliable rebloomer here in Ohio. To encourage rebloom, all the spent stalks should be cut to the ground after the regular bloom season ends. A second set of buds may appear about a month later, nearly equal in quantity and size to the first. Among the tall bearded iris, there are some very reliable rebloomers, which may flower again anytime from July until heavy frost. In a protected place, bloom will occasionally keep coming until November. Perhaps as its name implies, 'Immortality' will bloom almost continuously in favorable years. Dark purple 'Royal Summer' is often in bloom from July onward. The warm yellow 'Golden Encore' shares this habit, as does 'Queen Dorothy', a white with lavender edges. As with the Siberians, the bloom stalks should be removed when finished to help force the next set of buds.

Quite a few perennials have a very long bloom season because they keep producing additional branches and buds. A fairly recent introduction is *Coreopsis verticillata* 'Moonbeam'. This new thread leaf coreopsis makes a low, lacy mound covered with little pale yellow daisies over a very long period. Another similar variety, 'Zagreb', offers deeper yellow flowers on slightly taller stems. The short stemmed, pink-flowered evening primrose, *Oenothera speciosa* 'Rosea', also produces colorful blossoms on fresh stems all summer long. A hybrid form of the fern leaf bleeding heart, *Dicentra* 'Luxuriant', opens its showy pink flowers continuously through the growing season. One of the most prolific perennial rebloomers is

16

Aster x *frikartii* 'Wonder of Staffa', which opens lavender daisy-like flowers from July until frost.

Along with asters, in the same large family of flowering plants (Compositae or Asteraceae), are many other favorite long-blooming members. *Heliopsis*, the orange sunflower, keeps blooming on newly formed branches from July until frost. Two double-flowered forms of *Helianthus* x *multiflorus*, 'Flore Pleno' and 'Loddon Gold', are nice tall background plants for sunny locations, both of which bloom from July until frost. The deep gold flowers of 'Flore Pleno' are so doubled as to suggest dahlias or mums. 'Loddon Gold' is an anemone form with a

Certain perennials will give a second bloom season if. . . .

crested center surrounded by large petals of golden yellow. The 1988 All-American winning shasta daisy (*Chrysanthemum* x *superbum*), 'Snow Lady', is pretty much ever-blooming if kept dead-headed. It blooms from seed the first year, but the results are not completely uniform. Plant size, flower form, and ever-blooming performance vary from plant to plant.

Quite a few perennials will bloom all summer if the spent stalks are regularly cut back. Sea thrift, *Armeria maritima*, produces its main crop of rose-pink flowers in June, but will continue throughout the summer if trimmed. The common garden phlox, *Phlox paniculata*, blooms for many weeks if the main head of flowers is removed when it is finished blooming. Smaller clusters keep blooming from the side branches that develop after the main flower head has been removed.

Certain perennials will give a second bloom season if they are cut clear to the ground when the first bloom is finished. It takes some time for the plant to grow up again, but when it does, it re-blooms. Delphiniums may be the best-known example of this, but globe thistle (*Echinops* spp.) will also return to bloom. Often, however, flowers from the second blooming will be smaller and on shorter stems than the first.

Lavender and blue flowers are useful blenders of brighter colors. *Thalictrum delavayi* 'Hewitts' Double' grows a bit taller than catalogs indicate, and may need staking. This meadow-rue is worth the effort to get a cloud of double flowers; it looks much like lavender baby's breath and lasts six weeks or longer. This is one plant that blooms better and longer in partial shade. *Salvia* x *superba* (hybrid sage), with flowers in several shades of violet purple, will bloom on and off all summer. The Russian sage, *Perovskia atriplicifolia*, has narrow gray leaves and many branched, thin stems covered with small lavender blossoms for two months or more in late summer.

Most alliums bloom for a short time only, but there are several rhizomatous (having thickened storage roots) alliums that bloom throughout the middle of summer. Because they do not form bulbs, they grow all season, continuing to produce blooms as long as the spent bloom heads are removed. The lavender globe lily, *Allium tanguticum*, is similar to chives but much larger in both blossom and foliage. 'Pink Feathers', with fluffy lavender-pink heads, is the largest of these midsummer alliums. Besides long bloom, these plants share a distinctive odor of onions; the odor seems to repel most insects!

Any plant that's going to do double duty in one growing season must have good care. This includes being kept free of weeds and insects, having adequate moisture through the season, and being fed enough to make the extra growth necessary to flower again. Removing old blooms prevents the plant from setting seed, which in turn encourages it to make more flowers in order to try to reproduce. If we do a little searching and selecting for the right plants, we can all enjoy a long and colorful performance from our perennials, no matter where we garden.

NANCY GOODWIN is the proprietor of Montrose Nursery in North Carolina, specializing in hardy cyclamen and unusual border plants. She records the progress of her garden (USDA zone 7) through the seasons, emphasizing the marvels of the Southern autumn. Her property has been a garden for generations, and she prizes the heritage plants which abound there as much as her rare border perennials. Goodwin recently edited, with Allen Lacy, a manuscript left by the renowned garden writer Elizabeth Lawrence, *A Rock Garden in the South* (Duke University Press, 1990).

Signs of the Seasons
Nancy Goodwin

I have often wondered whether I could know the exact time of year by studying the cycles of plants. Stimulated by a query from Allen Lacy concerning plants that announce the arrival of fall, I began to notice which plants gave the first signs of seasonal change. Certainly one of the first indicators of fall is the germination of chickweed seeds, and summer is here when nut grass is at its height. But there are more welcome signs for which I search eagerly and which, when found, serve as harbingers of the next period. There are several genera, notably *Cyclamen*, *Galanthus*, and *Crocus*, which span three or more seasons, but are generally considered representatives of only one. Cyclamen are usually associated with fall, although there are species that bloom in each period. Both snowdrops and crocuses are thought of as spring-blooming plants, but they begin to flower in late summer and fall. And then there are species of many genera which tend to produce an occasional flower out of season. These are always exciting to see.

For years I dreamed of gardening in a location where the seasons would change gradually, without the violent fluctuations so common here. I imagined that if I could live where the summers would be cool and damp I might grow a really good perennial border in the English style. I have finally realized that this will not happen and have accepted the challenges and rewards of gardening in the mid-south. I have lived in central North Carolina for most of my life and have done all of my gardening here. It is considered zone 7 on the USDA hardiness map, although I discovered after years of disappointments that I cannot grow most zone 7 trees and shrubs; however, I can grow many zone 8 perennials, and have concluded that my location is excellent for year-round horticultural interest. Our summers are extremely hot and humid with prolonged droughts that create a stressful environment. We seldom have day-long rains from May through September, and must rely on sudden, brief thunderstorms to quench the thirst of our plants. We often have over 50 days with temperatures in the 90s and at least one spell of 100-degree days. The winters are relatively mild with the all-time record low of minus 12 degrees Fahrenheit testing our plants during the winter of 1985. Our average first day of frost is about the 20th of October and the last one may be expected about the end of April. We usually have snow once or twice a winter, but it is short-lived and cannot be counted on to provide that much-needed insulation against severe cold.

Anticipation is one of the joys of gardening and if you know how and where to look you can find signs of each season long before the calendar confirms it. Spring usually begins in February in the garden, but there are always galanthus in bloom in January and the swelling buds of *Adonis amurensis* 'Fukujukai' (amur Adonis) can be seen before January is over. One of our native witch hazels, *Hamamelis vernalis*, often reveals its twisted, thread-like blossoms in early January or late December, perfuming the air with a strange, spicy scent. This is the season when I think I can keep a gardening diary, as did Elizabeth Lawrence. Each flower in winter is reason for rejoicing. Every Christmas day I make a list of plants in flower. I reason that I must be able to see the stamens in order for the plant to be included on my list. The lovely, purple-flowered *Cheiranthus* 'Bowles' Mauve' (sometimes listed as *Erysimum* 'Bowles' Mauve') has made the list every year. Down in the woods is a patch of deep blue *Primula vulgaris* which can be relied on to have an early flower. In some years the shrub *Chimonanthus praecox* has a few delicate, pale yellow, fragrant flowers. And my first crocus of the winter, *Crocus sieberi*, can be located with its tightly clasped bud nestled in its emerging foliage; however, it rarely has a flower open and therefore doesn't make the list. The buds of *Cyclamen coum* will have been obvious to those who bend and look for them from late fall on, but I seldom find one in bloom on Christmas Day. The end of the calendar year is the beginning of the year for the gardener.

Anytime after the first of January we have spring alternating with winter, which often causes disappointments since many of the flowers that are tempted into bloom by a few mild days may be destroyed by sudden plunges of the mercury to zero degrees Fahrenheit or lower. At the same time there are always a few plants, the majority of which are bulbous, that can withstand these fluctuations. I have never seen galanthus hurt. These splendid little plants, after blossoming, leave me with a sense of sadness as their foliage yellows, for I think of the unknown trials of the seasons ahead that must be experienced before once again I can delight in their beauty.

I make a point of listening to three different weather forecasts each morning in hopes of hearing one that will tell me what I want to believe.

Among the reliable, early signs of spring are the reddish stems of *Anemone blanda* (Grecian windflower) which pull themselves up from the soil on the first slightly warm day. No amount of cold destroys their promise and a flower or two can be found under our pear tree by the end of January, even though they will not be at their peak until late February and March when *Cyclamen pseudibericum* comes into bloom. The spears of *Iris reticulata* leaves pierce the soil, pushing up through the leaf litter like needles through soft cotton. Finding the first flower is reward enough for the search. There are also a number of perennials that can be counted on to perform as beacons during the winter, but that reach their potential only in spring. By accumulating many strains of the Christmas rose, *Helleborus niger*, I have them in bloom by Christmas day and continuing through March; however, it is the first flower that is most exciting. When the whiteness of the flower can just be seen, I get a thrill of anticipation and hope that is greater than the satisfaction of a fully-opened flower.

There are clumps of an early-flowering, dark form of *Helleborus orientalis* that appear in the woods at the same time as *H. niger*. This form of lenten rose is nearly deciduous and new flowers can be seen just as the old foliage begins to wither. *H. foetidus* (bearsfoot hellebore) sends its chartreuse flowering shoots above deep green leaves in late fall. By the time cold weather has settled in, the fresh new foliage of *Arum italicum* has matured and I know that the arrow-shaped leaves with vivid stripes of cream will withstand the extremes of temperature. The red bark of our native dogwoods,

Cornus sericea, and the chartreuse bark of *Cornus sericea* 'Flaviramea' have attained their winter brilliance.

Because our springs are so long, it is difficult to decide just which plants are the leading indicators. There are years when we seem to have only fall, spring, and summer, with no real winter, and no day without something in bloom. The delicate leaves and flowers of rue anemone, *Anemonella thalictroides*, wait until spring is here on the calendar before making a definite show. However, the rue anemone is an imperfect indicator because throughout the summer and fall a few leaves and an occasional blossom can be spotted. The many species of columbine usually wait until after the 21st of March to open their flowers. Among the earliest of these are the many forms of *Aquilegia flabellata* (fan columbine), with their clean, glaucous foliage that is rarely marred by leaf miners, which prefer other species. Thanks to *A. buergeriana* and *A. chrysantha* (golden columbine) we have columbines blooming into summer. Only after the first official day of spring does *Phlox divaricata* (blue phlox) begin to show its carpet of blue in the woods and under the oak as well as in the wild parts of my garden. This is a plant which begs for study and selection, as the variety of its flower shapes is great and its shades of blue, mauve, and white are infinite. Some of the petals are rounded, each one touching the next while others are slender and separate; some petals are indented and others are smooth.

The major displays of primroses occur in spring with *Primula vulgaris* ssp. *sibthorpii* among the first. *P. sieboldii*, *P. polyneura*, and many candelabra types are among the last to appear. By the time spring is registered on the calendar our *Narcissus* have just about finished their bloom; there are only a few species left with their flower heads above the undergrowth of grasses that accompany them in the field. Flowering quinces have by this time had their flowers battered by the fluctuations of temperature, but they can usually be counted on for their major show close to the first official day of spring, shortly after which a hard, late freeze may brown their flowers yet again. There is one flowering quince here that continues to produce deep red flowers despite foul weather, and it is frustrating to know neither its species nor cultivar name. This remarkable *Chaenomeles* begins with a few flowers in fall, always has some at Christmas, peaks in spring, and continues into early summer. Hence, not all chaenomeles are true indicators of spring.

Summer is anticipated by a few early forms of hemerocallis, especially the diminutive daylily, 'Little Minor'. And verbenas which revel in the heat of summer begin to cover themselves with red to purple or white flowers from early spring on. I usually associate the noise of the cicadas with the fourth of July, but this year they spoke on the first day of summer, announcing the return of oppressive heat and humidity. The annual larkspur, *Consolida ambigua*, which are at their peak in late spring, look tired by the 21st of June, and are pulled out to freshen the garden for the summer display. Monardas come into their own and *Salvia uliginosa* begin to bloom. I know that the latter will be fresh and beautiful with its clear, bright blue flowers every morning until frost, making this an indispensable plant in the garden. Annuals begin to bloom. I don't have very many of them, but would hate be be without *Phlox drummondii*, with its small white, red, blue, or cream flowers. White or violet *Cleome hasslerana* (spider flower) open as the afternoon advances; they provide fresh flowers each day just when the heat has diminished the beauty of other plants that were fresh in the early morning. The sometimes perennial cupflower, *Nierembergia hippomanica* var. *violacea*, has violet flowers produced in abundance on low plants and the scarlet Texas sage, *Salvia coccinea*, lacks the gaudy, stiff quality of its relative, *S. splendens*, scarlet sage. White *Cosmos bipinnatus* with its fine foliage adds elegance to any border. Beginning in midsummer, *Abelmoschus manihot* (sunset hibiscus) produces large flowers of palest yellow.

I always carry the terrible dread of yet another record-breaking drought with the memory of those in recent years. Although our rainfall totals at the end of the year are about 40 inches, that isn't a comfort in midsummer when the earth is cracked and dry. I make a point of listening to three different weather forecasts each morning in hopes of hearing one that will tell me what I want to believe. It is usually late June before the pecan trees have their leaves fully expanded giving much-needed shade to the nearby borders. In this part of the world the primary challenge of a perennial garden comes at this season. We rely on long-blooming perennials, such as the heat-tolerant blue or white delphiniums (*Delphinium grandiflorum* and *D. tatsienense*). *Anthemis tinctoria* (golden marguerite) never fails to have pale yellow or white daisy-like flowers. The tall cupflower, *Nierembergia scoparia albiflora*, provides cool, white papery flowers every day. *Clematis integrifolia* is a sprawling, not climbing, sort that continues to send up new blooming stalks in the midst of skirts of ripening seed heads. A hybrid *Perovskia* that was formerly known as *P. atriplicifolia* (Russian sage) produces spikes of heathery, blue-purple flowers above pungent, gray-green leaves. The shrubby *Salvia greggii* (autumn sage) has small flowers in many hues of red, and *Caryopteris* x *clandonensis* (blue mist) adds more misty blue flowers to the summer garden. Grasses begin to make a show with *Pennisetum setaceum* 'Burgundy Giant' (crimson fountain grass), *Imperata cylindrica rubra* (Japanese blood grass), and some of the stately *Miscanthus* species.

Because of our intensely hot and humid summers, I rejoice at the coming of fall in the same way that most gardeners in New England celebrate the coming of spring. By the beginning of summer I look for the swelling buds of next year's dogwoods, azaleas, and camellias, and I check the berries on the hollies in anticipation of the winter display. Occasionally by the end of August we have clear days with low humidity and nights when temperatures fall below 65 degrees. I know then that I have three glorious seasons ahead. Fall is announced by the presence of colchicums and *Cyclamen hederifolium*. From late summer on there is always a patch of galanthus somewhere to be visited in hopes of finding an emerging leaf, bud or flower. The summer weeds begin to lose their grip and chickweed and henbit begin to appear. Seeds of violas and other perennials germinate, after resting all summer waiting for a drop in temperature. Because of the wonderful way in which the seasons overlap, it is often possible to find signs of autumn as early as June. I can always find a *Cyclamen hederifolium* blooming somewhere in the garden just as the old foliage dies and the seeds ripen, and by bending down can spot a new leaf and flower buds on *C. intaminatum*. *Arum italicum* waits until the cool days of late summer and fall to produce its new foliage, which will remain fresh and green and cream no matter how severe the winter. Witch hazels, *Hamamelis virginiana*, clothe their bare branches with yellow, fragrant flowers. *Sternbergia lutea* (fall or winter daffodil) with bright yellow vase-shaped flowers appears in the midst of *Ceratostigma plumbaginoides* (leadwort), which provides brilliant blue flowers from summer into the frosts of fall.

I find the earth in autumn a less hostile home for the many plants that have been nurtured in pots throughout the long summer. This is a time for rebuilding beds and for correcting those inevitable mistakes that shout at me throughout the summer. There are often tropical storms coming up from the Caribbean to soften the soil, and with their rains to help establish the plants. I plant trees, bulbs, and all sorts of perennials. And I watch the weather forecasters of folk wisdom, the woolly worms (banded caterpillars, *Isia isabella*), for although this is my favorite season, I feel uneasy about the possibility of a severe winter. I bring in bales of pine straw for emergency use when the temperature threatens to fall below five degrees. Plants are brought into the greenhouses; the cold frames and pit are packed with double layers of plants. The calendar year has ended. But the seeds of the cyclamen are germinating and that is a beginning. By this time the buds have swollen on *Jasminum nudiflorum*, and I can pick the stems with red-tipped buds, knowing they will open quickly in the warmth of the house. Honeysuckle, *Lonicera fragrantissima*, beckons me to come closer to enjoy its extraordinary fragrance. By the time I get around to raking and picking up the last leaves, I can see the new green shoots of the narcissus in the field. The year is an unbroken cycle full of successes and failures, new ideas for improvements, hopes for gentle weather, renewed energy, and that delicious feeling of anticipation that greets each day. Again I begin to wander through the garden searching for the first signs of spring.

SUSAN URSHEL is the head horticulturist at a private garden in Fort Worth, Texas. Her home garden shares the conditions that characterize Texas gardens (USDA zone 8): alkaline clay, brutal heat and cold, and gully-washing rains. Fortunately, she takes a positive pleasure in caring for her plants. Her interest in herbs, old roses, historical gardens, and heritage plants makes gardening an open-ended adventure.

A Method to This Madness
Susan Urshel

There is a certain madness that overtakes every gardener. A flower garden may be beautifully designed and planted. The bones — long lasting plants and design elements — may be laid out to perfection. The plant combinations may be well thought out and researched and each plant placed just so. The small plants begin to grow and bloom, and the picture begins to take shape. Then, the problems begin. Weeds appear. Plants get leggy. Insects chew the buds and leaves. In summer, we learn that the garden picture is not one we can just sit back and admire. Yes, flower gardens can be art, but gardening is an art that demands personal interaction. Some people call this "maintenance."

Garden maintenance has a bad name for many people, who think of weeding, watering, and deadheading as boring chores. Well, the reality is that without personal interaction with the gardener, plants don't thrive. This reality drives gardeners to madness, the madness of maintenance. Maintenance is the key that unlocks the perennial garden gate so that the picture may be viewed; without a method to our madness, the picture will not develop as we hoped and intended.

Which method you choose is less important than understanding the reasons and needs behind each interaction. Any of these jobs can be done well in many different ways. Every job well done brings us the pleasure of nurturing our plants, and the joy of coming to know more about both our plants and ourselves in the process.

I find it useful to think of maintenance as the continuing development or fine tuning of the design that was laid out so carefully in the beginning. When I go out into the flower yard to work, it is usually to weed, water, deadhead, and the like. It's both important and fun to do when treated as a chance for personal interaction with each plant in the garden. The point of every maintenance chore is to help our plants fulfill their potential. As we spend time in close contact with our plants, we learn how to grow them well. When we work to build the soil, we learn how to improve it. The more we know about the garden's environment, the more helpful we can be when problems appear. All the work and thought we put into our gardens is repaid many times, for we get back more than we give.

It takes time to make good soil, and some folks get tired of waiting.

The first year we had our front flower yard, my husband Paul and I worked hard on the soil. In this northeastern part of central Texas (USDA zone 8), I have found that the alkaline clay soil must be well amended before planting perennials. We tilled over and over, adding lots of rotting leaves, grass clippings, composted cow manure, aged and finely shredded bark, and wet peat moss to the soil. We learned to first get the peat moss thoroughly wet, since it is very difficult to wet peat well once it is incorporated with the soil. We mix peat with water in a wheelbarrow, or on the cement driveway, turning and stirring until it is totally wet. Then, we add it to the soil with the other amendments.

After the ground was prepared, the perennials were planted and mulched with wet newspaper topped off with pine needles. That kept the weeds down and held moisture in the soil. In Fort Worth's climate, the summer heat quickly burns the humus out of the soil, leaving it hard as a brick. When air and water can't penetrate, this hard, compacted soil drains poorly, especially in winter, and we lose plants like lavender (*Lavandula angustifolia*) to rot. We must renew our soil amendments repeatedly whether we mulch or not, but we find that with a good mulch the soil stays moist and rich with humus quite a bit longer.

It takes time to make good soil, and some folks get tired of waiting. A new madness grips them, and they are driven to make raised beds, or to dig out several feet of the dirt and replace it with a new soil mixture. Welp, I've tried both ways, and found that our intense summer heat means we must add new amendments regularly to keep the necessary air, water, and nutrients in the soil. Our flower garden has been planted for six years now, and we don't need the newspaper mulch anymore, because the plants cover the ground, but we continue to add pine needles and composted bark each year.

During the growing season, it is always beneficial to keep the soil worked up around the plants. I use a pointed hoe three inches by three inches, which is hard to find anymore, but well worth the trouble of searching for one. A flower bed is not a field of corn, so one must use an instrument that can be handled delicately and that moves easily in the small spaces between the spreading perennials. Early in the season, I watch closely to avoid cutting shallow roots near the small crowns. In midsummer, when the plants have grown so much that hardly any soil is visible, I prefer to work gently around each plant with a hand trowel. In late summer, I won't need to cultivate at all, because the plants have completely covered the ground. I might have to do a little weeding now and again, but nothing much, and now we really can sit back to enjoy our garden picture to the fullest.

Going out on a summer day to the front flower yard to weed, I may notice a cucumber beetle. Right then, I pick him and his friends off the plant and dispose of them. I have learned to act quickly when insects or diseases appear, using organic or sometimes chemical methods. If you don't recognize the problem, either talk with a qualified person or send a sample to your state extension service. I myself am more of a pick-off, wash-off type, and these methods work fairly well. Of course, right now there are no leaves on my mint (*Mentha* sp.) because of grasshoppers, but I am willing to lose a few minor battles. If you won't tolerate any pests at all, a preventative IPM (Integrated Pest Management) program can be very effective. If you do use sprays, whether organic or chemical, always read the label and always, always wear protective clothing. Madness might be all right in the garden, but not craziness.

After getting the cucumber beetles off the flowers, I begin weeding. The most common weeds I deal with are purslane (*Portulaca oleracea*) and Bermuda grass (*Cynodon dactylon*). Now, I don't pull all the weeds; I like dayflower (*Commelina communis*) and dandelions (*Taraxacum officinale*) and I even allow the occasional henbit (*Lamium amplexicaule*). Weeding soon leads me to those other elements of summer madness, deadheading and pruning.

Most folks know that deadheading means the removal of spent

flowers to encourage plants to make new ones. Over the years, I have learned to treat each perennial according to its individual growth habit, selecting where to cut so the new blossoms will emerge where they should. This form of maintenance madness sometimes calls for intensive shearing, and other times for delicate trimming, depending on whether the plant will bloom continuously or rebloom later in the season. With the aster 'Wonder of Staffa' (*Aster* x *frikartii*), I nip off the dead flowers on short stems, cutting just above a leaf or at a node, since this aster will then produce more flowers from leaf nodes all along its stems. I cut the Stokes' aster (*Stokesia laevis*) hard, taking off each bloomed-out stem at the crown, because I know that the old stalks' flowers would not be as large or prolific as those appearing later on new stalks. Spike gayfeather (*Liatris spicata*) calls for both methods. Some stalks get cut down to the crown, which may trigger renewed growth and more flower stems. Others are cut midway down to get several smaller flower spikes about six inches tall, a nice cut flower for a small vase. Don't be afraid to experiment with deadheading; it's all part of the summer maintenance madness, and the plants will look and grow better for it.

Later in the season, after most of our plants have bloomed and our ardent summers are well along, it is time for another madness: whacking back the perennials. Some people call this "pruning." It doesn't matter what you call it, but most perennials like to be pruned, and will renew themselves for the rest of the growing season. Leggy or overgrown plants, those with little rebloom, or those which are becoming invasive, should all be whacked back or pruned hard to get them back in shape.

In this part of Texas, I try to do my pruning in late June or early July, so the plants will have recovered and put on a healthy amount of new growth before the heat of August arrives. If I prune in late July, I don't cut as much or as far back on the stems. The plants seem to ne d that extra leaf surface to defy the heat and put on new growth. Even when you know the right time to prune, it is important to be sensitive to the weather and how the perennials are looking. You can sometimes manage to have a garden rebloom at a certain desired time, but don't prune your plants a week before a party and expect them to look as colorful on the big day as they did in spring!

Although I don't deadhead our native mealy-cup sage (*Salvia farinacea*), I do prune any leggy, falling-over stems by about two-thirds. You can deadhead it, or prune it to stay at any height you like, and it will never stop blooming. In fact, whether deadheaded daily or pruned once a year, this plant will bloom from late spring to frost, and it reseeds itself as well. Russian sage (*Perovskia atriplicifolia*) also blooms over a long period of time. The flowers fade about the time I prune the other perennials, so I cut back about two-thirds of the stems, which then send out new shoots that will be blooming by fall. I deadhead small-leaf catnip (*Nepeta mussinii*) throughout the growing season, and nip at the old undergrowth to keep it in bounds. When the whacking-back madness strikes, I remove two-thirds of the top growth, shaping the plants to rounded mounds. The only plants to be really cut to the ground are the 'Silver King' artemisia (*Artemisia ludoviciana*), the mints (*Mentha* spp.), and similar things that otherwise become too invasive.

Pruning gives each plant back its individual space, and keeps stronger plants from swamping more delicate ones. At first, it looks a bit severe, with bare earth showing once again, but in no time at all the new growth matures and the perennials re-create their garden tapestry.

After the whacking-back madness, the plants always need an extra boost to promote new growth. I often turn to Epsom salts (magnesium sulfate), bought at the local drug store. Epsom salts are used on our roses, on the shrubs, and on annuals as well as on the perennials; in fact, we use it on any plant that's been pruned. We scatter about half a cup around each plant, or add it to the whole bed as if it were granular fertilizer. It can also be used as a liquid, run through the siphon attachment of a watering hose. Plants need food all through the growing season, so we fertilize with a granular product—sometimes organic, sometimes chemical—early in the spring. Follow this up with a shot-in-the-arm booster of liquid fertilizer and you have some healthy flowering plants. Sometimes even with all those amendments and nutrients, the plants will turn yellowish. Well, in this part of the country, a dose of Ferriplus—if you can find it, and afford it—will give your plants a further boost of iron that will turn the leaves a deep, healthy green. There are other chelated iron products on the market that work, but be sure to use the Epsom salts at the same time. This will help by releasing nutrients locked in the soil, making them readily available to the plants. As with any granular product, water well before and after applying to avoid burning your plants. We have found that if the soil is well amended, full of humus and nutrients, plants need less additional fertilizer.

An important part of maintenance is experimentation. Deadhead here, cut back there, feed and water a lot or a little. Find out what works for you, for your plants, and for your garden. Making notes can help when memory fails; just how tall did the coneflower (*Echinacea purpurea*) get? When did it bloom, and for how long? Was it invasive? Did it get damaged by pests or diseases? For me, record keeping is fun, and I can't always remember the whens and wheres of gardening without notes. You may decide that, for you, the greatest joy comes from watching your plants grow without worrying over details.

For myself, I like having flowers to smell when I walk in the garden, flowers to cut for the house, flowers to share with friends. Having these in abundance proves the methods of my madness to be working well, and well worthwhile. As summer slows down and maintenance madness wears off, I look forward to the cooling breezes of fall, and the rebloom of fall flowers now on their way.

EDITH EDDLEMAN is an active garden designer who is also the volunteer co-curator with Doug Ruhren of North Carolina State University Arboretum perennial borders. Her special interests include native plants, plants with variegated foliage, winter-flowering trees and shrubs, and unusual bulbs. Although her home garden (USDA zone 7–8) is frustratingly tiny, it is crammed with a changing array of uncommon plants. Fortunately, her position at the Arboretum allows her to indulge her garden loves to the fullest extent.

Developing a Perennial Border
NORTH CAROLINA STATE UNIVERSITY ARBORETUM
1982–1988
Edith R. Eddleman

Nay sayers are everywhere: "The day of the 200-foot perennial border is over"; "I do not care for perennial borders, except in England where they are properly done"; "St. Gertrude of the Border is dead." I heard the last of these dire proclamations in a lecture given by Allen Paterson, the Director of the Royal Botanic Garden, Ontario, Canada. He was referring to Gertrude Jekyll and, though my respect for Mr. Paterson is immense, I beg to differ. St. Gertrude lives—her design principles are alive and well in the North Carolina State University Arboretum perennial border in Raleigh. Here, separated by 85 years and more than 3,000 miles, not to mention differences in longitude and latitude, flourishes a 370-foot by 18-foot border, a border for all seasons backed by a 20-foot tall holly hedge. Jekyllesque success is possible in America.

Today, a visitor admiring the well-developed border would not be aware of its rocky beginnings, the times of laughter and disaster that form the history of this border. To view its changes through the years is to see the accomplishments of many people. Elizabeth Lawrence wrote in *The Little Bulbs: A Tale of Two Gardens* (Duke University Press, 1986), "Gardening, reading about gardening, and writing about gardening are all one; no one can garden alone," and I do not. Newell Hancock makes sure that the border is watered, keeps the mulch coming, and holds the insects at bay. In 1985 Doug Ruhren joined me as co-curator. His creativity and gardening skill have added a special dimension to this garden, and his friendship has given a special dimension to my life. Over the years and transformations, members of the staff and their students have contributed countless hours of labor, digging, and replanting.

In 1977 no border or hedge existed, just nutsedge — of which we at the Arboretum are holders of the national collection. In 1978 the hedge began as one-gallon-sized hollies (*Ilex* x 'Nellie R. Stevens') planted at four-foot intervals. Gradually the hollies outstripped the nutsedge and the site was used for a wildflower research project. In 1980 the area was disked, treated with methyl bromide, and planted with 3,000 pink petunias. In 1981 the petunia plague gave way to a rose garden — the balling and burlaping exercise of an arboriculture class.

Salaried at $12.50 per week, I began my assault on the border.

In the fall of 1982, I was taking a planting design class in the NCSU Department of Horticulture. Various design projects were available for our final project, among them the design of the perennial border. Those selecting the perennial border project met with the Arboretum's director, Dr. J. C. Raulston, who showed us the site for the border — not the south-facing holly-backed rose garden site but a north-facing site only 200 feet in length on the opposite side of the arboretum. I suggested the border would be better sited in place of the rose garden, but Dr. Raulston vetoed this idea, feeling perhaps that asking a second arboriculture class to move the roses again might be risky to his health.

Undaunted, I chose to model my border design on that of Gertrude Jekyll's long border at her home, Munstead Wood. Using plants appropriate to our stressful southern climate (USDA zone 8), I attempted to follow Jekyll's color study, moving from gray-foliage plants combined with pastel pink, yellow, and lavender-flowered plants into deep intense red, yellow, orange, and purple-flowered plants; then returning to the pastels but with blue flowers replacing the lavender ones. (Jekyll preferred to separate purple and blue flowers; she felt that this combination failed to offer enough contrast and did not create an effective garden picture.) Dr. Raulston found the idea of the border as a color study an appealing one and my design was selected to be installed at the Arboretum.

A month later, Dr. Raulston told me he'd decided to move the border to the area occupied by the rose garden and asked if I would redesign my plan to suit this larger area, then 250 feet in length. Fortunately, the Arboretum contained a fine collection of ornamental grasses that I incorporated into the design, along with a number of seed-grown perennials. I asked Dr. Raulston if some other perennials could be purchased for the border and he agreed. I handed over the revised border design and my list of plants to be purchased along with possible nursery sources.

I was working on weekends so I couldn't be present for the installation of the border in March of 1983. Many students volunteered to help install the plants and, in one weekend, the border was completed.

The following Monday, I rounded the corner and was greeted by the sight of what appeared to be a mouse graveyard, with hundreds of plant markers, and huge 15-foot sweeps of Easter lilies (*Lilium longiflorum*) in full bloom. The Easter lilies were the legacy of Dr. August DeHertog's bulb research program, commandeered for the border by Dr. Raulston. In addition to the lily sweeps, many other plants had appeared that were not part of the original design. Every 15 feet were huge clumps of bronze-leaved hybrid cannas followed by swamp sunflower (*Helianthus angustifolius*), fronted by the Easter lilies, then the piece de resistance — clumps of variegated hostas arrayed in threes every 20 feet or so. Gone with the weekend was my carefully-envisaged color scheme, and in its place was something foreign to me. Despite the initial shock, I was optimistic. I kept walking and found one plant, the giant reed *Arundo donax* var. *variegata*, in the place I had specified. Well, one plant out of 2,000 isn't too bad; it was not, however, what I had had in mind. So, clenching my teeth, kicking my car's tires, I flounced, in fine Southern tradition, out of the Arboretum.

Two and a half months later, I met Dr. Raulston at the North Carolina Botanical Garden where he was giving a talk. He suggested to me that the border needed a caretaker and, since the Arboretum's budget was not large, I would be paid a minimum wage to work eight hours every two weeks. Salaried at $12.50 per week, I began my assault on the border. I removed the hostas, which had become crisp in the hot summer sun. I moved plants around to break up the border's profile, which resembled one giant stair step, all the plants being either two-feet tall or eight-feet tall. Because there was no mulch on the border, those 15-foot sweeps of Easter lilies had become 15-foot sweeps of weeds, most notably *Euphorbia maculata*, the insidious sidewalk spurge. Hence, I was able to occupy all my *free* time with its removal.

In five months the perennial border had filled in, but the muddle of colors still wasn't what I had in mind. I envisioned pastel clumps of the yarrow *Achillea millefolium* 'Rosea' drifting against *Coreopsis verticillata* 'Moonbeam' (thread leaf coreopsis) washing back to *Phlox maculata* 'Miss Lingard' (wild sweet William), with spires of the loosestrife hybrid 'Morden's Pink' (*Lythrum*), the hybrid speedwell *Veronica* 'Icicle', and *Yucca filamentosa* 'Golden Sword' (Adam's-needle) flowing back to clumps of the white sage *Artemisia ludoviciana* 'Silver King', green grasses, and the floating pink inflorescence of queen-of-the-prairie (*Filipendula rubra*) and a clump of *Miscanthus sinensis variegatus* (striped Eulalia grass). Plant groupings would deepen in color toward the center of the border where, in midsummer, against a rich green background of *Arundo donax* (giant reed), *Helianthus angustifolius* (swamp sunflower), and *Solidago rugosa* (rough stemmed goldenrod), masses of deep golden *Rudbeckia fulgida var. sullivantii* 'Goldsturm' (orange coneflower) would be accented by the glowing red spikes of *Lobelia cardinalis* (cardinal flower) which in turn would flow through clumps of rusty red and yellow blanket flowers (*Gaillardia*). Accompanying mounds of white-flowered *Boltonia asteroides* 'Snowbank' would brighten the whole.

I asked Dr. Raulston if we could completely renovate the perennial border and try again to bring the vision in my head to this piece of ground. Dr. Raulston agreed. Now a bit wiser, I began to plan again.

The new plan was drawn 20 feet to a sheet at a scale of one inch equaling one foot. The border was expanded to 300 feet in length and 18 feet in width. A work day was scheduled during which all the border's existing plants would be dug, labeled, bagged, and put in cold storage until the site could be prepared and replanted.

Typically, I was away during the scheduled work day, attending the New York Botanic Garden's first Perennial Symposium. Saturday morning, after a 5:30 a.m. flight to New York, I walked into the symposium just in time to hear the speaker, Fred McGourty, say "The day of the 200-foot perennial border is over." I was glad we were expanding ours to 300 feet! Then he said, "The cost of labor to maintain such a border is prohibitive," and I thought of my $12.50 a week salary.

From the symposium, I returned to Raleigh with renewed enthusiasm. The now empty border was plowed and treated with methyl bromide. Two weeks later, fertilizer was added and a string planting grid was laid down. All of this took some time. In November, exactly one month after the plants were removed, volunteers from the community and the University helped to replant the border. This time, taking no chances, I placed all the plants in the border where they were to be planted. The paths through the border were stamped down to mark their positions although the stone wasn't yet available for their construction. By the end of the weekend, the entire border was in place and we all breathed a sigh of relief. A premature sigh, as it turned out.

The fall of 1983 was unusually mild without hard frosts and the border plants, having spent a month of induced dormancy in the cooler, flushed into tender growth. Then on Christmas Eve, the temperature dropped from 70 degrees Fahrenheit to 5 degrees in four hours. Plants that normally would have no difficulty withstanding such a change in temperature were killed outright because they were not hardened off.

March 1984 found the border a desolate wasteland with only a few plants alive. And worse yet the Arboretum was to be opened on the second of June to the pre-conference tour of the American Rock Garden Society's 50th annual meeting. Panic ensued. However, there is a saying, "When the going gets tough, the tough go shopping," and I did. Armed with the plan and my checkbook I set out to fill in the border. With the help of more volunteers the border was replanted. Stone was ordered and the paths were laid. Dr. DeHertog's lilies came into play again. No, not the Easter lilies. This time various colored hybrids were grouped by color in threes and fives and planted throughout the border adding instant color. (To everyone's surprise, the lilies have become a permanent part of the border, blooming in early summer and adding delightful flashes of color as they rise above lower-growing clumps of perennials.) Once everything was in place, we began the arduous task of mulching the border; we finished about 8 p.m. on June 1st, only hours before the American Rock Garden Society arrived. By anyone's standards, the border was rather bare but to those of us who had seen the devastation caused by the freeze, it seemed truly remarkable.

The plants grew and prospered over the summer, and by September, the border appeared full of color and movement, with various asters, verbenas, and the ornamental grasses in full bloom. The following year, 1985, all of our efforts paid off as the border moved toward full maturity. The height of spring bloom comes in late May when the border is a study in pastel colors. These colors include the tender pale red-violet of *Penstemon smallii*, lavender *Verbena tenuisecta* (moss verbena), silver artemisia foliage, the fresh green and white of the emerging shoots of *Arundo donax* var. *variegata*, and the silken silver of the foliage of lamb's ears (*Stachys byzantina*). Spires of *Lythrum* 'Morden's Pink' (purple loosestrife) rise above a clump of dwarf Shasta daisy (*Chrysanthemum* x *superbum* 'Little Miss Muffet'). The shape of the *Lythrum* is repeated by the butter-yellow flower spikes of the hybrid torch lily, *Kniphofia* 'Primrose Beauty', and by the fluffy pink-beige flowers of *Calamagrostis acutiflora stricta*.

A springtime combination of particular charm centers around a planting of the large gray-leaved Bowles' mauve wallflower, *Erysimum linifolium*. Behind this are fans of an old deep purple bearded iris of uncertain variety (perhaps 'Amos') and of *Iris pallida* 'Aureavariegata' (sweet iris), whose cream-streaked foliage glows in the afternoon light. Framing the irises are clumps of *Euphorbia characias*. Raised from seed, these are variable in form; some have fat wide heads of chartreuse bracts while others have narrow green bracts. Rounding out this grouping are plantings of the hybrid *Chrysanthemum* x *superbum* 'May Queen'. (In our climate, this plant's name is misleading; it begins to flower in April.)

Elsewhere, ice blue *Phlox divaricata* (woodland phlox) and *Iberis sempervirens* (perennial candytuft) make a strong edging, punctuated by the narrow foliage and starry flowers of an unknown *Sisyrinchium* (blue-eyed grass). Behind this grouping, mounds of *Aquilegia canadensis* 'Corbett' (Canadian columbine) with its stubby, yellow dove-winged blossoms, contrasts with the narrow green leaves and steely blue flower clusters of *Amsonia tabernaemontana* var. *montana* (blue star or willow amsonia) and with the yellow and green marbled hummocks of *Sedum alboroseum variegatum*. Framing this combination, with its arching branches, is a form of the shrub *Kerria japonica* (Japanese rose), whose flowers are the color of heavy cream.

From midsummer until fall, masses of white flowers rise above the dusky foliage of *Euphorbia corollata* (flowering spurge). In September, these provide support for the arching stems of *Aster concolor*. The slender stalks of this aster are clothed in silvered leaves held upright against its stems, giving it the appearance of a dainty *Liatris* (gayfeather). Its true character is revealed when the buds borne in each leaf node begin to swell and open to deep violet-blue flowers and the stems arch gracefully forward. This tangle of white and violet bloom is complemented by the large, violet-streaked chalices of *Crocus speciosus* (showy crocus).

Another happy autumn marriage centers around the white-berried shrub, *Callicarpa japonica* 'Leucocarpa' (Japanese beauty-berry). This successful grouping features spires of sky-blue flowered *Scutellaria incana*, mounds of *Chrysanthemum* x 'Mei-kyo' with raspberry-stained pompoms which fade to pink before turning white, along with the white flowers of *Chrysanthemum uliginosum* (giant daisy) and the majestic standards of *Aconitum carmichaelii* (azure monkshood or fall-flowering aconitum). All these plants provide an elegant frame for the callicarpa.

Yes, over the years, we've had various successes. The story of the perennial border at North Carolina State University Arboretum continues. In 1988 the border was enlarged by an additional 70 feet. We were given the use of a former vegetable research plot in which to grow and evaluate new plants before including them in the border. Luckily, we have many friends in the nursery trade who have generously donated plants for evaluation. We are constantly adding new plants to the border and, blessed by the area's climate, we can work in the border almost year-round.

Not all is work; there have also been many moments of play. In 1987, the Arboretum hosted a show of sculptures, "Objects in the Garden." Among the objects were a five-member family of pink and blue plaid stegosaurus and a five-and-a-half-foot flamingo, creations of the Durham-based artist Emily E. Weinstein. The sculptures romped through the perennial border to the delight of our garden visitors. This delight caused later random placements of additional ornaments, a flock of pink flamingos and winter penguins. Yes, the perennial border offers year-round interest from late spring through winter; the inclusion of ornamental grasses not only gives the border an exciting winter profile but also provides the occasional canvas for the staff's alter egos, mad spray paint artists. (Examples of our spray paint work include the rare green and purple zebrinus forms of *Miscanthus floridulus*, and ever-pink *Calamagrostis*.) In winter, the border's flamingos fly inside while the painted grasses are joined by the flock of penguins. When spring returns to Raleigh, the penguins go into the cooler and the grasses receive a quick haircut from the rigid plastic blade of a weed cutter.

Although never planned within the color schemes at Munstead Wood, the possible combinations of flamingos with plants are endless. While I am unsure of her reaction to the lighter moments at the Arboretum, I believe St. Gertrude would smile at the success of our border. At its heart is the pleasure of gardening, the infinite possibilities offered us in terms of plant combinations, and the promise of gardening, all is possible, even a 370-foot English-style perennial border in America.

Part 2. COLORISTS

E dith Eddleman chose to illustrate Gertrude Jekyll's famous
color precepts, so often quoted and so rarely followed. She
succeeded so well that when Sir Geoffrey Jellicoe, the doyen of
English landscape architecture, visited the NCSU borders, he com-
mented, "This is an epic event in world horticulture . . . a heroic
border . . . it is beyond Jekyll." Other border builders have
elected to develop pleasing color runs by following varying sets of
rules. Often this means either eliminating or focusing entirely on
one particular color. Others partner plants according to the com-
plementary tints of the artists' color wheel, melding warm blues
and cool oranges, or mixing deep purples with chalky yellows.
Some resolve tonal difficulties by working with a limited palette,
usually excluding anything orange, magenta, or hot red. The bold
may decide to use only these hot, heavy colors, leavening them
with foliage of gray and gold. A few work intuitively, as Monet did
at Giverny, using any and every color freely, relying on an inner
sense of harmony to unite the whole mixed bag in a pleasurable
fashion.

All of these methods have their attractions, and most of us are
drawn to dabble with each in turn, hopefully in different beds or
parts of the garden. The all-white garden, dream child of the inex-
haustible Ms. Jekyll, was brought to life by Vita Sackville-West at
Sissinghurst Castle. Though this idea has been widely copied, few
of us have embroidered heavily upon the theme, enticing though
it is. White gardens, yes, but why not one in peach, salmon, and
apricot? Why not a purple garden, a red garden, a blue garden?
Think how magnificent a garden in cooper, bronze, and gold might
look, how lustrous a pearly one of lavender and purple, blue, and
silver.

Most of us plan such orchestrations for summer, but as always,
the visionary few urge us onward. Why not arrange similarly
sumptuous arrays for autumn? It is quite easy to find both flowers
and foliage in vivid reds and golds, but other schemes are also possible; white colchicum combines elegantly with silvery immortelle
(*Helichrysum petiolare*) and the opalescent snowberry, *Symphoricarpos*

x 'Mother of Pearl'. The pink and purple berries of callicarpas and the magenta ones of pernettya sing all fall when massed with dazzling nerine lilies (*Nerine undulata* and *N. bowdenii*) and shocking pink Kaffir lilies in front of 'Rose Glow' barberry (*Berberis thungerii*) or purple smokebush (*Cotinus coggygria*).

Next, we may decide to make the most of our winter-blooming hellebores, placing them near dwarf rhododendrons, evergreen ferns, hollies with golden berries or red twigged dogwood. This, of course, is the logical extension of colorist gardening, bringing it beyond the summer border to enliven the garden in every season. The idea is a natural where winters are mild, but the comments of a number of contributors throughout this volume point out the possibilities for those in cold winter climates as well.

JERRY SEDENKO is a garden designer who enjoys the challenge of working with "difficult" colors, experimenting freely to find combinations that bring out their finest qualities. After gardening in various parts of the country, he was won over by the year-round gardening climate of the maritime Northwest (USDA zone 8). He has written garden articles for several national magazines, and is working on a book about butterfly gardens.

No Time To Be Tasteful
Jerry Sedenko

One of the classic devices of the Japanese garden is the "borrowed view," whereby a distant hill or other scene of beauty is incorporated into the overall garden picture by artfully screening out visual offenses in the middle distance. Unfortunately for the modern urbanite, what with typical neighborhood densities, instead of a "borrowed view" we get stuck with an "imposed view" of some particularly loathsome object next door.

I am not overly fond of any of the purple-leaved flowering plums, an irrational personal bias, perhaps. In a garden of a certain scale, they can be used judiciously, in combination with, say, a glaucous juniper or golden yellow 'Frisia' locust, or with the myriad pale jade flowers of *Clematis ligusticifolia*. But in a tiny front yard, the bulky mass of matte leaves, the color of dried blood, overwhelm the scene—a foliar Black Hole. Wasn't I tickled to find such a beast lurking just over the property line from my new garden. I have long prided myself in my abilities as a garden colorist, but in the past have had the luxury of being able to choose my palette more freely, with a penchant for the tastefully safe tints: the pinks, lavenders, and blues, always white, with an occasional unobtrusive pale yellow. But this Thing next door created a real challenge. I decided to accept it as such. Actually, I had little choice, since beavers haven't been seen in this part of Seattle for quite some time, and a midnight injection of Paraquat would have created a bad-karma load.

There are two ways of tackling such a problem: either obliterate it, or feature it. The logic behind the second choice is that, with enough chutzpah, almost anything can be made to look intentional. This tree was definitely too large to hide. The choice was clear.

Planting other things with the same purply foliage as the plum was the most obvious trick I could use to integrate the tree into my garden picture. No longer would the tree's color stand out like the proverbial sore thumb, or, in this case, a bruised one. For edgers I used *Heuchera* 'Palace Purple'; *Setcreasea pallida* 'Purple Heart' (a relatively hardy perennial usually grown strictly as a houseplant); an unnamed *Oxalis*, looking like a maroon version of another houseplant, *O. regnellii*; and the lettuce-like purple form of the common lawn weed, plantain (*Plantago major* 'Rubrifolia'). A little farther back were 'Rubine' Brussels sprouts; *Clematis recta* 'Purpurea'; a five-foot plumy bronze fennel (*Foeniculum vulgare* 'Purpurascens'); and red orach (*Atriplex hortensis* 'Rubra'), a great leafy thing, sort of a red-leaved spinach on steroids. With just one color, and not even considering flowers, this garden was becoming pretty eclectic, containing everything from houseplants and herbs to vegetables and weeds.

I'm not about to let on that I didn't plan it that way.

Now that the purple of the tree looked integrated and purposeful, it was time to get really creative. Glaucous or gray foliage works wonders to lighten the rather weighty effect of so much darkness. Behind the plantain is a line of dwarf lavender-cotton (*Santolina chamaecyparissus* 'Nana'), for contrast of texture as well as color. The silver filigree of the low shrubby *Artemisia* x 'Powis Castle' and the rue, *Ruta graveolens* 'Jackman's Blue', serve as good foils for the *Heuchera* 'Palace Purple' and Brussels sprouts, and there's a furry rosette of the biennial *Verbascum bombyciferum* 'Arctic Summer'. Its second-year branched candelabrum, sprinkled with pale yellow blossoms, rises to an imposing six feet or more. (In this climate, hostas would have been naturals in a shadier site, but, as a further perversity of my nature, even if the site were shady, I probably wouldn't have chosen the easy way.) Golden foliage also combines well with purple, and there is a beautiful variegated lemon-balm I'm contemplating using, but as yet I've shied away from yellow-leaved things. Eclectic is one thing; chaotic, another.

Although I've come to appreciate the virtues of foliage more and more, and would love to do a garden of nothing but leafy effects, flowers add a punch to the border that is nearly irresistible. So, what to use? Certainly not the ethereal tints of my past experience. What was called for was something bold, something that would stand up to the richness of so much colored foliage.

Somewhere, years ago, I remembered reading about combining all those strong jewel tones, which are so hard to integrate into a color scheme, together in what the author (I think it was Graham Thomas) called a "Byzantine mosaic" of opulence. This notion had stuck with me, and if ever there was a time to experiment with it, this was it. Further encouragement for this idea was lent by a five-foot terra-cotta chimney pot that I had brought from my previous garden. Installed just in front and to the left of the plum, its form and color did much toward creating a focused picture in the corner of the garden. Obviously, flowers in colors relating to the chimney pot would be the way to go. All those scarlets (not the "cooler," more bluish crimsons), the oranges, and the golds, which cause the blood to race but can so easily overwhelm other colors, would find a place here. The effect of the scarlets and oranges interspersed with the murky purple foliage would be that of glowing coals on a hearth. In addition, red-violet flowers would relate to the purple foliage, and, if well chosen and of the same value as the scarlets, would combine with everything else to create a vibrant resonance. Weak-kneed self-styled aesthetes steer clear of such robust color. ("Far too brash, you know. No one in his right mind . . .") This, however, was no time to be tasteful.

Because of the height and mass of the plum tree, I needed to plant things that would be in scale, and not being a terribly patient person, I wanted sizable plants ASAP. Also, just because a garden is small doesn't mean the plants therein should be, too. You can find yourself constantly looking down on a collection of dainty niminy-piminies. Again, boldness called!

In my previous garden, I had placed a red-violet *Buddleia* next to the Michaelmas daisy 'September Ruby' (*Aster novae-angliae*), combining them with vibrant golds. I repeated the scheme here, knowing that the gray-green *Buddleia* leaves would be an added feature. Also, these plants can grow to eight feet and six feet, respectively, in one summer. A *Crambe cordifolia* (colewort) in front and to the side of the chimney pot disguised the base of that orna-ment with large, coarse leaves, blending it into the scene. And a *Crambe*'s six-by-six-foot cloud of sparkling white flowers certainly increases the scale of a garden. After the petals drop, the haze of bright green stems lasts for weeks, contrasting nicely with the plum. I don't cut these until the *Buddleia*, growing up through them, is ready to bloom in July.

Nearer the front of the border, just behind the rue and *Heuchera* 'Palace Purple', is a soon-to-be-gigantic *Ligularia* 'Gregynog Gold'. Its heart-shaped leaves, 20 inches across, give mass in an area where plant size often diminishes into the realm of cuteness. The six-foot cone of tousled orange daisy flowers adds a further emphatic bonus. Behind this is a collection of crocosmias, grown as much for the accent of their tall sword-like leaves as for their airy sprays of tropical-looking flowers. Clumps of *Crocosmia* hybrids 'Norfolk Canary', 'Citronella', 'James Coey', and 'Lucifer' front the asters, *Buddleia*, *Crambe*, and fennel, the crocosmia blossoms poised on angular inflorescences like floating tongues of flame. Another crocosmia variety, 'Solfatare', is included for the added plus of its bronzy foliage.

Other plants were also chosen for this same double duty of flowers and foliage. Next to the 'Palace Purple' are a few plants of *Lychnis* x *arkwrightii* 'Vesuvius'. The new leaves are a rich mulberry, setting off the vermilion flowers for an effect that is not for the faint of heart. Nearby is an experimental x *Lycene kubotaii*, a hybrid of *Lychnis* and *Silene*. It's quite similar to 'Vesuvius', but of a softer orange, and with a little less purple in the foliage. I'm eager to include *Lysimachia ciliata* 'Purpurea' (fringed loosestrife), with luscious dusky leaves and lemon yellow flowers. Next year. Just in front of the crocosmias is a clump of five-foot-tall hybrid *Lobelia* 'Queen Victoria', its gorgeous beet-red leafy stalks crowned by spires of incandescent scarlet flowers in late summer.

The dwarf non-stop golden-flowered daylily *Hemerocallis* 'Stella de Oro' forms a grassy clump near the *Heuchera* and *Lychnis*. Another dwarf daylily, an unnamed seedling, adds to this composition with grayish maroon flowers, virtually identical to the taller daylily 'Russian Rhapsody', which is behind and to the side. This odd color relates well to the other colors in the garden, and is precisely the color of the stems of the *Ligularia*; I'm not about to let on that I didn't plan it that way.

Geum (avens) and *Potentilla* (cinquefoil) are valued for their long season of brilliant flowers. 'Georgenberg', 'Starker's Magnificum', and 'Fire Opal' are the hybrid geums I grow here; the herbaceous potentillas are 'Flamenco', 'William Rollison', 'Fire Rim', and *P. atrosanguinea*. I do like the shrubby ones, derived from *P. fruticosa*, but opted for only the pale yellow 'Katherine Dykes', finding the orange-toned sorts inconsistent and disappointing.

To the left of the *Crambe*, next to the red orach, is a clump of *Phygelius* x *rectus* 'African Queen', whose towers of coral-scarlet are set off by lime green annual Bells-of-Ireland (*Moluccella laevis*) and *Nicotiana*. Another annual, *Bupleurum rotundifolium*, sows itself about, its airy chartreuse blossoms adding an astringent sparkle here and there. These green-flowered things, in moderation, contribute piquancy to any color scheme.

In early spring, the pink blossoms of the plum create a completely different feeling here. At this time, just about any color is welcome after our dull and dreary winters. But as soon as the riot of early season bloom is past, the color scheme gets serious again. The plum leaves are out now in their richest hue, and two late tulips pick out this color beautifully. 'Abu Hassan' is deep chestnut maroon, rimmed in gold, while the bouquet-flowering 'Wallflower' gives a lot of bang for the buck, in exactly the same shade as the plum leaves. The lavender-cotton, rue, and *Heuchera* are evergreen. Together with the tulips and the newly-emerging leaves—brilliant yellow daylily, purple *Crambe*, and blood red *Lobelia*—the show is on once again.

SOURCES
(See "Sources & Resources" appendix for complete addresses.)

Canyon Creek Nursery
The Crownsville Nursery
Lamb Nurseries

MARK HOUSER is a native of the Pacific Northwest whose first word was "flower." His garden career began over twenty years ago in Washington, D.C., with a packet of marigold seed; every one bloomed, and Houser never looked back. Now re-established in Pacific Northwest (USDA zone 8), his chief interests are in landscaping with shrubs and perennials. His current favorite combination involves placing black-leaved 'Japanese Bishop' dahlias in front of silver blue Colorado fir, *Abies concolor*.

Only You, True Blue
Mark Houser

N ewly-born gardeners often have a craving for color. Lots of color. Vast swaths of color. And color there will be: day-glo dahlias as big as basketballs, marigolds massed like lava flowing from Mauna Loa, red and white petunias crafted by Santa's helpers, spires of glowing gladioli, fields of searing red salvia, all bright enough to frighten cats and imitate the burning of Rome. Just when the garden has come to resemble a commando attack on a paint factory, the gardener installs five bushes of the rose 'Tropicana', a plant whose flower color can be described as Las Vegas lurid.

As the gardener matures and evolves, so does the appreciation of color. Bombast yields to planned restraint. Careful and coordinated waves of color come and go with the passing weeks on the floral calendar. Endlessly flowering marigolds now seem like guests who play the stereo too loudly and won't go home.

When sizzle gives way to subtlety, the gardener comes to cherish the delightful variations in foliage. We dote on blue-green, dark green, yellow-green. Yellow, red, and silver plants brighten a winter day or combine with carefully chosen summer flowers. Plants that otherwise might be dogs are selected for their bark.

Lester Hawkins, the late California plantsman, has described a gardening method you may find especially effective: Use flowers in bays among trees and shrubs. Each planting could feature a small group that flowers at the same time. Flowers backed by conifers and shrubs project with more impact, and evergreens offer all-season utility. Large island beds composed only of flowers have merit, but they can leave the spirit marooned in a Wisconsin winter. This planting strategy gives the garden a series of "events" spaced over many months and provides the ideal opportunity to experiment with flower and foliage colors.

Blue and Not Blue

The gardener is a giraffe-like creature who alternates between staring at the ground or staring at the sky. Unless these movements are coordinated perfectly, the gardener steps on an emerging lily shoot, or is impaled on a barbed-wire blackberry. With practice, the gardener learns the technique of bending over to inspect a plant while placing one foot firmly on a serenity-threatening slug. Seen in this position, the gardener is often mistaken for a pink flamingo.

While gazing skyward, the garden muralist may contemplate the fascination and frustration of blue. We may begin with the optimism expressed by Eleanor Perényi in *Green Thoughts: A Writer in the Garden* (Random House, 1981), who loved blue "more than any other color." Her love of blue extended from precious stones to cobalt skies, from ocean seas to Moslem tiles, and definitely embraced any and all blue flowers, regardless of merit.

However, the gardener quickly learns that no other flower color offers so much reward—and chagrin. Too often, plants described as blue turn out to be gray-blue, lavender, mauve, or purple. *Echinops ritro*, the very useful globe thistle, may be briefly blue but quickly turns gray. The evergreen *Azalea* 'Blue Danube' is a lurid magenta-purple, which reminds me of something I once drank at a high school party. *Ageratum houstonianum* 'Blue Blazer' is the victim of too much bleach in the washing machine. *Petunia* 'Blue Picotee' is a pleasing purple. For you the hybrid 'Blue Bird' clematis (*C. macropetala* x *C. alpina*) may sing off key. Gardeners who spend good money on these promises may wish Congress would pass a Truth In Seed Catalogs Act.

If you cannot trust the description, surely a nice glossy photo will do. Not so! Derek Fell, the garden photographer who has authored an excellent book on plant photography, explains how even the camera can be fooled. In his *How to Photograph Flowers, Plants & Landscapes* (HP Books, 1980), he explains the "ageratum effect." To a far greater degree than the human eye, the camera lens is sensitive to the red side of the spectrum. Slides or prints of a blue *Vinca minor* may appear pinkish or violet.

Seeing a blue plant in bloom is often the only way to avoid disappointment. My own knowledge of gardening derives entirely from reading, visiting gardens and nurseries, and failing. Failures in life and in gardening are the spiritual pointers given to us by the Higher Power. If emotional pain is the touchstone of spiritual progress, then failing with the gentians or with the Himalayan blue poppy (*Meconopsis betonicifolia*) allows us to learn acceptance and to say, "Well, that's show biz."

Standing alone, it looks like a frozen nudist in the middle of the road.

Blue plays another trick. Only through trying and failing can you know which shade of blue will be recessive and which shade will project from a distance. Consider the annual lobelia. The variety 'Cambridge Blue' is a true and bright color, visible from across the street. Much darker and harder to see is the variety 'Mrs. Clibran'. On this count, I still remember one of my worst gardening mistakes. A large rock garden above and behind a perennial bed was carpeted with *Lithodora diffusa* 'Grace Ward', a low-growing evergreen shrub "known" for its blue flowers. Unless the sun shone brightly, the flowers were invisible. But had I used the light, brighter shade of *Geranium* x 'Johnson's Blue', the color would have carried effectively.

For every gardener who wishes to look at the world through Gainsborough's eyes two lessons must be learned. First, blue flowers may require massing for impact. Second, some blue shades are so recessive that they can only be used in containers or other close-up situations.

Of Slugs and Shrubs
Or Blue Across the Land

Cool blue flowers can demand growing conditions that are moist and cool. Hybrid pansies offer some of the best and truest shades of blue, but many Americans can grow them only as winter or spring annuals. Given our harsh national climate zones, we may

51

have to admit that those lush scenes in British coffee table books are hard to duplicate in Kansas, Arizona, or South Carolina. An appropriate science fiction title would be *Dallas Does Delphiniums*.

Cool temperatures also suit the hardy geraniums. *Geranium himalayense* is a purple-blue paragon that spreads rapidly and self-seeds. It creeps, weaves, climbs, and is valued as a groundcover in large tree and shrub beds. I have had fun mixing it with white and yellow *Viola cornuta*. The hybrid *G.* x 'Johnson's Blue' is a lighter color, close to blue. It blooms about two weeks later and forms solid clumps. Its flowering season matches late peonies, mountain laurels, and multi-hued rock roses (*Helianthemum nummularium*).

Here in Puget Sound country (USDA zone 8) we experience a climate that varies between damp/chilly and dry/cool. From year to year there will be sharp variations in the number of sunny days. Much of the time the early growing season can be a long run of 52-degree Fahrenheit temperatures, seed-rotting drizzle, and weather forecasts promising sunbreaks. Think of us as having America's longest April. Although we grow an extraordinary range of plants, our choices are limited by Ugh the Slug. We suffer year-round slugs the way others endure fire ants, chiggers, and black flies.

Never understood is why Ugh and his brood will avoid certain plants such as annual lobelia (usually) but will cannibalize campanulas, devour delphiniums, and lunch on lupines. In the especially wet year of 1981 I grew blue and white Russell hybrid lupines. One morning I found a plant festooned with no fewer than 14 slugs, a necklace of death. In my yard slugs chew Siberian iris but ignore the Japanese sorts. It's weird. Even so, I can't fault a creature that has the good taste to eliminate dwarf marigolds.

We have weedy predators, too. Our local Nazi is the Himalaya blackberry, an imported menace like the kudzu vine in the South. In many areas it has lashed up in a pact of steel with that Viet Cong of weeds, the wild morning glory (*Calystegia sepium*), a.k.a. bindweed. I once asked a nurseryman what chemicals would stop the blackberry. "Bulldozers," he replied. "Or you might keep a few goats."

Complain I won't. For 11 years I lived in Washington, D.C. Among the taxes imposed by the capital on gardeners are heavy clay, blasting heat and smog, and monsoons fierce enough to pulverize a staked dahlia. Leaving the Gomorrah-by-the-Potomac was addition by subtraction.

I left behind, however, two of the best blue-flowered shrubs, ones that can be grown only with sufficient heat. *Hibiscus syriacus* 'Bluebird' is a charming subject, marred only by tatty foliage and gourmet appeal for the Japanese beetle. For a visual tonic on a torrid August day, try *Vitex agnus-castus* (the chaste tree); elegant, lavender spires adorn this plant, whose size is often proportional to the heat it receives.

Plant freaks have no native habitat. In the Pacific Northwest they dwell among dahlia and rhododendron monocultures. We have rhododendron gardens, rhododendron nurseries, and rhododendron breeders cranking out cultivars at an assembly line speed only equaled by daylily hybridizers. Rhododendrons suffer in parking strips, sunburn in southern exposures against buildings, and squat sullenly near fast food restaurants, their roots suffocated by a too-deep layer of bark.

Happily for gardeners in other parts of the United States, some of the best flowering blues are comparatively hardy. Usually they are hybrids of *Rhododendron impeditum* and *R. augustinii*, and they tolerate temperatures down to five below zero or lower when sheltered from winter sun and wind. Among the best are *R.* 'Blue Diamond' (lavender-blue flowers on a dense upright grower), *R.* 'Crater Lake' (as intense in color—brilliant lavender-blue—as its namesake lake), and *R.* 'Blaney's Blue' (a prolific bloomer with blue-purple flowers).

My own favorite is the dazzling 'Blaney's Blue'. What you get is a compact rhododendron with good winter foliage and flowers that project electric blue over a long distance. Companions for it might include flowering cherries, leopard's bane (*Doronicum*), Fosteriana hybrid tulips, and narcissus. If you want to try 'Blaney's Blue' or any of these rhododendron cultivars, the Greer Gardens mail order nursery in Eugene, Oregon, publishes a catalog that lists hardiness ratings for each selection.

Away from California and southern Oregon it may be difficult to grow the spectacular ceanothus or California lilac, surely among the most noble of the true blue shrubs. The plants grow very rapidly, are prone to wind rocking, and dislike heavy summer watering. One of the best is the award-winning *Ceanothus* x 'Julia

Phelps', a six- to ten-foot beacon of blue in May. My own dinner with Julia ended in 1984 when a bad freeze made her look as if she had stayed overnight in a microwave.

As much as I like the robust blue of *Hydrangea macrophylla*, the poor thing often suffers from malnutrition and perverse planting. Standing alone, it looks like a frozen nudist in the middle of the road. Plant it in groups, in partial shade, and among deciduous and herbaceous neighbors. Woodland plants by nature, the hydrangeas are hungry critters that associate with ferns, Japanese maples, and shade perennials such as astilbe, bugbane (*Cimicifuga*), and monkshood (*Aconitum*). The yellow *Hypericum patulum* 'Hidcote' (Hidcote Goldencup St. John's-wort) is a shrubby companion that also appreciates some shade. My own hydrangeas grow on the north side of a fence near *Koelreuteria paniculata*, the golden-rain tree.

How to feed and "blue" a hydrangea has occupied many garden pages. What works best for me is to mulch them heavily with pine needles in the autumn. Hydrangeas take to pine needles the way a rose responds to chicken manure; spring growth surges at an almost audible rate. 'Nikko Blue' is perhaps the hardiest and most commonly sold bigleaf hydrangea, *H. macrophylla*. The very stable true blue of its flowers projects a long distance. More tricky are the lacecap varieties such as 'Blue Wave' and 'Bluebird'. To give their best these hydrangeas want a shaded woodland. Lacecap hydrangeas may require a year or two to settle down before their true spectrum blue shade becomes evident.

Rating Flower Effectiveness

How do we evaluate flowering bulbs, annuals, and perennials? We use just about every criteria except the one factor of most concern to the garden muralist: effectiveness. Height, color, hardiness, blooming season, soil preference, and exposure can usually be learned. What we frequently lack — except by trying and failing — is knowledge of how flowers will look and how they will combine with others.

Climate and garden backdrops play a key role as well. Hot, light-saturated days can make purple more visible than blue, especially when the flowers are seen against surfaces other than green foliage. Wooden fencing tends to show off purple but mute the blues. Finding enough purple for your garden can be easily achieved with petunias, salvias, clematis, heliotropes, and verbenas. In Washington, D.C., I grew that oddity of a floribunda rose, *R.* 'Angel Face', a fragrant lavender-purple.

Because blue is a recessive color, effectiveness varies enormously. For example, I am fond of *Felicia amelloides*, the blue South African daisy. But the color is shy. To be noticed it must be massed or used close up, such as in a container. It likes cool weather and may cease blooming just when you want it most.

Falling into the subdued/massing category are three grayish-blue perennials: blue Cupid's dart (*Catananche caerulea*); the blue varieties of Stokes' aster (*Stokesia laevis*) such as the lavender-blue 'Blue Danube' or the deep blue 'Wyoming'; and caucasian scabious (*Scabiosa caucasica*). Drums and trumpets they are not, but all of them sing as cut flowers. *Stokesia laevis*, a native American plant, is much appreciated for adding blue to late summer and autumn bouquets.

"True blue" is how one of America's leading seed companies advertises *Scabiosa caucasica* 'Fama'. Penalize them 15 yards for illegal use of the adjective. Nice, but not quite true blue, 'Fama' wants to consort with the pink shades in the border. "It has taken me a long time to learn to grow it successfully," British author Beth Chatto admits of scabiosa in *The Damp Garden* (J. M. Dent & Sons Ltd., 1982). Resenting climate extremes, the plant wants an odd combination of light, limy soil and generous watering. For many areas the pincushion flower may be too prickly to handle.

Seen rarely in the Pacific Northwest is one of the most telling of all blue flowers, the annual morning glory. *Ipomoea purpurea* 'Heavenly Blue' is just that. Like the zinnias, morning-glories need heat to get jump-started, and in our climate they sulk. Cool weather yellows the foliage.

Closing up shop early is a trait shared by two richly colored blue perennials, flax and spiderwort. Before living in the nation's capital I had never seen blue morning-bloomer, *Tradescantia* x *andersoniana* or the Virginia spiderwort. One afternoon I took a lady friend to see a mass planting of it in the National Botanic Garden. When she looked at me curiously, I could only mumble, "Jeez, it was here earlier today." *Linum perenne*, the perennial flax, is one of the world's best plants for imparting light and airy effects; its flowers are sky-blue.

Of similar sky-blue color is an annual airy delight, *Cynoglossum amabile*, the Chinese forget-me-not. It is charming when massed, and the clinging seeds make me think of it as the pantleg plant.

True, strong blue is the color of the annual bachelor's button or cornflower, *Centaurea cyanus*. But it is a taxing creature. Tall forms such as 'Blue Diadem' may become bare at the base and may become martyrs to the first moderate wind. To spare us the need to think, ever-vigilant seed companies now offer dwarf strains such as 'Jubilee Gem'. Growing the tall sorts behind shrubs is one answer. I have found another.

Have you noticed how many of the best planting schemes show a strong talent for inventing and improvising? Maybe we invent because all gardeners are defiant, as noted garden writer Henry Mitchell suggests. I have the mechanical aptitude of a doorknob; more than a few times I have felt inferior, and depressed by another's cleverness in the garden. Then I found a solution for growing tall, floppy plants such as geums and coneflowers. Nearly all garden and hardware stores sell the common three-ring or four-ring tomato cage. Holy hollyhocks, I realized one day, THAT'S IT. These simple devices work wonders to prop up unstable plants; my favorite method is to use the four-ring kind with the bottom loop removed. Chancing on this solution made me feel like Walter Brattain, my great-uncle who earned the Nobel Prize as the co-inventor of the transistor.

Another blue flopper, an ideal candidate for the tomato cage, is *Aster* x *frikartii* 'Mönch'. British garden books tell you it needs no staking, but a Midwesterner, accustomed to severe thunderstorms, may argue otherwise. 'Mönch' benefits from early pinching to make it more compact and to multiply the floral effect, and this variety's cool lavender-blue daisies go well with anything. Further down my street lives an elderly couple whose August and September garden features 'Mönch' playing in an ensemble with yellow dahlias, pink Imperial Crimson lilies, red poppies, and orange-brown heleniums. It works.

You don't have to be a plant snob to want certain things in your garden when they are blooming, but consigned to another yard when not in flower. For me this ambiguity occurs at lilac time. For others it may happen in late spring when *Anchusa azurea*, the Italian bugloss, erupts with its breathtaking electric blue display. The bugloss is a baseball player that hits .375 in the spring but finishes the season with a .225 average on a last place team. When it's over, it's over.

Bells and Spires in the Garden Cathedral

Because blue is a recessive shade, it follows we should seek out plants that bloom in masses or that have large spires. Herein lies the fatal attraction of that relentless seducer that botanists could call *Delphinium frustratum*, if they truly wanted to give us helpful nomenclature. To erect a Pacific Giant hybrid is to invite every slug and thunderstorm in five states. In the movie *Patton*, actor George C. Scott talks of his persistent nightmare. "I dream there's a bullet aimed right at my nose," he confesses. Maybe Old Blood and Guts was a closet delphinium grower.

Disaster, Henry Mitchell reminds us, is the normal state of gardening. In his book *The Essential Earthman* (Indiana University Press, 1981) Mitchell writes, "Wherever humans garden magnificently, there are magnificent heartbreaks." Growing delphiniums may give you an instant humility transplant. Recently hybridizers have taken to tinkering with *D. grandiflorum*, a dwarf species. Varieties include 'Blue Mirror' (gentian blue, two feet high) and 'Blue Butterfly', and both are highly commendable.

More adaptable to America's rigorous climate are two lesser known and scarcely available members of the great campanula family. Campanulas aren't true blue, but most of them do a fine job of projecting gray-blue, lavender, or violet. *Campanula lactiflora* hails from Russia and packs the same wallop as the giant Soviet boxer in *Rocky IV*. Here you have a supernova of a plant, a whole galaxy of lavender-blue flowers atop stems that can rise to six feet. My plants grow against a fence to permit easy staking. How surprising that no garden books mention the sweet clover-like fragrance of this splendid campanula. On warm June mornings it gives a heady start to the day.

Familiar to more gardeners is *Campanula persicifolia*, the peach-leaved bellflower. Closely related is a more robust campanula with significantly different traits. Previously known as *C. latiloba* or *C. grandis*, and frequently offered under the old names, *C. persicifolia* ssp. *sessiliflora* has larger, flatter flowers, is more sun resistant, and will quickly become an effective groundcover. The blooming season parallels that of delphiniums; both the size of the flowers and their three-foot spikes make this campanula a worthy alternative. My plants of the deep purple-blue 'Percy Piper' were obtained from the Canyon Creek Nursery in Oroville, California.

No garden is proletarian if it has a lot of spikes and spires. Now that *Time* magazine has named Mikhail Gorbachev as its "Man of the Decade," I may grow several plants of *Perovskia atriplicifolia*, the Russian sage. This hardy and sun-loving plant wants a hard trimming in spring, and the gardener is rewarded with dense spikes of lavender blue in mid to late summer. Looking best in groups, its form and color make it an ideal companion for dahlias, crocosmias, and Japanese anemones. I promise to remove the Russian sage from my garden if Gorbachev does anything maliciously unwise.

I use *Kniphofia*, or red hot poker, as a color contrast against blues/purples. Five plants of the hybrid *K.* 'Gold Mine', an amber yellow, are placed directly adjacent to a trellis filled with the purple-blooming *Clematis* x *jackmanii*. In another part of the garden I have the canary-yellow hybrid *K.* 'Vanilla' mated with the rich violet *Salvia* x *superba* 'Blue Queen'. Perennial salvias make terrific cut flowers. Chopping back 'Blue Queen' sharply after she's finished her first reign will give more bloom in late August, just in time to hold court with *Rudbeckia fulgida*. The deep shading of the orange coneflower works effectively with purple. Blue might be too passive.

The flowering time of the veronicas lasts from May to September; this is a perennial family of garden spikes given to tangled branches and tangled nomenclature. A lot of them are grayish-blue and shy. Prince Charming is *Veronica teucrium* 'Crater Lake Blue', one perennial that is absolutely true blue. Dark flowers with white eyes appear in dense spikes during late May and June, and this Hungarian speedwell cultivar combines well with ledebour globeflowers (*Trollius ledebourii*) 'Golden Queen', geums, Siberian irises, and rock roses (*Helianthemum nummularium*). In my experience 'Crater Lake Blue' was reluctant to rebloom, a factor to consider if your garden is small.

With each year of my gardening experience I become more and more convinced that Siberian irises are indispensable. Not only are the Siberians a bridge plant between spring and summer, their persistent foliage enhances any landscape. For blue the best shade I have seen is the remarkable *I. sibirica* 'Cambridge', a nearly pure color with slight shading of gray. In floral arrangements there is no better companion for the first yellow roses. My plants also mix well with the neighboring mountain laurels.

Islands of Blue

There are, I believe, certain plants that show better in containers than in flower beds. One example is *Hyacinthus orientalis*. Growing five bulbs of the variety 'Delft Blue' in a small pot brings the color and fragrance closer than if the bulbs were scattered in small clumps in the flower garden. Beyond the advantages of easy placement for effect or appreciation, containers also allow the introduction of spectacular non-hardy blues. The agapanthus positively croons in confinement; this South African native blooms best when root bound. (Sure, to Californians they are a common plant, but to northern eyes they are exotics thought to be beyond reach.) Deployed in a container, agapanthus will not lean awkwardly and can be used as a conversation starter on the patio or deck.

If you ache for agapanthus, if you go ape over the plant's giant blue clusters, then have them! Do not settle for the puny dwarf types. Go with the really giant *Agapanthus africanus* (lily-of-the-Nile), and watch amusedly as visitors drool over the four-foot-high pompoms of clear blue flowers. Nothing in my garden causes as much comment as the three 15-inch tubs from which rise strong stems in July and August. The flowers are like blue aerial bombs.

I grow divisions of a single agapanthus plant purchased in 1978. Using a planter with a saucer facilitates watering and moving. When growing actively the plants are very thirsty; it's my belief the size of the flower heads corresponds to the supply of water. In the spring I feed them with liquid fertilizer until early June. As the frosts approach the plants are moved into the garage and then watered only slightly over the winter. When dormant, agapanthus wants dry soil and just-above-freezing temperatures. Every few years I use heavy lopping shears to cut open the containers and divide the very thick roots with a butcher knife or pruning saw. On several occasions the powerful roots have actually cracked open the plastic tubs. Growing these fine blue plants in portable tubs brings your Hawaiian vacation back to New Jersey.

Gardeners epitomize the human trait of wanting something we can't have, be it tropical plants in New Jersey or a garden filled with true blue plants. Be willing to experiment and to fail. Try some of these blue-flowered plants. If you cannot find them at local garden centers, consult the nursery source book recently published by the Brooklyn Botanic Garden, *Perennials: A Nursery Source Manual.* It's excellent! Be ready to learn. Be willing to fail. To fail is to be given opportunities to grow new mysteries. And when you and I finally get it right, we will both be 87 years old and ready for the great compost pile in the blue, blue sky.

SOURCES
(See "Sources & Resources" appendix for complete addresses.)

Canyon Creek Nurseries
Carroll Gardens
Greer Gardens
Andre Viette Farm and Nursery

KAREN JESCAVAGE-BERNARD has designed and renovated gardens, lectured on plants and gardens and is now a garden writer. Her wide interests include conservation, minimal-maintenance gardening, xeriscaping, native plants, shade gardening, and garden history. In her own garden (USDA zones 5–6), she enjoys finding ways to bring out the best in unpopular colors, and likes plants that make her see red.

Seeing Red
Karen Jescavage-Bernard

Although we no longer surround mounds of scarlet sage with bright yellow marigold rings, Americans still have trouble using red in the garden. "Harsh," "glaring," and "screaming" are some of the words the experts aim at red; they go on to advise us to tone down red with white, pale yellow, and light blue companions.

Part of our problem is that we are confused by red's split personality. One persona is jungly. Red takes us straight to the sensuous tropics, where brilliant flowers shimmer under indigo skies. Thanks to this association, a velvety carpet of red impatiens rolled out under our temperate trees has a thrill far out of proportion to what we expect from so simple a planting.

Red's other, completely opposite, persona is strictly formal. Geometric rows and rings of red flowers have been a feature of classical French gardens for hundreds of years. Red flowers are also indispensable in municipal plantings in England, which bequeathed them to us. In America today we still see masses and mounds of scarlet sage doing their civic duty in front of museums, town halls, and traffic triangles, vestigial floral appendixes which have outlived their public purpose.

Once we clear up the color confusion inherited from gardens in other places and other times we can think seriously about red. What does red really say to an American? Red makes us think of fast cars, fire engines, and fashion ads for slinky dresses and lipsticks. Red means excitement, adventure, and danger. To "see red" is to rage; to "wave a red flag at a bull" is to dare. The sense that red is aggressive is more than just a feeling: since the focal point of red lies slightly behind the lens of our eyes this color really does come right at us and makes us back off.

How much of this excitement can a garden handle? It depends on the viewing distance. Red flowers flanking the front entrance or paralleling the sidewalk can be dramatic. But in that part of the garden dedicated to relaxation and recreation, reds can get too close for comfort. The only place where overuse is impossible is the winter garden, where our color-starved eyes feast on red berries, red bark, and the bright red birds that replace our vanished flowers.

Whether to use red at all is hotly debated by garden designers. Is it tasteful or vulgar? Sophisticated or naive? Dramatic or just distracting? Limiting the discussion to right or wrong misses a critical design consideration: the color of the background. A white background makes every color brighter, while a dark background makes it more intense. The visual impact of a red border backed by a white picket fence, a white house, or a hedge of silvery artemisia is utterly different from the effect produced by a red planting in front of a stone wall, a house painted gray or blue, or a yew hedge. Still more important is the quality of light in the garden. In nature, red flowers are usually found in open, sunny places and there they are found en masse. We are probably 50 years too late to see wild red lilies and phlox carpeting our American prairies but the gardener who sees a French field of corn poppies (*Papaver rhoeas*) in person or in a picture grasps this point intuitively. But for the misguided efforts of professional hybridizers, we would rarely see red flowers in shade, and I never see red astilbe smoldering under the trees without wanting to head for the hose and yell, "Fire."

Most of America is blessed with the bright blue skies which red flowers require for best effect. The crisp summer light of New England, the sultry Sunbelt skies, the brilliant blue shimmer over the prairie, the dry, clear California light — all these regions provide perfect conditions for red flowers. Only the Pacific Northwest, whose gray hazy skies so closely resemble England's, has real problems with red. It's true that red flowers in a cloudy climate look as lurid as volcanos erupting against smoky skies. Good English garden design strives to minimize this awful effect by limiting the population of red flowers and toning them down with pale companions. Why we Americans continue to follow this advice is a mystery, since our climate gives us so many more options. We can harmonize, contrast, highlight, punch red up or play it down, but the rightness of red in our gardens is not an issue.

When and how to use red, however, pose real questions. The answer to "When?" lies outside the garden fence, in weed lots and wildflower plantings. In nature, color schemes are seasonal. Spring's shades of white, blue, lavender, and light yellow evolve into the blues, pinks, and brighter yellows of early summer. In high summer, color heats up in tandem with the weather. Yellow turns gold, blues darken, orange appears, and red really comes into its own. Autumn in America is the regal season. Red reigns supreme in flowers and foliage, and imperial purple asters and goldenrods join the final procession of the year. Nature has had 10,000 years since the last ice age to work out these color schemes and rhythms and gardens which take her advice are the ones which feel right and speak most eloquently of the *genius loci*, the "spirit of the place."

> . . . **I never see red astilbe smoldering under the trees without wanting to head for the hose and yell, "Fire."**

It is sometimes said that nature never makes mistakes in taste. While it's true that only human beings plant candy pink flowers next to mustard yellow ones, it surely was bad judgment to allow crimson bee balm (*Monarda didyma*) and yellow-orange *Rudbeckia hirta* (Gloriosa Daisy hybrids) to bloom at the same time. Similar mismatched red/yellow pairs can be found in most of our gardens in most seasons of the year. Spring sees the gruesome duo of pinkish-mauve *Rhododendron mucronulatum* with chrome yellow forsythia; summer offers awful possibilities among the daylilies, phloxes, purple coneflowers, and black-eyed Susans; autumn ends the gardening year with a carpet of chrysanthemums as yellow as lemon rinds rolled out under our red maples. These glaring pairs get right to the heart of Americans' real problems with red in the garden.

Pure red, whatever that may be, splits immediately into two families, the yellow-reds, which shade away through salmon, and coral toward orange, and the blue-reds, which head off in the opposite direction toward crimson, magenta, and maroon on their way to purple. Like Hatfields and McCoys, the red families never meet without causing trouble and tragedy. (Any gardener inspired to try a mass planting of geraniums in mixed shades of red, salmon, and magenta learns this lesson once and forever.) What we have not learned yet is that this deadly antipathy extends to flowers outside the two red families. Cream, yellow, gold, and orange flowers stay loyal to their flame-colored neighbors and wage constant warfare with the whole tribe of blood-red crimsons, while pink and purple want nothing to do with the scarlet family across the spectral street.

Why do we have so much trouble seeing two separate reds? One reason may be that advertising has trained our eyes to see only the scarlet half of the family. (Gardeners old enough to remember the color of fire engines before the discovery of High-Visibility Yellow will know what I mean by "scarlet." Color psychology supposedly proves that red sells, but blue doesn't. Any unscientific survey of magazine ads will turn up more red products than blue ones. The reds will all be eye-popping, but whether the product is soap or sports cars, its hue will probably not be blue-red. Thanks to our expert consumer training, when we say "red" we only see "scarlet" and this keeps us from seeing all the other shades of red in our gardens.

Another reason for our poor color perception may well be the lack of terms to describe many of the shades of blue-red. Besides crimson, we have rose, magenta, maroon, mauve, and fuchsia. Is anyone really convinced that "magenta" covers both the silvery flowers of the 'P.J.M. Hybrid' rhododendron and the fiery sparks of rose campion (*Lychnis coronaria*)? What color is the purple coneflower, *Echinacea purpurea*? Or *Rhododendron mucronulatum*? The nursery catalogs have settled for "rose-pink," but none of these tints, hues, and shades look like any roses, pinks, or pink roses that I have ever seen. A fascinating historical footnote to this dilemma is that Latin, whose dead hand lies so heavily on our own language, was rich in words for red, yellow, and purple and poor in words for blue and green. English seems to have inherited this defective color vocabulary, though how far it affects our ability to perceive blue-red is open to question.

Traditionally, English gardeners hold the blue-reds in low esteem and especially magenta, probably because it is one of nature's favorites. Magenta is an alpha and omega color, the undifferentiated dab that first faces the professional hybridizer and the final failure that claims the careful work when rigorous deadheading is not observed. Thalassa Cruso called magenta "Garden-of-Eden" since it surely must have been the primal color there. In our own ecologically-aware age we value nature's work more highly and human's "improvements" less, and so magenta has come into its own. But we still think of it as a "difficult" color, though the fault lies in ourselves and not in our flowers.

Since the experts disagree on just what red is and what to do with it, what is the poor gardener to do? First, we need to train our own eyes to see these colors clearly. The best way to do this is right on the job. Vita Sackville-West carried flowers around her garden and poked them into existing plantings to test for color harmonies. A more practical approach for a smaller American garden might be the simple Red Test. Necessary materials include a color wheel (available at an art supply store), several seed catalogs, and a letter-size piece of bright yellow paper. Clipping color photos of red flowers from the catalogs and checking their effect against the yellow background is a fast way to learn the difference between scarlet (or yellow-red) and crimson (or blue-red). Repeating the experiment with pictures of cream, yellow, gold, orange, blue, purple, and pink plants will identify all their respective allies. Flowers that look fine against yellow should stick with scarlet, but any that scream in protest should stay with crimson. Comparing the tests results with the color wheel is a quick course in the basic principles of harmony and contrast. Harmony comes from pairing near neighbors, contrast from combining colors on opposite sides of the color wheel.

A harmonious planting for scarlet flowers could include nasturtiums in flame, salmon, coral, orange, yellow, and cream, while a contrasting color scheme could use light and dark blue flowers untinged by purple. One essential harmonious companion for scarlet is the daylily. *Hemerocallis* provides unlimited variations on the yellow/orange/red theme, plus tonal refinements like contrasting throats and marginated or striped petals. Gloriosa daisies, Mexican hats (*Ratibida columnifera*), and such summer bulbs as gladioli and dahlias also offer solids, stripes, splashes, speckles, spots, and circles of subtly related colors. Scarlet's summer- and fall-blooming yellow and gold neighbors include various stonecrops (*Sedum*), yarrows (*Achillea*), columbines (*Aquilegia*), *Coreopsis*, *Craspedia*, chrysanthemums, goldenrods (*Solidago*), lupines, and loosestrifes (*Lysimachia*). Creams could include wild white indigo (*Baptisia leucantha*), foxglove (*Digitalis*), and *Yucca*. Orange offers various sneezeweeds (*Helenium*), Chinese lanterns (*Physalis alkekengi var. franchetii*), and butterfly weeds (*Asclepias tuberosa*). A wholly different effect would emerge from a planting contrasting scarlet with the varied pure blues of *Aconitum* (monkshood), *Agapanthus* (African lily), *Anchusa*, *Baptisia australis* (false indigo), *Ceratostigma* (leadwort), *Eustoma grandiflorum*, *Platycodon* (balloon flower), and *Tradescantia* (spiderwort). Blue-flowering varieties of *Aquilegia*, *Aster*, *Campanula*, *Centaurea*, *Delphinium*, *Liatris* (gayfeather), *Lupinus*, *Penstemon*, and many salvias and veronicas also belong in this contrasting palette.

The size of the planting can confront the gardener with an either/or decision. A big border or bed has room for both harmony and contrast, but a small planting can only accommodate one or the other. Red, orange, yellow, and blue crammed into tight quarters look jumbly, as if the designer hemmed and hawed and couldn't make up his or her mind. Where contrast and harmony are wanted and space is small, the trick is to add a few really intense red flowers (*Crocosmia* is one example).

Contrary to basic British advice, white is rarely right with scarlet since it makes the planting look as stark as a flag. A rare exception is the time-honored duo of *Gypsophila elegans* (baby's-breath) and *Papaver orientale* (Oriental poppy), which manages to look hazy rather than strident. White will look lovely near lilac, pink, and rose on the light side of the blue-red spectrum and dramatic with dark crimson and maroon. But white should stay away from magenta, mauve, and fuchsia in the middle, since it makes these flowers look like dingy lingerie. Silver foliage plants are also a mistake; they will turn the whole planting into cheap plastic.

A silver surround for the blue-reds is, however, a stunning choice, and anyone who sees the flowers of rose campion *Lychnis coronaria* 'Atrosanguinea') set off to perfection against its own sparkling leaves will get the idea right away. Nothing beats the artemisias here, either for a back border or a front facing. Silver-leaved herbs like lavender and Russian sage (*Perovskia atriplicifolia*) combine beautifully with all the blue-reds. So do lavender cotton (*Santolina chamaecyparissus*) and strawflower (*Helichrysum bracteatum*), if the gardener can devote time to removing their yellow flowers. Often overlooked is the combination of crimson, magenta, or pink perennials with a backdrop of shrubs and small trees with dark purple leaves. Planting light blue flowers next to the lighter blue-reds (mauve, pink, rose, and lilac) is one of the few ways to achieve the misty romance of a classic British border in our severe climate. Mixing intense shades of blue, blue-violet, and purple with flowers at the dark end of the blue-red continuum produces a rare and lovely Persian carpet. (Such a design does call for a light hand with bright reds.) Except for pairing them with silver plants, the best thing you can do with blue-red flowers is keep them close to home; don't let them wander around the color wheel. The pure blue perennials listed above work well with the whole spectrum of blue-reds. So will the many blue flowers tinged with violet or purple.

Repeating the Red Test with black and white backgrounds is tremendously helpful in planning a red bed or border. Placing color cutouts of perennials against both backgrounds will reveal the hidden mood of each flower and prevent expensive and discouraging design errors. Gardeners still unsure of their color schemes should order only those red perennials necessary for happiness and sanity and plant out the rest of the border in annuals. Winter will silence any false notes, mistakes with annual flowers are relatively cheap, and the gardener will not be taxed to find space elsewhere for a perennial that grates on the eye. The first season will not be lost, since what has grown and flourished is the designer's knowledge and understanding.

A perfect planting is a living tapestry and whether the design favors contrast or harmony, perfection can be a long time coming. Every border requires repair and reweaving, and none more so than a pattern of reds, which calls out all the gardener's sensitivity and skill. However carefully drawn the paper plan, there is just no shortcut to painting, and repainting, the garden picture in place. With red, seeing is believing.

CINDY GILBERG is the co-proprietor of Gilberg Perennial Farms, located near St. Louis, Missouri (USDA zone 6). There, she fills display gardens with a changing array of perennials, demonstrating the possibilities of various combinations to her customers. Although all colors find their places in her borders, she values the unseen — green — as much as the flamboyance of flowers. Her emphasis on foliage colors and textures reminds us that flowering plants require a firm setting in order to be displayed effectively.

Foliage as an Important Dimension for Your Sunny Garden
Cindy Gilberg

Much of gardening results in happy serendipity — and, if not, then disasters must be viewed not as failures but as lessons for next season's planting. In discussing perennials with customers at our nursery, I've discovered that it's not just beginners who become confused and overwhelmed by the challenges of gardening. Even experts have moments when they lose confidence and don't quite know where to start or what to plant in certain situations.

We're very fortunate in being able to use our display gardens for testing plants and experimenting with design. These gardens provide our customers with many ideas on plant combinations in addition to showing them what does well in our area. We founded Gilberg Perennial Farms on family property in western St. Louis County. Ours is primarily a perennial retail center with a customer base that includes the St. Louis metropolitan area, although some of our loyal regulars come from outstate Missouri and other nearby states.

The farm is in the foothills of the Ozark Mountains, fairly rough, hilly countryside that is not particularly productive. We have to add a lot of organic matter to the soil which is clayey and rocky. Our climate puts us at the northern edge of USDA zone 6, a designation that tells too little about the extremes of hot and cold (20 below to 100 above zero), wet and dry that we face every year.

When Gilberg Perennial Farms first opened, perennial gardening was not very well known or much practiced in the St. Louis area. We have reintroduced many plants that enjoyed popularity years ago and introduced even more that have never before been grown here. Therefore, in many cases, we've had to learn the envirnomental requirements and limits of many species and cultivars.

Gardening with perennials has more possible combinations than the state lottery. What then separates the average garden from a truly great garden? One aspect of garden design that is vital to a good garden design is the use of plant foliage for texture and color.

We gardeners sometimes are blinded by plants' flower qualities. As we've mastered garden design with flowers, we have often found something is still missing. That missing quality may well be the artistic use of plant foliage as a major design element.

Even experts have moments when they lose confidence.

To be sure, one of our ambitions in gardening is to create substantial drifts of flower colors that complement each other and delight the eye. But many of our favorite flowering perennials, such as phlox, asters, shasta daisies, and coreopsis, have medium texture and medium green foliage. What will the garden look like when the plants aren't in bloom? Textural differences can provide new dimensions to make a garden stand above the ordinary.

Plants that deviate from this middle-of-the-road type foliage add special qualities and help to break up what I call the "sea of green." The characteristics that distinguish these from other perennials are gray, blue-green, bronze, gold, or variegated foliage, and also large or boldly-textured foliage. Unusual or striking growth habits can also add interest. Ornamental grasses are good examples of plants with an unusual growth habit and foliage that is attractive in its own right. The Scotch thistle (*Onopordum acanthium*), up to ten feet tall with large silvery leaves that are prickly and deeply toothed, is bold in many respects.

Through the years, I've come to love the textures of plants as much as the flowers. Each year I've tried new plants and new combinations. Some worked out well in my garden designs; others did not. And sometimes when I thought a garden was quite successful, a critical eye would reveal that something was not quite right. The planting might be fun, with blasts of color through the season, but then, quite frankly, it would be just plain boring when nothing special was in bloom.

As I searched for cures, various plants happened into my garden.

A planting of *Artemisia* x 'Powis Castle' settled in between some dark-leaved *Heuchera* 'Palace Purple' and the late-blooming double pink *Anemone* x *hybrida* 'Whirlwind'. The result was striking! Silver foliage has a way of softening or cooling the overall effect, making a pleasant foil for blue or pink flowers and a delightful contrast to more ordinary foliage.

Other favorite silver-leaved plants are beach wormwood (*Artemisia stellerana*) and a selected form of the common wormwood, *A. absinthium* 'Lambrook Silver', with foliage similar to *A.* x 'Powis Castle'. Russian sage (*Perovskia atriplicifolia*) with its silver-green shrubby growth is covered with soft, sky-blue flower spikes in mid- to late summer. *Dianthus* x *allwoodii* 'Alpinus' performs well for me, providing a low, gray-green, spiky mound with fragrant summer flowers in varying shades of pink to white. Others with silvery foliage that flourish in our midwestern climate include the yarrow *Achillea* 'Moonshine', snow-in-summer (*Cerastium tomentosum*), basket-of-gold (*Aurinia saxatilis*), Siebold stonecrop (*Sedum sieboldii*), and lamb's-ears or woolly betony (*Stachys byzantina*). All the silver-gray plants in my garden perform best when if given a midsummer trim, after they've bloomed.

Another cure for garden boredom is the use of plants with variegated foliage. A section of garden in front of one corner of our very dark-colored house seemed to be crying for help. A handsome clump of green-and-white striped *Miscanthus sinensis variegatus* provided relief and did much to visually soften the lines of the house. This ornamental grass has grown into a graceful fountain over five feet tall and about four feet wide that now serves as a focal point for that part of the garden. An added bonus of *M. s. variegatus* is that it does fairly well in partial shade. This *Miscanthus* and others, most notably *M. sinensis* 'Gracillimus' (maiden grass) and its varieties, form elegant arching clumps of thin leaf blades. From a distance, these grasses have a vase shape that is topped in the fall with soft plumes.

Tender yet lovely is the green and gold variegated cultivar of the common culinary sage (*Salvia officinalis*) that I use in both herb and perennial beds. Planting this sage in a protected corner and providing extra mulch in late fall helps it survive through the winter. I grow the green and gold showy stonecrop, *Sedum spectabile* 'Variegatum', exclusively for its foliage since I don't find the flowers particularly interesting either in color or form. Either one of these will complement white- or yellow-blooming perennials with finer foliage textures, such as *Coreopsis verticillata* 'Moonbeam' or *Geranium sanguineum* 'Album'.

The green-and-white striped iris, *Iris pallida* 'Variegata', is a plant that I expected to be weak. I had never seen it growing in our area and had seen too many variegated "gems" burn or lose their variegation in our climate. Nonetheless, I first planted it in a hot dry area to give it the real Midwest test. It performs beautifully, holding its foliage and color well through the season. The soft lavender-blue flowers are a late spring bonus. Adding plants with variegated foliage is an easy and extremely effective way to add new interest in any area of the garden.

Large or boldly-textured foliage can enliven the overall look of the garden. One of my favorite additions to a perennial garden is late-flowering *Anemone*, either the Japanese anemone, *A.* x *hybrida* (*A. japonica*), or the grape leaf anemone, *A. tomentosa* (syn. *A. vitifolia*). They have been consistent in holding up through our summers with a late summer blooming period as an additional reward. The leaves are large enough to provide good contrast with fine-textured perennials.

We have used garden rhubarb (*Rheum rhabarbarum*) in mass where our plantings tend to have an abundance of finely-textured perennials. Large leaves atop darker red-green stems make rhubarb ideal for background or contrast plantings. While the edible rhubarb has ornamental relatives (*R. palmatum* with deeply lobed leaves, *R. p.* var. *tanguticum* with darker foliage), garden rhubarb is easier to find and grow. I have found that perennials that flower in white, light pink, or pale blue blend best with the brilliant red stems of the rhubarbs. A few suggestions are New York aster 'Boningale White' (*Aster novi-belgii*), white perennial flax (*Linum perenne* 'Album'), pink baby's breath (*Gypsophila paniculata* 'Pink Fairy'), and hardy ageratum (*Eupatorium coelestinum*).

The giant butterbur (*Petasites japonicus* var. *giganteus*) is a plant with huge round leaves (three feet by two feet) and invasive roots that is commonly used at water's edge and in bog gardens. We have tucked it in the corner of a boggy raised bed in our waterfall area where it is easy to control. It makes a handsome contrast to cattails

(*Typha* spp.), horsetail (*Equisetum* spp.), Japanese iris (*Iris ensata*, syn. *I. kaempferi*), and other bog plants.

Scotch thistle (*Onopordum acanthium*), previously mentioned, is a real eye-stopper for not only is it absolutely huge (eight to ten feet high), it also has large downy silvery leaves that are deeply cut and spiny. This plant could be used as an architectural focal point. Once it goes by in late summer, it can be a giant eyesore; therefore, I have placed it next to a high screening fence where it can be chopped out and the site shielded by late-blooming companions such as coneflower (*Echinacea*), boneset (*Eupatorium*), or *Anemone tomentosa*.

The plume poppy (*Macleaya cordata*) is another impressive silvery-green giant, often ten to twelve feet tall. Its large rounded leaves flutter in the breezes to reveal downy white undersides. It does come with a caution, however: Be sure to remove all spent flowerheads, for the plume poppy can reseed heavily. We placed it on a large berm that separates our parking lot from display gardens, where it is very effective with *Hibiscus moscheutos* 'Southern Belle' and a border of the ornamental grass *Pennisetum alopecuroides*.

Spiny bear's breeches (*Acanthus spinosus*) has large, deeply cut foliage that is dark, glossy green. It flowers in early to midsummer with four-foot spikes of lavender and white. The individual one-inch flowers are cupped in shiny bronze-green bracts tipped with spines. Place it where it can be clearly seen as its foliage truly is fascinating, a bold note to play against plants with run-of-the-mill foliage or against light-colored fences or walls.

Filipendula rubra 'Venusta' is a fine cultivar of our four- to seven-foot American native that has large rosy flower plumes. This queen-of-the-prairie has large pinnately compound leaves and forms a sizeable clump. In hot dry summers these plants will suffer if not provided with a deeply tilled, water-retentive soil and, of course, irrigation water.   For bold texture and late bloom, I use the hardy hibiscus or rose mallow (*Hibiscus mosheutos*) which is available in several handsome cultivars, including 'Disco Belle Rosy Red', 'Disco Belle White' and 'Southern Belle'. The flowers are often well over six inches in diameter, an impressive sight. It resembles a shrub but is completely herbaceous; note that it is very late to appear in the spring. The leaves as well as the flowers are boldly large.

There are a few plants that have dark red to bronze foliage, adding yet another dimension to the palette of foliages. Some of the dark-leaved sedum varieties are among the most familiar. These are very effective when used with lighter-colored stones or pebbles. Red and bronze foliage is striking when intermixed with plants that have light green, grayish, or silver foliage. The large, dark-red leaves of *Heuchera* 'Palace Purple' provide a pleasant contrast in foreground plantings when it is backed by dull or ordinary greens. Its flowers are inconspicuous, but I think that's an acceptable compromise. To explore beyond this short list of plants with foliage potential, one need only walk into a garden. Let your eyes wander over the different foliages and then ask yourself "What catches my eye?" Nine times out of ten, it will be a plant with one or more of the qualities mentioned here. Make note of great combinations and, most of all, experiment!

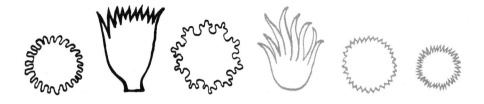

Part 3. REGIONALISTS

The search for a national garden style has been going on for some time now. The excitement dies down, then flares again as yet another unilateral concept is proposed. A few of the ideas get considerable media play, but very few gardeners have cleansed their gardens of all but native plants, or reduced their plant palettes to a few fashionable favorites. Media pressures notwithstanding, garden makers know that the generic American Garden is strictly a novelty item.

Apparently, the idea is to refine American style into a reproducible essence. Questionable as this goal may be, developing an all-purpose plant palette that works all across the country is even more ridiculous. The inevitable result is a homogenized reductionism, for pursuing the least common denominator is a losing game. By exploring and exploiting legitimate regional differences, we move away from an archetype toward the personal. Celebrating regional diversity also celebrates the quirky individuality of each gardener. Rather than playing it safe within a strict framework of plants and design rules, why not work toward melting pot gardening, mingling precepts and lessons from other traditions with our own notions, borrowing freely and experimenting often. This may lead to anarchy, and it's a dead certainty that some perfectly dreadful gardens will be made, but so what?

Formalists are horrified at the prospect of so much potentially bad taste thus unleashed, but life is always a messy process. Look what it takes to make a simple omelet. If our gardens are to be living ones, our tradition in the making a lively one, then surely a few broken eggshells along the way are a small price to pay. After all, garden revolutions are less dangerous than most other kinds, involving chiefly the question of good taste. For some reason, Americans are readier to accept fashion dictates in the garden than anyplace else. This is too bad, for lapses of accepted taste may lead to significant departures from the common run of design. Not all will be advances, certainly, yet uncomfortable as they often are, radical concepts shake us out of complacency, forcing us to question all that we assume.

In the garden, as elsewhere, our preconceptions blind us to reality, and limit the possibilities. When Monet first made his garden at Giverny, the most influential gardeners of his day regarded it as a hideous, self-indulgent blot. To this day, few sophisticated gardeners will openly admire Monet's garden, yet it has enormous populist appeal; it is colorful, simple and obviously achievable. In this volume, we artfully dodge the question of taste; it is an entirely individual affair. We do, however, hope to encourage the kind of questioning that leads the gardener away from the safe and simple to examine thoughtfully the more complex puzzle of what is regionally and personally appropriate.

In a sense, of course, all of our contributors are regionalists, learning to garden where they live. For some, the enforced alteration of garden plans and plants comes hard. Some abandon the old wholesale to embrace the new, employing native plants to the exclusion of anything else. Others stubbornly strive to coerce old favorites to thrive in unsympathetic terrain. Resistance to native plants often stems from the mistaken belief that the garden will be entirely filled with roadside weeds. It's true that few wild flowers look as prepossessing as a well-grown border perennial, yet it is amazing what good culture can do for a plant. Here we might take advantage of research conducted by the English and the Germans, both of whom have sifted a sizeable chunk of the North American flora for good-looking, well-behaved winners. Curious gardeners will want to try lesser known natives as well, but the wise will evaluate newcomers in nursery beds rather than the garden proper, where rampant takeover tendencies or other unsociable habits may be discovered without risking disaster. Regional nurseries and seed companies, or native plant societies, are likely to prove good sources of information, plants, and seed, providing as well the company of the like-minded.

Regionalists don't necessarily confine themselves to native flora, but they do select exotic plants according to their own native conditions. Though the USDA zone maps are useful to some degree, they can't begin to compare with specific local knowledge. As contributor Stephanie Spencer notes, plants that grow just fine in the Pacific Northwest may die in the Carolinas, though both areas are nominally USDA zones 7 and 8. Hot nights stress plants accustomed to cooler climes. Similarly, ornamental grasses that grow equally well in both locations will flower magnificently in the Carolinas and little or not at all in maritime Northwest, where the accumulated daytime heat is insufficient.

Regionalists spend a lot of time in other people's gardens, looking at what thrives and fails, comparing microclimates, listening to the experiences of others, then experimenting on their own. Regionalists make the most of what they have. Dreadful soil and alkaline water, biting winds and torrential rains, bitter frosts and tropical heat can be daunting to plants and gardeners alike. By seeking out and selecting for plants that thrive under the worst conditions, by staying flexible and adapting their techniques, regionalists may succeed where traditionalists fail.

WILLIAM WELCH is a landscape horticulturist, teacher, and writer, and an expert on plants that tolerate the extreme conditions that characterize the Texas Gulf Coastal Plain (USDA zones 8,9,10). His recent books, *Perennial Garden Color* (Taylor Publishing Company, 1989) and *Antique Roses for the South* (Taylor Publishing Company, 1990) are invaluable regional resources. Dr. Welch enjoys his plants broiled medium rare.

The Broiled Border
or Gardening in the Gulf Coastal Plain
William C. Welch

As a professional horticulturist, writer, and teacher, I have devoted a lifetime to that frustrating, sometimes absorbing, often rewarding question of just exactly which trees, shrubs, and plants will thrive on the Gulf or Southern Coastal Plain, the area generally considered to extend 150–200 miles inland from the Gulf of Mexico. Here in zones 8, 9, and 10, plants must overcome a combination of very high temperatures and generally high humidity; our summers don't just fry vegetation, they broil and steam it overnight. If plants don't succumb to the heat during the day, diseases caused by our nighttime heat and humidity usually finish them off.

To be considered gardenworthy, not only must a plant survive under these conditions, it must also bloom, grow well with minimal care, and make a good display in the garden. Among the perennials, the majority of plants that fulfill these criteria are natives, native hybrids, or very special imports.

Choosing the right cultivars is essential to success, but finding commercial sources for the plants is a major problem. There is a very welcome movement afoot in the nursery trade to satisfy the public demand for more adapted plants, so the situation is improving. Until the nursery trade meets market demand, the gardener must rely on swapping and gathering.

Since division is a necessity for many perennials, quite often the difficult-to-find plants can be obtained by sharing these "extras" with friends and neighbors. Other excellent cultivars can be obtained by "swapping" with experienced local gardeners, and through market bulletins and magazines.

79

Seed gathering is another way to obtain regionally adapted native plants. When in bloom, the wild plant should be clearly and permanently marked. When the seed ripens, you can return to gather it and, for most perennials, sow it soon afterward. In this way you can know what the plant will look like and preserve it in the garden while conserving the wild population.

I have always had a special interest in dooryard and cottage gardens throughout the South. Often the product of very limited resources, these plantings teach valuable lessons in traditional garden design, plant choice, and cultivation methods, all tried and true over years of hardship, climatic and otherwise. The classic cottage garden is an enclosed front dooryard, surrounded by a closely-clipped privet hedge or wood fence, with a brick, stone, or packed dirt walk to the front door. Blooming annuals, perennials, and roses, packed closely together, positively erupt from the yard. This sea of flowers often includes small fruit trees and ornamental vegetables as well as colorful vigorous roses and vines on trellises and fences. The plants of this mini-paradise are some of my favorites, and often fulfill my admittedly difficult criteria for plant selection.

In the cottage garden, past and future meet. The gardeners who tended humble pioneer dooryards did not have modern garden hoses and sprinkler systems. Today, the catchword in the drier parts of the South and Southwest is "xeriscape"—a concept that promotes the use of plants and landscape design practices that require little irrigation water. With increasing emphasis on conserving our water resources, this is a relevant topic indeed. Water needs should be one criteria of plant selection.

On the whole, cottage garden plants are tough, self-reliant survivors worthy of twentieth- (and twenty-first!) century rediscovery. In the following paragraphs I have listed a few favorite cottage garden plants, including natives and native hybrids, along with some of their characteristics.

Yarrow (*Achillea millefolium*) is a fine perennial with ferny foliage and drought tolerance; the newer colored sorts have more garden value than the white type. The common name "sun fern" aptly describes the appearance of yarrow, but, of course, ferns do not flower. Few plants are as useful inside the house, as either fresh or dried blossoms. My favorite colors are the rosy purple ones, like *A*.

millefolium 'Fire King', although their rich colors fade to pink and lavender during the heat of our summers.

Aquilegia, the columbines, seem delicate but some are widely naturalized or are native to springs and seeps of the Hill Country and Big Bend regions of Texas. The golden columbine (*A. hinckleyana*) is my favorite; it is a short-lived perennial or reseeding biennial in most of Texas. The red and yellow wild columbine (*A. canadensis*) is also useful, but not as spectacular in the garden because of its more subdued colors. Both may be readily started from seed in the fall and are especially useful as sources of color in shady and partially shaded areas.

In the cottage garden, past and future meet.

The best perennial aster I have grown is similar to *Aster* x *frikartii*, but blooms only in the fall. *A. oblongifolius* is popular from eastern Texas to far western Texas and is occasionally available in nurseries and garden centers as *A.* x *frikartii* or autumn aster. Flowers appear in mid- to late October and cover the mounding plants with small lavender-purple flowers. Plants are started by division in the spring. These, with mums, marsh mallows (*Althaea officinalis*), and obedient plants (*Physostegia virginiana*) give color to fall gardens in the Gulf Coastal Plain.

I like the old "wild" perennial wormwood or western sage, *Artemisia ludoviciana*, which multiplies by underground runners and colonizes waste places and old house sites. It has exactly the same clean scent as common wormwood (*A. absinthium*), but survives with almost no care. Pinching promotes branching and prevents floppiness later in the season. The gray foliage is a welcome addition to the garden but the plant is so vigorous that it can become a pest in good soils. Southernwood (*A. abrotanum*) is less vigorous, but equally nice.

Five perennial wildflowers, coreopsis, cigar plant, boneset, coneflower, and Indian Blanket, are all good garden subjects. The cultivars of lance-leaved coreopsis (*Coreopsis lanceolata*) and tickseed (*C. grandiflora*) are best and include new dwarf kinds like 'Baby Sun' and 'Sunray'. Selections of thread leaf coreopsis, *C. verticillata*, such as 'Zagreb' and 'Moonbeam', offer beautiful finely-textured foliage, but these are more dependable where night temperatures and humidity are lower, 100 or more miles inland from the Gulf. (The immediate coastal climate, unfortunately, sets up an environment favorable to fungal root rot.)

Two of the *Cupheas* are natives of Mexico and are valuable in Gulf Coast gardens. *Cuphea micropetala*, sometimes called "cigar plant," attracts multitudes of hummingbirds with its red and yellow tubular flowers, which appear in September. *C. hyssopifolia* is known as Mexican heather and flowers throughout the warm season. It is not, however, as cold hardy as *C. micropetala* and is actually an annual for all but zone 10 and the southern part of zone 9. Drought tolerant, both species are at home in our long, hot summers.

Boneset is the common name for our tall wild ageratum (*Eupatorium coelestinum*), which grows from white underground roots and blooms in late summer and fall. In the eastern parts of our area, it inhabits ditches and boggy places, but can do with less water. It can be overly aggressive in well-prepared soil.

The purple coneflower (*Echinacea angustifolia*) of our fields and pastures is the narrow-leaved kind, but the garden cultivars of *E. purpurea* like 'Bright Star' succeed almost as well. White forms like 'White Lustre', however, have not been as vigorous in my garden. Purple coneflowers are among the most long-lasting and useful cut flowers to be grown in Southern gardens.

The native "Indian Blankets" (*Gaillardia pulchella*) so abundant along our roadsides are mostly annuals. However, *G.* x *grandiflora*, a garden-worthy hybrid blanket flower, is sometimes perennial in Texas and the Gulf South. One of the best cultivars is 'Goblin'; its warm red-orange petals end in bright yellow tips. The daisy-like flowers of 'Goblin' add color to the garden until frost.

Hamelia patens or firebush has become very popular in the San Antonio area. It is a tropical shrub that has been grown for many years in a few South Texas and Florida gardens. The flowers resemble large red woodbine honeysuckle blooms. Reliably root-hardy only in zones 9 and 10, firebush provides lots of color with little care, even in the hottest and driest of conditions, from late spring until late fall.

The jewel-like colors of modern daylilies are wonderful, but I still have a fondness for their ancestors, *Hemerocallis fulva*, the tawny daylily, and *H. lilioasphodelus* (syn. *H. flava*), the yellow form. 'Kwanso Variegata' is the double orange form that is also ancient.

These are found in old gardens and appear to be the most insect- and disease-resistant of all. The newest daylilies have the advantages of repeat flowering, miniature as well as large-growing types, and a wide color range. I like to see gardens in which a wide mixture of colors is used to provide a kaleidoscopic effect.

The huge white spider lilies (*Hymenocallis* spp.) are bulbs I would like to see used more often in our gardens for their exotic flowers and lush tropical foliage. They are, admittedly, difficult to find in commerce. A cultivar of unknown origin, now commonly called 'Tropical Giant', can often be found in old gardens in the Gulf Coast states. It bears large umbels of flowers in late June and early July and is one of the finest foliage plants available for Southern gardens, growing readily wherever adequate moisture is available. The large, dark green foliage and fragrant, white flowers make an excellent accent in the garden.

Upland parts of our region, less humid than the Gulf Coastal Plain, have better luck with the tall bearded irises, while the Louisiana and spuria sorts do well over the entire South. Nurseries that specialize in irises carry the best selections. Mallows are excellent plants that are too often neglected. *Malvaviscus arboreus* var. *drummondii* may be the most useful of all the native mallows. The small, red-turbaned flowers occur throughout the growing season and thrive in sun or shade. *M. arboreus* is the giant Turk's cap or wax mallow. It has larger flowers, often reaches five to six feet in height, and is root-hardy into zone 8. Both mallows attract hummingbirds, butterflies, and bees.

Narcissus is a much-loved denizen of the cottage garden, and some of the old species, hybrids, and cultivars are our first presages of spring. My favorites are the "paperwhites" (forms and varieties of *Narcissus tazetta*), the Chinese sacred lilies that bear clusters of small white miniature daffodils, including the hybrid 'Grand Monarque'. I also enjoy the common jonquil with golden yellow flowers (*N. jonquilla*), and its hybrid (*N.* x *odorus*), the campernelle. Another hybrid (with the tazetta narcissus) is *N.* x *intermedius*. These persist in cemeteries and waste places all over the older inhabited sections of the Gulf Coast, where they thrive and multiply. Their bright colors and dark green foliage along with wonderful fragrance are especially cheering to a gardener after the gray days of winter.

There are several native penstemons I have learned to appreciate, especially *Penstemon tenuis* (Gulf Coast or sharp-sepal penstemon), which has small lavender cupped bells. It gives an airy feeling to the garden, especially when planted between larger, more coarsely-textured plants. *P. tenuis* is not very particular about drainage.

An old-time favorite is summer or garden phlox, *Phlox paniculata*. The magenta-pink form is by far most common and is found all over the South. If summer rainfall is adequate, phlox can bloom most of the summer and into the fall.

The obedient plant received its name because its flowerheads remain wherever they are moved on the stalk. Native with us, *Physostegia virginiana* blooms in August through November in a mauve pink. The white cultivar, 'Summer Snow', blooms earlier in my garden. Obedient plants like wet locations and thrive even in poorly drained soils.

The tender pale blue *Plumbago auriculata* (Cape leadwort or blue plumbago) is root-hardy in zones 9 and 10 and may be used as an annual elsewhere. Drought and heat tolerant, its color persists over a very long season; the flowers need not be removed to continue a tidy appearance.

There are several forms of the wild or Mexican petunia that are among our toughest perennials. *Ruellia brittoniana* is native to Mexico and has escaped cultivation in the Gulf Coastal Plain of Texas and the South. It has broader foliage than the equally common *R. malacosperma*. Both plants reach three to four feet in height and bloom with lavender-purple petunia-like flowers spring through fall. A lower-growing form is often sold as "Blue Shade" in the San Antonio area and is sometimes used as a groundcover.

The crinum lilies, *Crinum bulbispermum* and its hybrids, are historic Southern beauties that require little care and have large scapes of pink, white, or striped flowers from late spring until frost. Known regionally as "milk and wine lilies," they are often found in old cemeteries and home sites. New hybrids and old ones are all fine, but finding them through commercial sources is often challenging.

A very old-fashioned favorite in cottage gardens is the *Dianthus* species. Dianthus requires very good drainage and will die if kept too wet. Otherwise, all but the alpine varieties do well. My favorite, probably a form of *Dianthus caryophyllus*, is a red carnation with a long history of cultivation by old German families of Central Texas. It blooms practically year-round and roots readily from stem cuttings in the fall. Dianthus tend to be short-lived and usually last two to three years in my garden. Keeping a supply of rooted cuttings coming along is an easy and practical way of perpetuating these beautiful plants.

Our perennial salvias are really garden mainstays. *Salvia greggii* (autumn sage or cherry sage) is a fine native plant with rose-red flower spikes and rosemary-like foliage. Other colors — pink, white, and salmon — have recently been made available from plants collected in Mexico. The mealy-cup sage (*S. farinacea*) comes in white or violet-blue and is equally successful. 'Indigo Spires' is a new hybrid that seems to have inherited the sage's rugged constitution, but has larger flower spikes. *S. leucantha*, Mexican bush sage, is primarily a fall bloomer, but is a wonderful garden subject for South Texas.

The Mexican mint-marigold or sweet-scented marigold (*Tagetes lucida*) is the only member of its group that appears to be resistant to spider mites in our area. It is a drought-tolerant perennial in zones 9 and 10 and has handsome single golden flowers atop its stems from October through November. Its foliage is used like tarragon for cooking and is also popular as a tea; the flowers are a source of yellow dye.

With these dependable heat-tolerant flowers, our long summers can be less bleak for the garden and the gardener. While the concept of an old-fashioned cottage border may not be practical for every town and city dweller imprisoned by rows of variegated privet or pittosporum outlining the house foundations — take heart! A few of these perennials massed in front of such foundation plantings can add pockets of color and individuality to the most ordinary of landscapes.

SOURCES & RESOURCES
(See "Sources & Resources" appendix for complete addresses.)

Antique Rose Emporium (Perennials and old roses)
The Fragrant Path (Seeds of old fashioned perennials and annuals)
Louisiana Market Bulletin
Ty Ty Plantation (Crinum lilies and other bulbs)

PATTI HAGAN has written garden articles for numerous national publications, and is currently a regular contributor to *The Wall Street Journal*. Her horticultural interests include clematis, of which she grows nearly a hundred kinds, as well as conservation and wild flower gardening. Hagan lives and gardens in Brooklyn, New York (USDA zone 6), but the hostile urban environment she describes so well might be relegated to the Twilight Zone.

Gardening
Countering the Crack Attack
Patti Hagan

Brooklyn, N.Y.

It's spring in the city, April in New York, and the crack gardeners—the ones who draw their horticultural inspiration from the dirt-cheap, lethal cousin of cocaine—are back working the soil and the street. Plant muggings on this block already include a purple primrose by the roots and three hyacinths by the bulbs. Crack gardeners finger plants for their resale value. A vial of crack goes for $2.50 or so in this borough: An azalea is two vials of crack, a rose three or four.

According to a June 1988 *Time* cover story, quite a lot of Americans are into gardening these days, and, according to a *Time* cover just a month earlier, quite a lot of Americans are also into crack. *Time*, however, failed to make the crack/gardening connection. I will, because my Brooklyn street garden is situated smack on the frontier of this new urban American gardening trend.

Crack gardeners care about ornamental plants only in so much as the plants can be cashed for crack, and so they prefer upscale shrubs and perennials. In inner-city neighborhoods such as mine, crack gardening has given rise to counter-crack gardening. For this reason, urban gardening must be reckoned among the most advanced of our indigenous gardening schools. (Nevertheless, counter-crack gardening has yet to be acknowledged by any experts on urban gardening.) Counter-crack gardening requires a radical change of style. My street gardening has become combative, thorny and downright offensive—I am plotting a plot of thoroughly vicious plants.

A year ago the first crack gardeners hit my neighborhood, tearing apart the charming street garden of a floral designer. Over the course of a week, working weeknights, they stole a weighty terra cotta planter filled with herbs and flowers; a flatsworth of lettuce; a white azalea; and roses, among them a blooming, pink 'Betty Prior'. They hacked at the limbs of a Rose of Sharon and left the branches dangling by a thin bark skin. They uprooted a border of 24 pink wax begonias. They cut the chains securing some large, top-of-stoop planters and disappeared them.

An azalea is two vials of crack, a rose three or four.

Across the street and around the corner the MIAs included: three azaleas, one *Pieris japonica*, euonymus bushes, roses and three 'Enchantment' lilies. Crack gardeners are not mere blossom snatchers — they appreciate the higher resale value of the whole plant, and always steal the roots.

At the height of the crack gardening spree, officer Bert Marrero of Brooklyn's 77th Precinct told me: "I just locked up a guy for stealing some shrubbery. He was a crack addict, trying to sell the shrubbery to the merchants on Flatbush Avenue . . . Crack is an inexpensive drug. With a few bucks they can make a buy. So they're rippin' little things off . . . Don't be surprised if they take your plants and we don't get the perps."

I did not much like 'Cary Grant', the rose, when we met at the 1988 New York Flower Show — an orange-juice colored, fragrantless modern. But crack came into the garden and my neighbor lost a rose. I suggested 'Cary' — a hyper-thorny hybrid tea, a brass knucks of a rose. 'Cary Grant' lasted two weeks in Brooklyn.

It is possible that the nursery business will do as well by the crack epidemic, considering the garden fallout, as has, inadvertently, the baking soda biz. For instance, a gardening friend, fed up with crack plant predators, last spring ordered 100 'Simplicity' roses from Jackson & Perkins, which guaranteed the protection of "100 feet of Simplicity Living Fence." A year later, 37 'Simplicity' roses remain. In the interim, various of the crackheads who had done the stealing approached the gardener with excellent buyback deals.

This woman had begun the garden in 1986 to give street kids

something to do. By 1988 she knew that several of her little gardeners also were working as crack runners. She lost some kindergarteners when she decreed: "Either garden or run drugs—you can't do both!"

Last year during fall "bulbing," instead of squirrels digging up her bulbs, crack-heads dug them—and tried to sell them back to her. And one autumn day the crack gardeners made off with a hand truck, seven spades, 17 trowels, hand cultivators and shovels. "I am not ready to put my life on the line for gardening tools," my friend informed me.

Crack is a pestilence for which there is no pesticide. Urban counter-crack gardeners begin to envy suburban gardeners their kinder, gentler pests—aphids, grubs, bugs, slugs. Nowhere in Ursula Buchan's British *Bouquet of Garden Writing* (David R. Godine, 1987) do I find Gertrude Jekyll, Vita Sackville-West, William Robinson, E.A. Bowles or Reginald Farrer complaining of anything more noxious than slugs and snails. Nor do any of the 13 authors in the Pests and Poisons chapter of *The American Gardener* (Farrar, Straus & Giroux, 1988) deal with anything more pesky than children and apple tree borers.

Some counter-crack gardeners dream about booby-trapping the petunias. A neighbor recalls the tactical value of upfront blackberries in his East Harlem youth, "Blackberries! That's the thing! Nobody'd touch those vicious bushes!" Enraged urban green thumbs suggest glass-shard and razor-wire mulches. Appraising your plants in terms of crack, you realize that not only must you "plant down," you must plant mean. (This garden won't be entered in the National Peace Garden competition in Washington, D.C.)

Considering there were 697 murders in Brooklyn last year, and 1,896 citywide, crack gardening is a mere blip on the city's crime screen. It is really up to counter-crack gardeners to help themselves, mindful of garden guru Christopher Lloyd's dictum that we need to be aware "of the uses to which armed plants can be put as offensive weapons." This spring my defense-procurement plant contracts have been let, solely on the basis of each plant's reputation for viciousness, and the heck with competitive bidding. Even now the following defensive-garden weapons systems are in the pipeline.

For the rear & side defensive perimeter: Hardy Orange (*Poncirus trifoliata*) — a wickedly thorny shrub that, according to *Taylor's Encyclopedia of Gardening*, "forms impenetrable, defensive hedges"; Hawthorn (*Crataegus*); Blackberry (*Rubus*); the Sweetbriar rose (*Rosa eglanteria*) — "the stems bristly, and with strongly hooked prickles," *Taylor's* says; Father Hugo's rose (*Rosa hugonis*) — quoth *Taylor's* "beset with flattened, straight prickles and bristles"; the equally prickly Scotch rose (*Rosa spinosissima*).

For the front defensive perimeter: Barberry (*Berberis*); Prickly Pear cactus (*Opuntia compressa*); and, in extremis, Poison Ivy (*Rhus toxicodendron*). For the defensive interior: Scotch thistle (*Onopordum acanthium*); a Sea Holly *(Eryngium yuccifolium*, a.k.a. rattlesnake master); Burdock (*Arctium lappa*); Stinging Nettle (*Urtica dioica*) and Deadly Nightshade (variously *Solanum nigrum* or *S. dulcamara*). These plants are plenty nasty enough for the offensive gardening necessary to the counter-crack attack, even if the garden will paint a pretty prickly picture.

PAT HAYWARD is the customer service manager at a nursery in Brighton, Colorado (USDA zone 4), and a gardener who enjoys experiments. The Flatiron mountains outside Boulder make a dramatic backdrop for her home garden, where she and her husband grow native and alpine plants as well as a wide range of border perennials. Hayward has contributed garden writing and photography to national nurserymen's publications as well as those of the American Rock Garden Society.

Colorado Perennials
Pat Hayward

When I tell people from out of state that I live in Colorado, they generally picture one of two things: ranges of snow-covered Rocky Mountains or cowboys riding the great Southwest. Both images are accurate, but there's even more to the picture. That's the attraction of this state; Colorado, because of the Rocky Mountains, is one of the most topographically and vegetatively diverse states in the union. Though this state claims over 50 peaks exceeding 14,000 feet elevation, it is also home to hundreds of square miles of grassland and sagebrush and all vegetation zones in between. The selection of plants native to this region is as exciting as the area is diverse.

My husband (and fellow gardener) Joel and I moved into our new house in Lafayette during the winter of 1987. Our household currently consists of two dogs, a rabbit, indoors and outdoor fish, a Quaker parakeet, a tarantula and one child on the way. Lafayette is a small, older mining town with many young families. Many people in the newer developments work in Denver, 20 miles to the southeast, or Boulder, only 12 miles west. We selected this house as much for its lack of landscaping as anything else. (Our realtor never quite understood that when we said we didn't want any trees on the lot, we really meant NO trees.) We wanted to start with our own ideas, our own plants, and our own surprises.

In our gardens we've planted both plain and fancy varieties of perennials, trees, and shrubs, and even in the short three years since we've started we have moved, removed and added many plants. Joel and I met over six years ago at work (a large, wholesale nursery) where he was assistant field manager, growing and managing 50 acres of field trees. I was (and still am) in charge of customer service and inside sales. He has since moved into outside sales and now we often act as a family sales team for the company. Because both Joel and I are in the nursery business, we tend to be very demanding gardeners. If something doesn't perform up to our expectations, there's always a stand-in in the wings, awaiting a trial performance.

Our biggest challenge as Colorado gardeners has been learning to work with the unpredictable climate. The fifteen inches of moisture we receive each year comes in the form of sporadic but drenching rainfall, or as snow, usually three feet at a time! Our growing season here in the high plains lasts about four months, but early and late frosts are so common

Our realtor never quite understood . . . we really meant NO trees.

that most years we don't know what to expect. And though we are officially listed as USDA zone 4, because of our erratic winter temperatures we often need to search for hardier plants. Last February, during a week of 70 degree days, the earliest shrubs began to leaf out and bloom. The following week we hit record lows with temperatures below minus 20! Summers, however, are quite pleasant for both people and plants.

Other climatic challenges we face include high winds, over 100 miles per hour in winter at times. Plants that do best in naturally windy areas tend to be low and compact, "buns" as they are referred to by local rock gardeners. Sunshine, considered in many parts of the country to be a blessing, can sometimes cause problems near the "Mile High City." Our almost constant sunshine in winter prevents us from using many broadleaf evergreens such as holly and rhododendrons except where they can be protected from winter sunburn.

All these challenges (or opportunities, depending on your attitude) combined with the naturally clayey and alkaline soil, set the stage for gardening in Colorado. Though we are limited in natural resources, these limitations can be overcome artificially, very often quite simply. For example, water and compost are easily applied to a garden, but try growing our Rocky Mountain alpines in soggy England and just see how hard it is to deal with too much of a good thing.

Now, to introduce you to our gardens: our 70- by 100-foot lot runs north and south lengthwise. The north side, or front gardens, have been the easiest to build and design. (Joel calls these "Pat's gardens" since the goal of this area is to be a low-maintenance perennial border and I'm very involved with perennials at work.) An existing irrigation system for the lawn has been slightly modified to accommodate these sweeping perennial and shrub beds. The most dynamic part of our yard, though, has been in the back, where the majority of the beds are very hot and dry. We have five distinct areas in the back, consisting primarily of plants native to the areas between southern Montana and northern New Mexico and Arizona. Weekends from spring through fall are spent traveling or gardening. We have collected seeds, cuttings, and occasionally, plants from all over this region for the past five years.

The garden I'd like to describe is actually older than the rest. For two years we had been renting a house three miles from our present home. Joel and I had gradually built up a sizable collection of native plants there, and when it came time to move, we brought everything with us, including the rocks. It was February and I remember very clearly hours of chipping away at ice to get some of the stuff out. Right before the final move it snowed and we were wheelbarrowing pots and plants and rocks uphill through six inches of snow to get the whole garden moved before our lease expired. Luckily, almost everything made the trip successfully and has flourished.

This oldest, driest garden began when Joel was temporarily working for a construction company that owned a gravel pit. One of the first things we did after moving in to our new house (besides digging up the atrocious junipers lining the driveway) was to remove the sod and dig out an area 16 by 30 feet to a depth of about 18 inches. We then brought in pea gravel and sand (hand carried by the bucketful because there is such limited access to the backyard). This was mixed with the existing soil to make a planting mix that's 60 percent sand and gravel and 40 percent clay soil.

The garden is roughly rectangular with four main, odd-shaped berms. It is outlined with steel edging to keep the surrounding buffalo grass at bay. A short gravel path bisects the garden horizontally, while larger stones have been set in north to south for plant observation and from which to work. Each berm rises about six to fifteen inches above grade. Most edges slope gently downwards, but on the east side we have set in rocks to form miniature "cliffs," even though they may only be ten to twelve inches high. The rocks are primarily rounded, native red sandstone from Boulder County; given to us by Mary Maslin, they were leftovers from Paul Maslin's famous rock garden in Boulder.

Since there is no irrigation in this garden and we wanted some privacy from the neighbors year round, we planted a five-foot piñon pine in the southeast corner. This has also given us a much-needed, but small area for dry shade plants. Some of the native shrubs we've planted to set the backbone of the garden are: Curlleaf mountain mahogany (*Cercocarpus ledifolius*), a small-leaved evergreen that grows mostly upright; New Mexico cliffrose (*Cowania mexicana*), another somewhat evergreen, rounded shrub with pale yellow flowers; several species of yucca; and antelope bitterbrush (*Purshia tridentata*), similar in leaf to the cliffrose but shorter and bushier. A number of nasty-spined cacti from Colorado and New Mexico were planted at strategic points along the edge to encourage our dogs to stay out of the garden. So far this has worked both for dogs and visiting children as well!

The drama in this garden comes, of course, from the spectacular color displays all season long. The colors seem more intense and the bloom time longer on many of the plants here than in all the other sections of our garden. Some of the plants we've had great success with in this non-irrigated, very well-drained area are:

Aquilegia barnebyi (**Barneby's columbine**) A dryland columbine found near shale outcrops and cliff walls in the northwest portion of Colorado. When grown dry it has steel blue, petite foliage that forms a mound six to eight inches tall and is attractive in all seasons. (We've grown this at the nursery in heavy clay with irrigation and it tends to be rather weedy.) The flowers with their orangey-red spurs and yellow central petals are pretty, but not exceptional. It's quite unlike its famous relative, *A. caerulea*, the Rocky Mountain columbine, which loves moisture and whose blossom is elegant. Grow Barneby's columbine for the excellent texture of its foliage.

Calylophus hartwegii (**Hartweg's sundrops**) is a day-blooming relatively large-flowered member of the evening primrose (Onagraceae) family. We got it from a nursery in Santa Fe. It's native to the Southwest (probably further south than here) but it has lived three years for us. The lemon-yellow flowers are two inches

93

across with crinkly petals and the trumpet-like corolla is almost two inches long. The flowers fade to orange and contrast with each set of new flowers appearing daily throughout the summer. It's a magnificent bloomer for hot, dry gardens. The only drawback, for people like me who work all day long, is that it is a day bloomer and closes up by evening. I make a special point of walking through the garden early each morning to see some of these beauties I might miss later that day. *Calylophus hartwegii* can also be sprawling so it needs more room than many of the other plants.

Melampodium leucanthum (**blackfoot daisy**) This a long-blooming, four- to six-inch-tall plant from the roadcuts and semi-arid plains of southern Colorado and further south. It starts blooming in June and continues through August. The white flowers are about one inch across with mustard-yellow centers. It is a tremendous performer in the dry garden, but so far, it refuses to be propagated commercially. Since it is a profuse self-sower, we often transplant seedlings into small pots for our friends and visitors. It's difficult to grow in the nursery for some reason, so is rare to find for sale.

Zinnia grandiflora (**paper flower**) Another native plant of the Southwest that grows along with *Melampodium* many times. It refuses to do anything in our garden until things really heat up, but then it performs non-stop through the summer. It, too, is only four to six inches tall and self-sows throughout the garden. The mustard-yellow ray flowers surround reddish disk flowers. The leaves are more needle-like on *Zinnia* than *Melampodium* and the flowers dry to an attractive tan. We have this on the south end interspersed with *Sphaeralcea coccinea* (cowboy's delight), and the combination of bright orange and yellow is very pleasing.

Penstemon **spp.** We figure we've had over 60 species of penstemon in our gardens, and many have been quite showy for one reason or another. *Penstemon alamosensis* is another plant we picked up at a nursery in Santa Fe and have never found since, either in the wild or at any other nursery. It is reported to grow native in a canyon near Alamogordo, New Mexico. It's particularly special because both foliage and flowers are attractive. The coral-red, tubular flowers appear on open stalks ten to twelve inches above the basal rosette of silvery-blue leaves. Remove the flower stalks after blooming and a second set of blossoms often appears. The leaves are evergreen and take on an even bluer silver tone in the winter. In a garden on the south side of the house we have this planted below *Chamaebatiaria millefolium* (fernbush), an almost evergreen, white-blooming shrub and next to *Cercocarpus intricatus* (littleleaf mountain mahogany). This corner spot looks great both in summer and winter.

The Chihuahuan phloxes (*Phlox mesoleuca* varieties) have been local sweethearts ever since Paul Maslin of Boulder rediscovered several varieties back in the 1970's. Two favorites of ours are 'Mary Maslin', an intense vermilion-colored phlox with a yellow eye, and 'Arroyo', a carmine-rose. The Mexican or Chihuahuan phloxes are stout, creeping plants with vividly-hued blooms that appear all summer long. Their natural habitats are the arid lands of northern Mexico and surrounding areas. Many varieties and colors can be found in limited quantities at local nurseries and all are quite choice. You'd think the pink of 'Arroyo' and the orangey-red of 'Mary Maslin' would be almost gaudy planted next to each other. But in the heat of summer, that spot is the brightest in our garden.

These six plants are just a few of the stars of our native gardens. Despite (or is it because of?) drought, heat, wind, and sun, many native plants have adapted themselves to perform only in the most challenging conditions. By carefully re-creating natural plant habitats, gardeners in many areas can enjoy Southwestern natives at their best. And once established, these local players actually prefer to be left to their own devices. Why fight Mother Nature?

SOURCES
(See "Sources & Resources" appendix for complete addresses.)

Old Farm Nursery
Plants of the Southwest

CAROL BORNSTEIN and **LAURA BALDWIN** worked together at the Santa Barbara Botanic Garden in coastal California (USDA zone 10.) Bornstein, director of horticulture at the Botanic Garden, designed the native plant borders discussed in the following piece. Her areas of expertise include native and other drought-tolerant plants as well as historical garden restoration. Baldwin, a horticultural writer who was the editor of the SBBG newsletter, wrote this article to inspire interest in native perennials.

Perennial Borders for the Best of Both Worlds

Laura Baldwin and Carol Bornstein

Tall pink inflorescences weave among ground-hugging mounds of clear blue blossoms with accents of saffron yellow. Tiny white flowers cluster over close mats of gray-green leaves, and fragrant whorls of small purple blossoms ring stalks of soft gray foliage. The rounded forms of tall evergreen shrubs create a backdrop for the whole, leading the eye to the hills beyond the garden. A description of a classic English garden, right? Wrong. This is one of two experimental plantings at the Santa Barbara Botanic Garden; the plants are not care-demanding imports but rather perennial, drought-tolerant California natives.

Many California gardeners have recognized for decades the advantages of native trees and shrubs: low water use, resistance to disease, and low maintenance. However, native perennials (equally desirable, and perhaps more diverse) remain under-used and await discovery as garden-worthy plants. At the Santa Barbara Botanic Garden, the goal was to develop plantings that would kindle public enthusiasm for these potential garden standards. The borders were needed to show how native perennial plants, both woody and herbaceous, could offer solutions for local gardening challenges while providing waves of year-round color and season after season of interest.

The Santa Barbara Botanic Garden is in the foothills (700-foot elevation) of the Santa Ynez Mountains, about three miles from the ocean. In our Mediterranean climate, we experience cool, wet winters and warm, dry summers. At the Garden, average winter temperatures range between 47 to 66 degrees Fahrenheit, whereas summer temperatures are typically between 62 to 77 degrees Fahrenheit (USDA zone 10). Our average yearly rainfall is 21.2 inches, most of which falls between November and April. Some additional moisture is available to plants from coastal fog, which usually is a late spring phenomenon. Two of the biggest challenges confronting gardeners in this area are the almost total lack of natural precipitation during the long, warm summer months, and the fact that gardening is a twelve-month undertaking. Gardeners from regions with cold, snowy winters may not, upon settling here, initially realize how these climatic factors place demands on the planning, installation, and maintenance of a garden.

All our educational efforts would be in vain if gardeners . . . failed with natives in their own gardens.

We wanted to use only plants that would help gardeners conserve water yet maximize effects of color and foliage texture. A particular joy of these plantings is that they undergo seasonal changes. The public, by returning to view these beds at different times of the year, can learn how different plants will dominate the garden as the seasons progress. We designed the beds on an accessible scale to demonstrate how people might incorporate these plants in their own gardens.

Another factor we had to consider was the importance of matching the plants' cultural requirements to the site. Plants with different water requirements should not be interplanted. Some natives require summer watering while others cannot tolerate it. Many gardeners who have tried to use natives have come to grief by making this critical mistake. All our educational efforts would be in vain if gardeners, excited by the plantings, failed with natives in their own gardens.

The first experimental border was planted in the area of the Santa Barbara Botanic Garden known as the Manzanita Section. Several of the manzanita (*Arctostaphylos* spp.) specimens were past their prime and ready for removal. The remaining manzanitas, along with the established oak trees and naturally occurring boulders, provided the background and structural "bones" for the site as well as creating opportunities to use both shade- and sun-loving plants.

REGIONALISTS

After removing the declining evergreens, we recontoured two planting beds on opposing sides of a pathway, to take better advantage of the striking rock formations. We amended the soil with organic material and covered it with a layer of wood chips to hold moisture in the soil and to discourage weeds.

The bed along one side of the path features gray-leaved plants. During winter and spring, their foliage creates subtle patterns of light and dark; in early summer, the plants burst into yellow, pink, and white flowers. Species of native buckwheat, *Eriogonum*, are featured here, and their pleasing mounded forms echo the shapes of the round boulders. The flower sprays of the different species offer diverse color options: cream (Santa Barbara Island buckwheat, *Eriogonum giganteum* var. *compactum*); yellow (saffron buckwheat, *E. crocatum*); and rose or pink (red-flowered buckwheat, *E. grande* var. *rubescens*). Buckwheat is particularly appealing when its flat sheets of bloom (in reality, thousands of tiny flowers) turn russet or warm sienna as summer and fall progress, giving seasonal variety to the garden.

Planted with the various *Eriogonum* are purple sage (*Salvia leucophylla*); a prostrate form of coastal sagebrush, *Artemisia* 'Canyon Gray', introduced by the Santa Barbara Botanic Garden; Matilija poppy (*Romneya coulteri*) with its huge and fragrant white flowers; and many species of live-forever (*Dudleya*). The succulent rosettes of the *Dudleyas* are particularly effective at brightening up the shadier portion of the bed. We also planted a blue-gray form of California fescue (*Festuca californica*), to soften the rough sandstone boulders at one corner of the bed.

Across the path are several species of penstemon—the clear blue azure penstemon (*Penstemon azureus*), and the pink to purple foothill penstemon (*Penstemon heterophyllus*). Visitors will also find the less familiar pink cups of checkerbloom (*Sidalcea malviflora*) and the mass of pink flowers offered by the wishbone bush (*Mirabilis californica*). Even more unusual are the little yellow flowers of rush rose (*Helianthemum scoparium*), a very fine-textured chaparral plant. Lining the paths are wands of southern goldenrod (*Solidago confinis*). Drainage is fast in these beds due to the light-textured soil. Although the various plants are drought tolerant, we water bi-weekly during the summer to improve the appearance of the display.

One very appealing combination that works well in this area is red-flowered buckwheat (*Eriogonum grande* var. *rubescens*) and southern goldenrod (*Solidago confinis*). The buckwheat's soft pink flowers (its common name is misleading) intertwine with the goldenrod's large, somewhat floppy inflorescences, and the plants support each other. They bloom together in mid- to late summer for several weeks, when most of the other flowers have faded. An added bonus is the volunteer buckwheat seedlings that appear each year. When small, they can be transplanted to other spots.

The second experimental border planting is in the upper Meadow. Here, our design idea was to integrate a pathway border with the main Meadow by mixing striking clumps of native grasses with colorful flowering plants. In this area, an overgrown collection of *Mahonia* was in decline and no longer useful as a botanical collection. After we removed the evergreens, the Meadow edges could be reworked to form an undulating pattern of grasses and herbaceous perennials. The soil in this border has a fairly high clay content; therefore, summer watering is minimal. Most drought-tolerant California natives will succumb to root-rotting fungi if watered out of season when grown in heavy soils.

Planted in late 1987, the pathway borders do not yet possess the majesty of maturity. However, small clumps of delicate grasses (species of *Bouteloua*, *Stipa*, *Melica*) already provide a harmonious link with the more spectacular bunchgrasses sweeping across the expansive Meadow. Scarlet-bugler (*Penstemon centranthifolius*) produces spikes of red tubular flowers, and woolly blue-curls (*Trichostema lanatum*) add touches of fuzzy purple-blue. Both plants are very intolerant of summer water, and bloom in late spring through early summer. Chaparral yucca (*Yucca whipplei*) makes an effective gray accent here, and coyote mint (*Monardella villosa*) — a low, rounded shrub — adds purple flower clusters as well as fragrant foliage.

Perhaps the most striking display occurs in late spring, when the visually arresting penstemon, *Penstemon spectabilis*, begins to bloom. Last year it looked fantastic with a ten-foot-tall western redbud tree (*Cercis occidentalis*) as a backdrop, the latter's limbs clothed with pink pea-shaped blossoms. Nearby is a colony of the blue-leaved form of California fescue (*Festuca californica*), which deepens the visual intensity of the pinks.

REGIONALISTS

Changes are always occurring. Just as the new native perennial borders replaced older waning collections, not all plants in the experimental beds will remain. We are testing some plants outside their normal range, including several species from California's higher elevations. Will mountain-pride (*Penstemon newberryi*) thrive? Will the temperamental woolly blue-curls (*Trichostema lanatum*) survive?

Gardeners visiting the Santa Barbara Botanic Garden will find exciting alternatives to traditional garden plants. Native perennials come in every flower and foliage color, in varied textures, and with a delightful choice of growth habit. California's native aster, *Corethrogyne leucophylla*, hugs the ground in spreading mats while the foliage of Catalina silver-lace (*Eriophyllum nevinii*) sways waist-high. Matilija poppies (*Romneya coulteri*) explode in large, showy white blossoms. The deep purple flowers of Douglas iris (*Iris douglasiana*) enrich the spring garden, and later, yarrow (*Achillea millefolium*) offers its soft pink corymbs and ferny foliage. No color need be absent from a garden of native perennials.

Borders of water-conserving natives are a successful alternative to the frustrations of traditional plantings. However, a new challenge may face gardeners wanting to try these perennials: where to buy them? For the moment, many of these wonderful plants are not widely available in the nursery trade. But they should be. Create supply through demand!

SOURCES
(See "Sources & Resources" appendix for complete addresses.)

C.H. Baccus
Bay View Garden (Iris rhizomes)
California Flora Nursery (Trees, shrubs, & perennials)
California Native Plant Society
Callahan Seeds (Trees & shrubs)
Forestfarm Nursery
Russell Graham (Specialty bulbs, natives, & perennials)
Larner Seeds (Trees, shrubs, & wildflowers)
Las Pilitas Nursery
Moon Mountain Wildflowers
Native Sons Wholesale Nursery (Trees, shrubs, & perennials)
Theodore Payne Foundation (Native trees & shrubs, wildflower seeds)
Plants of the Southwest

Clyde Robin Seed Co., Inc (Wildflower seeds)
Robinett Bulb Farm
San Simeon Nursery (Trees, shrubs, perennials, & ferns)
Siskiyou Rare Plant Nursery (Alpines & Northwest natives)
Tree Of Life Nursery (Trees, shrubs, & perennials)
Wildwood Nursery (Wholesale: trees, shrubs, & perennials)
Yerba Buena Nursery (Native Trees, shrubs, and ferns)

ROBERT STREITMATTER is a landscape architect with an abiding interest in perennials. He particularly enjoys championing those which are undervalued, yet which perform brilliantly in the Midwest. His own garden (USDA zone 5) holds an extensive collection of herbs as well as numerous sterling examples of his favorite underdog perennials. His garden writing has been published in *American Nurseryman*.

Perennials that Play in Peoria
Robert Streitmatter

P
erennial gardening is challenging in the Midwest but well within our abilities when we use appropriate plants. The Midwestern climate, more specifically that of Peoria, is characterized by bitterly cold winters with little snow cover to protect plants, by hot, dry summers, and by very erratic temperatures in spring and fall. It seems intolerable, yet all this fades to insignificance with the first delicate snows of winter, the woodland flowers of spring, the blazing color of the summer border, or the familiar blue asters and goldenrod of fall. My garden is in Princeville, Illinois, a small town fifteen minutes from Peoria, at the southern edge of USDA zone 5. The garden rests in a shallow, wide-spreading swale, bordered by a pasture to the west, woods to the north, a neighbor's property to the south, and a street to the east. Conditions within the garden vary greatly, from clay soils to rich loam, dry to moist, and full sun to full shade. The garden layout includes a south-facing entry garden, an east garden room, a woodland garden, an herb garden, and a west garden room. In a sense, I'd like to stroll with you, through my garden and point out the perennials performing particularly well.

Starting with the entry garden, there is a clump of sea lavender (*Limonium latifolium*), a plant that enjoyed the 1988 drought. It is slow to establish itself and does not appreciate division or transplanting because of its very long roots. Sea lavender has a basal rosette of glossy leaves that turn burgundy-brown in fall. The foliage, which appears shabby when young, improves greatly with plant maturity. In July, branched scapes hold aloft a cloudlike mass of tiny lavender flowers, creating the same effect as baby's-breath (*Gypsophila paniculata*). Its flower scapes usually need minor staking, best accomplished with a well-branched twig. The flowers dry to a soft, silvery gray and can be used in dried arrangements. The scapes are best cut when most of the flowers are open. All in all, sea lavender is a beautiful alternative to baby's-breath, which occasionally fails to survive the winter.

Tucked between a bayberry shrub (*Myrica pensylvanica*) and the sea lavender is a drift of butterfly weed (*Asclepias tuberosa*). Despite the awful common name, it is one of the most stunning native prairie plants. Butterfly weed has bright orange or orange-red flowers between mid-June and August. With maturity, the number of flowers increases as does the length of bloom. It requires full sun and likes a poor soil with little or no water. There is little problem with disease or insects, though it does attract butterflies; hence its common name. Monarchs are the most frequent visitors, but I have noticed sulphurs, whites, swallowtails, and admirals as well. Butterflies or even moths add a great deal to the feel of a garden. They animate the garden and give it a warm, inviting quality. As a relative of the common milkweed, butterfly weed forms a narrow, seed-filled pod after flowering. If left to ripen, the seeds will be eaten by birds, and any remaining seeds will germinate to produce small seedlings. These can often be moved to another spot if their roots remain intact. A long, fleshy taproot seems to explain the plant's drought resistance; however, it makes mature plants impossible to move or divide. Propagation of butterfly weed is most successful in the spring, using seed or two- to three-inch root cuttings. I have good luck with both. It's best to mulch these new plants in winter, as they are susceptible to frost heave. They come up late in the spring, so cultivate carefully and give them some time before probing around the crown, although I am aware of how difficult that is for an anxious gardener in the spring.

> **Covering plants must be done on the spur of the moment; it just wouldn't be right to plan ahead and do it without complete darkness and 35 degree temperatures.**

The genus *Salvia* is crowded, as it includes culinary sage, clary sage and annual salvia, so meadow sage (*Salvia* x *superba*) is often overlooked. I only started using it last year in borders. Erect spikes of intense, violet-blue flowers last from June to August. If the old flower heads are clipped every couple of weeks, the plant will flower longer. As with most salvias, full sun and well-drained soil are required. I have noticed it has a good tolerance for drought. Meadow sage works well in herbaceous or mixed borders, particularly as an accent among prostrate and dwarf evergreens.

I have planted a clump of small globe thistle (*Echinops ritro*) next to George, a spruce named after my grandfather. It seems appropriate to name a plant after my grandfather since he loves to garden. At 86, he still spades his entire garden and produces the finest onions and tomatoes ever seen. Anyway, globe thistle has a gray-green, thistle-like foliage. This striking foliage is best used with the calming effects of fine textures. *Echinops ritro* makes a spectacular focal point or specimen. Spherical blue flowers appear in July and August and can be used in dried arrangements. Globe thistle needs a well-drained soil with medium to light moisture. Since it is a large plant with long roots, established plants are hard to move, and special care should be taken in placement and planting. Unless the garden is particularly windy, it isn't usually necessary to stake the plants. *Echinops ritro* 'Taplow Blue', a cultivar with great potential, has a larger flower with a more intense blue. I'd strongly recommend using this cultivar if you find space for globe thistle in your garden.

In the east garden room, *Rudbeckia fulgida* var. *sullivantii* 'Goldsturm' forms a drift against a backdrop of garden phlox (*Phlox paniculata*) and a couple of outstanding 'Illini Warrior' peonies. (The peonies are a must for any Illinois graduate.) 'Goldsturm' is a magnificent plant for massing or specimen use. I have seen masses of this orange coneflower that literally stop traffic. The flowers are deep yellow with a slight orange cast and brown-black centers. They bloom almost continuously in late summer, between mid-July and mid-September. The foliage forms a neat mounded habit and remains glossy and pest-free all season. Unlike most other *Rudbeckia*, 'Goldsturm' does poorly in dry soils. However, generous mulching eliminates this problem and the plants will remain quite hardy and dependable.

Scattered throughout the east garden, as well as in the remaining garden, are clumps of peony (*Paeonia lactiflora*). Each time a peony catalog comes in the mail, I pledge not to order any more. However, an order always mysteriously finds its way to the mailbox.

Part of the attraction lies with the peony's ability to last for years with little or no maintenance. Peonies bloom in mid-May to June, around Memorial Day. By using early-, mid- and late-season cultivars, you can greatly extend the flowering period. I prefer the single flowers. The heavy double-flowering types are prone to wind damage. As for color, I lean toward pastels, finding them easier to blend into color schemes; however, I have many of the deep rose, magenta, and maroon cultivars, introduced by Edward Auten. Gilbert H. Wild and Son of Sarcoxie, Missouri, and Klehm Nursery of South Barrington, Illinois, both carry an impressive selection of new and old peony introductions, including many from Auten. Between 1931 and 1956, he hybridized peonies in Princeville. My grandmother worked in peony fields during the war, and she still has the fern-leafed peonies given to her by Auten. The peony fields have long since been replaced with cornfields, but we still have the peonies.

Peonies do best in rich, well-drained soil and full sun or light shade. Since they are very long-lived and dislike being moved or divided, planting procedure is very important. In late August to early September, plant them with generous amounts of organic matter and a handful of bone meal. Most importantly, the uppermost eye on the root must be one and one-half to two inches below the surface. If planted at the incorrect depth, either too deep or too shallow, the peony may not flower. Peonies have a few problems; they are susceptible to botrytis and phytophora blight. However, these diseases can largely be prevented by removing and burning the dead foliage in late fall. To further prevent the spread of disease, I dip my pruners in a ten-percent bleach solution after cutting back each plant. The stems often carry huge flowers and usually need additional support. Peony hoops, circular rings atop stakes, work best. They can remain in place all year and the plants grow up through them in the spring. When given support, peonies offer handsome foliage all season and are ideal planted in masses, as accents, or as informal hedges. I often underplant with crocuses or daffodils to add a bit of spring color when peonies are just getting started. A friend edged her circular drive with 'Sarah Bernhardt', a rose-pink double flower. In May, they are so spectacular that cars are kept off the driveway so tea can be served on the drive among the peonies. The fragrance is incredible. Recently a "peony bench" has been installed to provide permanent seating for this event. During tea, obvious non-gardeners drive by looking very confused. They're not sure what has caused this driveway gathering.

Nestled between the north side of the house and the woods is the woodland garden. My intention was to bring the woods up to the house, and, all bias aside, I think I have succeeded. The plantings include trillium, Virginia bluebells, bloodroot, American ginger, false Solomon's-seal, woodfern, ostrich fern, woodland phlox, hosta, and a variety of shrubs. One of my favorites is the Virginia bluebell (*Mertensia virginica*). These are not the easiest perennials to use, but once established, they spread and become more spectacular with each passing year. In April to May, the small pink buds open to periwinkle blue, bell-shaped flowers. They require light shade and a moist, well-drained soil, rich with compost or leaf mold. The major drawback is that the foliage dies back in May or June, leaving a void. Virginia bluebells should be underplanted with hostas, ferns, or daylilies to hide the passing of the foliage. They are best planted in drifts in a woodland garden or as accents in borders or rock gardens. Once established, they should remain undisturbed. If necessary, division or transplanting is best done in early fall. Remember to mark the plant locations unless you enjoy the sport of randomly digging holes.

Hostas are one of the finest and most indispensable perennials for shaded sites, woodland gardens, and mixed borders. In a mass, they make a fine ground cover or edging. I often combine them with plantings of spring bulbs, as well as Virginia bluebells. Hosta's bold foliage contrasts well with the fine textures of astilbe, sweet woodruff, fern, and bleeding heart, or with the linear textures of daylily, iris, and ornamental grass. Hostas prefer moist, well-drained soils, rich in organic matter. Generally they require light to full shade, although light requirements vary with the specific cultivars and the ability of the soil to remain moist. If you have a good moisture-retentive soil, rich in organic matter, a plant can handle an eastern exposure with five to six hours of morning sun. If exposed to excessive sun or too little moisture, the plant's telltale sign is browning margins. Overall, hostas have few drawbacks. For neatness it is best to trim the old flower scapes. The lowly slug is the hosta's only major enemy. There are a few chemical slug repellants that work, but I have seen good results from spreading sharp sand or diatomaceous earth around the plants. Also, you may try the old method of placing lids filled with beer around the base; I suspect they prefer dark imports over light beers.

There are numerous hosta cultivars, with different sizes, leaf color, leaf variegation, leaf texture, leaf shape, and flower color. With so much to choose from, it is difficult to see why only a few cultivars are widely used. One of my particular favorites is *Hosta* 'Francee'. This hybrid has a deep green, heart-shaped foliage with narrow, refined white margins and lavender flowers in late summer. In comparison, 'Francee' is far superior to the overused *H. undulata* 'Albo-marginata' with muddy, white margins.

Hosta plantaginea 'Royal Standard' has a glossy leaf and beautifully fragrant, white flowers in late summer. I have some planted along a path where the fragrance can be easily enjoyed. This cultivar is often touted as tolerating full sun, but I have yet to see a hosta that looks happy planted in full sun. Around July, brown margins start to appear on the foliage and the entire plant looks shabby. One of the finest gray-foliage cultivars is *H.* 'Krossa Regal', with its frosty gray-blue leaves. When young, its foliage remains rather upright and odd in appearance. However, after a few years the leaves become more horizontal and form a stately mound. In late summer 'Krossa Regal' has lavender flowers atop towering four- to five-foot scapes. Just outside my office, the flower scapes have surpassed four feet on four-year-old plants. I have noticed in several gardens that *H. sieboldiana* 'Elegans' and *H. sieboldiana* 'Frances Williams' are susceptible to late frost. The damaged leaf margins remain annoyingly visible throughout the season. This problem, however, can be easily solved by covering the plants during a frost. I generally wait until I see the frost warning on the news. Around 11 p.m. I head out with a flashlight and one of the good bath towels (the kind that aren't supposed to get dirty). Covering plants must be done on the spur of the moment; it just wouldn't be right to plan ahead and do it without complete darkness and 35 degree temperatures. Since observing these problems with 'Frances Williams', I use *H. fortunei* 'Green Gold' or *H. fortunei* 'Aureo-marginata'. They are both a bit smaller in stature, have a more refined gold margin, and lavender flowers in August. *Hosta sieboldiana* 'Elegans' is so uniquely striking that it is difficult to replace with any other cultivar. Two outstanding hybrid cultivars that equal and even out-perform 'Elegans' are

H. 'Blue Angel' and *H*. 'Big Daddy', but they are not widely available yet. However, Klehm Nursery in South Barrington, Illinois, does carry many of these newer introductions. 'Elegans' has huge, round, powdery, blue-gray leaves, which become more textured with plant maturity. The best blue coloring is obtained in full shade. In June, short, thick scapes with large white flowers will form, just above the foliage. It has been a long time in coming but I've finally begun to appreciate the gold hosta cultivars. After several years of observation, I think that *H*. 'August Moon' and *H*. 'Piedmont Gold' seem to perform best. They must have some sun, preferably an eastern exposure, to remain yellow. Around midsummer, they both have white flowers. 'August Moon' sometimes has flowers lightly frosted with lavender. Yellow foliage is a striking accent and should be used sparingly.

In the herb garden, flanked by a massing of boxwood and a 'Harison's Yellow' rose, is blue false indigo. *Baptisia australis* is an underused perennial that merits more attention. It forms bright blue flower spikes from late May to early June. The flowers change to green, leguminous pods by the latter part of June. The pods will dry to rich steel gray and can be used in dried arrangements. *Baptisia*'s attractive blue-green foliage stays healthy and disease-free all season. The plant grows well with full sun and poor to average, dry soil. Being rather long-lived, *Baptisia* is rather slow to establish and does not care for division or transplanting. It does, however, germinate very easily. If any matured seed pods are left over winter, you will find scattered seedlings. These can be moved successfully only if the root is undisturbed, which is easily done if you use a stout spade and get a large ball of soil. The flowers or pods often become too heavy for the stems but a peony hoop can alleviate the problem entirely. Considering the plant's height, *Baptisia* is best placed towards the back of the border, thus hiding the hoops or supports. It seems to work well in both mixed or herbaceous borders.

At the base of a beautiful 'Hansa' shrub rose, mother-of-thyme or wild thyme (*Thymus serpyllum*) forms a lush ground cover. The name *Thymus serpyllum* is often mistakenly used to identify a number of different plants, all of which should be classified as different species or varieties of subspecies. I use *Thymus praecox* ssp. *arcticus* (also known as mother-of-thyme and often listed as *T. drucei*) most often. It thrives in an average to poor, well-drained soil. With soft, fragrant foliage, this thyme deserves to escape the herb garden more often. It is spectacular when tucked into crevices of stone work, planted among stepping stones, or drifted through rock gardens and mixed borders. The species is drenched with lavender to rosy-purple flowers around mid-June to July. Other cultivars can have pink, red, white, lavender, or purple flowers. It spreads at a controllable pace, unlike others in the mint family. *Thymus prae-cox* ssp. *arcticus* can be easily propagated from roots that form at nodes that touch the ground. The new plants very often vary in flower color. This variation would explain the many varieties and cultivars. Beyond the different flower colors, there are different variegated or textured foliages, and there are even different scented varieties of thyme. Unlike the species, these specialty forms often require winter protection and should be used sparingly as small accents or specimens. A couple that I find useful are the lemon-scented thyme, *T.* x *citriodorus* and woolly thyme, *T. pseudolanugino-sus*. The latter forms a dense mat of silvery-gray foliage. It does require division since it has a tendency to die out in the center.

The west side of the herb garden is home to a prairie border, planted with yarrow, switchgrass, little bluestem, butterfly weed, aster, purple coneflower, and the white-flowering shrub, *Ceanothus americanus* or New Jersey tea. Purple coneflower, *Echinacea purpurea*, acts as a backdrop for the New Jersey tea. The coneflower carries rose-purple flowers with orange-brown center cones from July to September and is especially interesting when paired with an orange flower like daylily or butterfly weed. The orange in the coneflower centers is picked up by the orange flowers to create a very strong grouping. It thrives in well-drained soil with full sun to partial shade. The flowers are very long-lasting and often fade to a dull mauve, at which time I usually remove them. The cultivar 'Bright Star' has a brighter rose color that seems to last much longer. There are even two white cultivars of *Echinacea purpurea*, 'Alba' and 'White Lustre'. Rather than true white, I consider the petals of these coneflowers to be a dull oyster color. You will find that they all self-seed very easily if the flower heads remain over winter. I always dig a few coneflower seedlings to share with friends.

A recent addition to the west border is cushion spurge, *Euphorbia polychroma*. (In many catalogs it is listed as *E. epithymoides*.) It prefers full sun and an average, well-drained soil. The flowers are inconspicuous and form small clusters within bright, yellow-green bracts. These bracts are very showy and last through May. It keeps a tight mound-like habit, making it a wonderful plant for edging or the front of a border. I have admired its use in other gardens and a recently expanded border has finally given me some space to include it in mine. I'm rather anxious to see the red fall color, which is often mentioned in descriptions I have read. If you purchase or acquire euphorbia, make certain you are not receiving *E. cyparissias*, cypress spurge. Cypress spurge is used as a groundcover in some regions, but in the Midwest, it should be considered a weed. It has a narrow, linear leaf as opposed to an ovate leaf and spreads with vigor. It is a mistake that is difficult to eradicate since each fragment of root can produce a plant.

Also in the west border, Siberian iris (*Iris sibirica*) is used with a dwarf Norway spruce as a facer plant for a star magnolia (*Magnolia stellata*). This iris prefers a rich, moist, well-drained soil in full sun or partial shade. It flowers in late May to early June, with white, blue, lavender, or deep violet cultivars available. In comparison to bearded iris, the color selection seems rather limited. I grow two common Siberian iris cultivars, 'Caesar's Brother', a deep purple, and 'Sea Shadows', a mix of turquoise and blue. The 'Caesar's Brother' is planted near a large massing of light orange daylilies. The combination sounds dreadful, but I have used it in a number of other gardens and it works great. Siberian iris forms a stately clump that contrasts well with the large foliage of hosta and rhododendron, or with finely textured evergreens.

The fine, grass-like foliage of *I. sibirica* alone is a valuable asset. The finer foliage seems to hold its appearance better than the floppy, coarse foliage of the bearded iris. In about August many bearded irises brown along the margins, while Siberian irises, at the worst, only brown at the leaf tips. If allowed to remain, the leaves of Siberian iris turn to a rich chestnut-brown in winter. Also, in comparison to the bearded iris, *I. sibirica* is not as susceptible to the iris borer and soft rot, and it requires division less often; division is best done in early spring after six to seven years.

For four years I have been observing the performance of the perennials in my own garden, and in gardens I have designed and gardens I have seen in Central Illinois. During this period, I have compiled a list of perennials that do well in the area. This is merely a rough outline of recommended genera; one cannot begin to list all the available species and cultivars. You may notice that some perennials you might expect to find on the list are conspicuously missing; they have been omitted because problems with hardiness, disease, insects, or invasiveness outweigh their benefits.

SUN: *Achillea, Alchemilla, Anaphalis, Anthemis, Arabis, Artemisia, Ascelpias, Aster, Baptisia, Carex* (grass), *Centaurea, Clematis, Coreopsis, Deschampsia* (grass), *Dictamnus, Digitalis, Echinacea, Echinops, Erianthus* (grass), *Euphorbia, Filipendula, Gypsophila, Heliopsis, Hemerocallis, Hibiscus, Hyssopus, Iris, Liatris, Limonium, Lysimachia, Lythrum, Miscanthus* (grass), *Nepeta, Oenothera, Paeonia, Panicum* (grass), *Phalaris* (grass), *Phlox, Physostegia, Platycodon, Rudbeckia, Ruta, Salvia, Sedum, Solidago, Sorghastrum* (grass), *Spartina* (grass), *Stachys, Thymus, Tradescantia, Verbascum, Veronica.*

PARTIAL SHADE: *Alchemilla, Amsonia, Aruncus, Astilbe, Baptisia, Bergenia, Brunnera, Carex* (grass), *Clematis, Convallaria, Coreopsis, Dicentra, Digitalis, Epimedium, Filipendula, Geranium, Hemerocallis, Heuchera, Hosta, Iris, Lysimachia, Mertensia, Paeonia, Phalaris* (grass), *Phlox, Physostegia, Platycodon, Polemonium, Polygonatum, Smilacina, Thalictrum, Tradescantia.*

SHADE: *Adiantum* (fern), *Aruncus, Asarum, Asperula, Brunnera, Convallaria, Dicentra, Dryopteris* (fern), *Epimedium, Heuchera, Hosta, Matteuccia* (fern), *Mertensia, Polemonium, Polygonatum, Smilacina, Trillium.*

Peoria has a long and glorious reputation of having a tough crowd to please. All things considered, I think this rather demanding or critical approach is necessary when selecting perennials. By sharing some of my experiences, I hope you will be better prepared to make the right choices and to create a perennial garden suited for the Midwest. I wish you many years of gardening success. There are few things that equal the fleeting, but rewarding, beauty of a flower.

BIBLIOGRAPHY

Cox, Jeff and Marilyn. *The Perennial Garden.* Emmaus, Pennsylvania: Rodale Press, 1985.

REGIONALISTS

Giles, F.A.; Keith, Rebecca; Saupe, Donald C. *Herbaceous Perennials*. Reston, Virginia: Reston Publishing Company, 1980.

Nehrling, Arno and Irene. *The Picture Book of Perennials*. New York: Arco Publishing Company, Inc., 1977.

Thomas, Graham Stuart. *Perennial Garden Plants*. London: J.M. Dent & Sons, Ltd., 1976.

SOURCES
(See "Sources & Resources" appendix for complete addresses.)

Klehm Nursery
Gilbert H. Wild and Son

BARBARA PERRY LAWTON has been a garden and horticulture writer for nearly twenty years, yet she still loves plants. In her Kirkwood, Missouri garden (USDA zone 6), where plants are exposed to extremes of weather and temperature, she finds that a wide variety of perennials handle the tough conditions with aplomb. Native plants that thrive without fuss are among her favorites, but she has suffered passions for all sorts of perennials, including daylilies, iris, and many others.

Garden Inspiration from Native Plants
Barbara Perry Lawton

How many times have you driven along highways or country roads and marveled at the flowers of field, roadside, and woodland? Who has not seen an entire field from fence to fence glowingly painted by goldenrod in fall? Or splendid summer clumps of yarrow swaying gently, defiant of both drought and poor soil? Plants that flourish and flower from year to year no matter what the growing season may bring—that's what we all strive for in our perennial gardens. We can covet nature's success while we continue to pamper poorly chosen delicate perennials, or we can learn from these roadside visions!

Oddly, human nature is such that we often value plants imported from other countries more than our own handsome natives. For example, it took the English to recognize the beauty of our goldenrods and breed them into the forms of *Solidago* that Americans admire—and import. North America has long provided a treasure trove of ornamental plants. European travelers, explorers, and plant collectors gathered the ancestors of many of our favorite perennials and took them home, where plant breeders created splendid new cultivars for royal gardens. From Colonial times to the present, many of these improved varieties have been returned to the land of their origins, some so changed as to little resemble their North American ancestors. Yet, the vigor of our American wildflowers remains in the sturdy modern cultivars of asters, helianthus, filipendulas, rudbeckias, verbenas, solidagos, achilleas, and gaillardias, to name just few.

Only in recent years has there been a resurgence of interest in the wildflowers of our own woods, fields, and meadows. We are now free to choose the best of both old and new worlds. Success will be ours in the garden if we carefully choose plants that are genetically programmed to succeed in our climates, in other words, the native plants and their domesticated relatives.

Native North American plants and their cultivars offer enough variety in texture, size, bloom, and bloom time to create magnificent gardens. They offer spectacular opportunities for perennial gardens. They will thrive in our demanding climate, given a modicum of care and decent well-drained soil. While purists may prefer to grow only the original natives, I like to choose the best from both originals and improved varieties. Both philosophy and taste guide my following selection of perennials:

Achillea millefolium, the common yarrow, is a highly visible plant that blooms from June to late summer in fields and roadsides. Although originally from Europe and western Asia, this *Achillea* has been in North America for hundreds of years, probably brought here for use as a medicinal herb. The ferny foliage is strongly pungent and the flowers, tiny white ray flowers surrounding yellow disks, are carried terminally in flat clusters.

Offering more color and less invasive growth, cultivars have flowers of pink through red on 18- to 24-inch plants. 'Cerise Queen' has rose-pink flowers. 'Crimson Beauty's two- to three-inch flowers are bright red. 'Fire King' has flowers of rose-red, and 'Red Beauty' bears crimson flowers. 'Rosea' has pink flowers and 'Rubra' has dark pink flowers. 'Paprika' is a new cultivar with handsome orange-to-red flowers. Clearly, there's plenty of choice.

The species, quite weedy, is most effective in meadow plantings or other naturalized sites where its invasive growth habit is an asset. The cultivars are better choices in massed plantings of three or more plants, in beds or borders. Also highly worthy of inclusion in sunny perennial gardens are other achillea species and cultivars, including the dwarf, eight-inch *A. tomentosa* 'Aurea' and the popular hybrid 'Moonshine' from the renowned English plantsman, Alan Bloom. 'Moonshine' offers sulfur yellow flowers above gray foliage; 'Aurea' has yellow flowers and woolly gray foliage. In the garden, the flowers of *Achillea* hold for several weeks and also serve the gardener well as cut or dried flowers.

Asclepias tuberosa (butterfly weed), a milkweed relative with orange to red and, more rarely, yellow flowers, attracts butterflies like nobody's business. Native to eastern and central North

America, this species is an excellent choice for meadow plantings or sunny gardens. It usually grows about two feet tall but may reach a height of three feet under ideal conditions. The foliage is sturdy and dark green. The flowers are long-lasting; both flowers and seed pods are good choices for fresh or dried arrangements.

The deep taproot of *Asclepias tuberosa* makes it difficult to transplant successfully, but I have found it an easy plant to grow from seed. Spread the seeds to areas where you want more plants as soon as the seed pods ripen. This native is a real survivor in full sun, even under drought conditions.

While purists may prefer to grow only the original natives, I like to choose the best from both originals and improved varieties.

Aster novi-belgii (New York aster or Michaelmas daisy), a native to the eastern United States, has splendid violet-purple flowers in late summer to fall. Clusters of two-inch flowers top tall plants that may reach a height of three to five feet. The species and taller cultivars require staking if they are not to flop over onto neighboring plants. Full sun and well-drained soil are a must for this handsome American.

One of the finest cultivars is 'Professor Kippenburg', which has masses of half-inch lavender blooms atop foot-high mounded plants. Other good *A. novi-belgii* cultivars are 'Ada Ballard', 36 inches tall with semi-double, lavender-blue flowers; 'Boningale White', 40 inches tall with yellow-eyed, double white flowers; and 'Violet Carpet', just ten inches high with violet-blue flowers. Cultivars of varied heights are available in shades that range from reds through pinks and whites to blues and lavenders.

Plan to divide asters every two to three years to increase vigor and control spreading. Asters can be pinched regularly through mid-July to increase branching and promote compactness. For the wildflower purist, there are many native asters that offer great beauty in their unimproved forms including the shade-tolerant *A. divaricatus* (white wood aster) and the large New England aster, *A. novae-angliae*.

Cimicifuga racemosa (black snakeroot or bugbane) is a three-to-eight-foot plant with long pale flower spikes that appear in mid-summer here in Missouri, in early fall further north. *C. ramosa*, a handsome relative, has white branched flowers while the variety 'Atropurpurea' has white flowers rising from a basal clump of dark purple-green foliage. A native woodland plant in the eastern United States, *Cimicifuga* can be grown in sun to partial shade. Unlike other drought-tolerant natives, *Cimicifuga* requires rich, moist, but well-drained soil for top performance.

Snakeroot can be massed along a stream or pond, naturalized in wooded areas, or used as a stunning specimen for large perennial borders in partial shade. As a rule of thumb, the hotter the climate, the more important it is for snakeroot to be shielded from afternoon sun. Since its growth habit is not rampant or invasive, this plant can be left undisturbed for many years.

Coreopsis verticillata (thread leaf coreopsis), a native perennial of the southeastern United States, has finely cut palmate leaves and yellow daisy-like flowers. The species grows two feet tall in a dense erect clump and blooms from late spring through summer. Easy to grow, the thread leaf coreopsis and its cultivars thrive in full sun and dry conditions. Poor drainage is about the only thing that will jeopardize its vigor.

A good subject for naturalized areas, dry perennial beds, or sunny wildflower gardens, the thread leaf coreopsis is truly a superior plant. Although slow to begin growth in the spring, it soon makes up for lost time and may become invasive when grown under ideal conditions. Since it's easy to pull out of the ground, its vigorous growth is not a problem.

'Golden Showers' is a tall, two- to three-foot cultivar of thread leaf coreopsis with bright yellow star-like flowers. 'Zagreb' is small, producing yellow flowers on plants only 12 to 18 inches tall. Most favored among the cultivars is 'Moonbeam', which has creamy yellow flowers densely covering two-foot mounded plants. A new star, 'Rosea', is beginning to appear in nurseries. 'Rosea' possesses all the pluses of 'Moonbeam' while providing flowers of a soft rosy shade! Encourage vigorous reblooming in these cultivars by pruning several inches of growth when the first flush of flowers begins to dwindle.

Echinacea purpurea (purple coneflower) is a tough, two- to four-foot native of open dry land in the eastern and central United States and is an ideal low-maintenance plant for sunny dry sites. A daisy-like member of the plant family Compositae or Asteraceae, the coneflower has purplish disk flowers surrounded by drooping ray flowers of purple or lavender to, rarely, white or off-white shades. Light, filtered shade or at least late afternoon shade will increase the brilliance of the flowers, which last for many weeks each summer.

The foliage is coarse and the stems erect, making this a good plant to combine with softer-textured plants such as the floppier yarrows. Let yarrows lean against coneflowers. *E. purpurea* is great for meadow or prairie gardens. It is somewhat susceptible to leaf spots and Japanese beetles but, all in all, it is an easy plant to grow. Clumps can be easily divided every few years.

The coneflower has been bred into several fine cultivars. *E. purpurea* 'Magnus' is a new European cultivar with vivid pink flowers. 'Bright Star' has two- to three-inch blooms of rosy-red with maroon centers, and 'White Swan', a smashing new cultivar, offers creamy white petals surrounding a rich lime-green disk. Excellent for long-lasting cut flowers, the coneflower cultivars make great additions to perennial beds where they offer strong vertical growth; I doubt if you would ever have to stake these handsome plants. Coneflowers are stars of the summer garden.

Oenothera speciosa (showy evening primrose) lives up to its common name. It is extremely showy and, with correct pruning, it will bloom and rebloom throughout much of late spring and summer. Native to the central United States from Missouri to Texas and hardy well into USDA zone 6, it has two-inch flowers of a delicate pink or, rarely, white, on plants about a foot tall. Like the thread leaf coreopsis, it can be encouraged to rebloom by pruning several inches of foliage when the first big flush of flowers begins to wane.

This *Oenothera* can be invasive, spreading by both seed and runners, but the flowers are so lovely that it's worth planning a little extra weeding time in case the plants go beyond reasonable bounds. Naturalize this plant at the edge of woods or use it in the border where low perennials are needed. Both the original pink species and the newer white variety, 'Alba', are increasingly being grown by perennial nurseries. Look for other new varieties, including dwarf types, in the future.

A few of the other genera that offer great potential for American gardens and naturalized plantings include *Filipendula* (meadowsweet), *Helianthus* (sunflower), *Monarda* (bee balm), *Physostegia* (obedient plant or false dragonhead), *Rudbeckia* (coneflower) and *Trades-cantia* (spiderwort).

Unless you have a local grower who specializes in native plants, and there is an increasing number of these specialists, you may have some difficulty in finding natives for your own garden. More and more of the major mail order catalogs now include a section on native plants and wildflowers.

Since North American natives often are regionally unique, help can be gained from local plant societies, state conservation groups, departments of natural resources, chapters of the Audubon Society and the Nature Conservancy. Nearly three dozen native plant or wildflower societies, their contacts, and dues information are listed for the United States and Canada in Barbara Barton's excellent source book *Gardening By Mail* (Houghton Mifflin Co., 1990), a publication that you should be able to find in libraries and in bookstores. The Brooklyn Botanic Garden has published *Gardening With Wildflowers and Native Plants*. This handbook lists societies and sources.

Gardeners who live in the eastern half of the United States may wish to check the plant lists of Holbrook Farm and Nursery and Native Gardens. In the Midwest, there is Gilberg Perennial Farms. These mail order nurseries feature native plants and wildflowers. If you cannot find a nursery source, consider marking desirable plants and returning to collect the seed. This is the best way to bring wildflowers into your garden without violating conservation bans on digging plants.

Clearly, growing native plants is not as easy as buying cabbage starts at the local garden center, but the research is fun and you are sure to meet others with common interests as you travel down the wildflower path. Look to your roadsides, fields, and woods to find a new highway to success. Preserve, multiply, and grow our native perennials. They demand little yet offer countless opportunities in a new world of gardening.

SOURCES
(See "Sources & Resources" appendix for complete addresses.)

Brooklyn Botanic Garden
Gilberg Perennial Farms
Holbrook Farm and Nursery
Native Gardens

BETTY BARR MACKEY, a free-lance writer, has learned that, though the rules are decidedly different in Florida (USDA zones 8, 9, 10), the pleasures of gardening are the same anywhere. A dedicated organic gardener, Mackey found that tropical pests and plant problems gave new meaning to the word "control," but achieving peaceful coexistence with the native fauna has made her appreciation of the floral possibilities all the deeper. Her newest book, written with Pat Kite, is *A Cutting Garden for California*.

Florida Gardening
THE RULES ARE DIFFERENT HERE
Betty Barr Mackey

Hi! If you are a newcomer and you want to grow flowers in Florida, just think of the state's advertising slogan: "The rules are different here." In the ads the message is that, in Florida, you are allowed to have fun all the time. In the garden, the message is, watch out for the unexpected! Florida's gardening conditions can be a shock to people who, like me, learned their gardening skills in states to the north.

When I stepped off the plane, I looked forward to learning to grow wonderful new plants like orange trees and bougainvillea. It was going to be fun. Easy, too. After all, I grew up in rural Maryland, gardening in dense red clay that didn't seem too great, but I coped. Then I lived in Hopewell, New Jersey, in a house built in 1899. When they redid our antique septic system, the contractors dumped subsoil all over the yard. Undaunted, I rebuilt the soil and made a legendary 200-foot perennial flower border and an adequate herb and vegetable patch.

However, my gardening experience did not prepare me for Florida conditions. For one thing, the insects are immense. There are five-inch green grasshoppers and four-inch brown, hard-shelled flying palmetto bugs, for instance. With experience, I ignored the palmetto bugs; they are not very energetic and probably prefer table scraps to flowers. The grasshoppers are something else. Once I got so mad about the damage that I threw one into the street; it was so big and fat that the very thought of stepping on the creature was repulsive! Later I learned to recognize them in their immature stages (they are black with red markings) and control them with rotenone, pyrethrum, and the sole of the shoe before they reached unusual proportions.

The bugs did not cause my early failures at gardening in Florida. I moved in during July, one of the hottest months in 1983, an unusually hot year. I planted some annuals from the garden center and some seeds I had saved from the New Jersey garden. (There were no seeds for sale at the center, which should have told me something.) Nothing grew. I tried again. The plants were miserable. I decided it must be the soil, which looked kind of sandy. I added fertilizer and peat moss, but the results were not much better.

Eventually I bought a soil test kit to see what was the matter, but the readings showed nothing. Couldn't I follow the directions? I tried again. Nothing. At last it dawned on me. I was testing inert silicone with no nutrients, trace elements, pH, or organic matter, and trying to garden in the equivalent of silver beach sand. I would have to add *everything* in order to turn it into soil. For me, this insight was the key to success. I learned to till in soil builders equal to the volume of soil in the top foot of the bed—anything organic: grass clippings, compost, weeds, wood chips, manure, peat moss, peanut hulls, and oak leaves; to fertilize the bed liberally; and to add clay in the form of clean kitty litter. (If they had been available then, I also would have added wetting agents like Agrosoke R, to help the soil hold onto moisture.)

Progress came in two more stages. After some research on planting times, I learned to plant during cool seasons, not hot. (The seed packets returned to the garden centers in the fall.) Practically anything can be grown in Florida if it is planted at the right time of year. Once I understood the soil and climate, I could successfully adapt the plants I had grown elsewhere to the perplexing Florida conditions. Next, I researched what to plant. Driving around the older neighborhoods, I would see a wealth of beautiful flowers. The botanical gardens (Leu Botanical Gardens, Marie Selby Botanical Gardens, and horticultural displays at Walt Disney World's Magic Kingdom) were helpful too, and they put name tags on their plants. Finally, I used old-fashioned trial and error. Besides trying out my favorites if I thought they had a chance to succeed, I planted mixed packets of flower seed, just to see what types would grow in the conditions I offered.

One more obstacle was the presence of root knot nematodes in the soil. Shallow-rooted annual and perennial flowers were most seriously affected by them. Shrubs and larger perennials grew deeply enough to avoid heavy damage. However, actively tilling the soil and exposing it to the sun helped clean up the soil. Enriching it with compost and manure (a friend of mine had a horse) seemed to weaken the effect of the nematodes, too. I also had good luck growing plants in clean potting soil in containers. The chemical Vapam, now banned for home garden use, was used commercially to fumigate nematode-infested soil, although it was against my mostly organic outlook.

There were no seeds for sale at the center, which should have told me something.

In my part of Florida, central Florida near Orlando in USDA zone 9, November is the best time for planting hardy seeds or plants outdoors, despite the likelihood of frost. In North Florida, September and October are better, and in South Florida, December and January are best. This way, seedlings and young plants are set in during cool weather at the time that insects are least active. Water seedlings twice a day if temperatures climb into the 90s or above and shower all leafy plants at midday if they begin to droop. You can save yourself at lot of trouble by growing things at the right time of year, including some things that people say won't grow in Florida. Plant hardy annuals in late fall and grow them as biennials. Do this for those perennials, like columbine (*Aquilegia*), that do not withstand hot weather, too, and replant seeds each year. For less work, stay with the hardy but heat-loving plants like butterfly weed (*Asclepias tuberosa*). Unless you live in a cold part of the state, avoid peonies, bearded irises, and other plants that need chilling in winter.

To me, a garden is not right without lots of flowers to cut for bouquets, so in my yard even groundcovers and shrubs tend to serve double duty. One of my favorite Florida combinations was my big red poinsettia bush in front of a white camellia tree (cultivar unknown). They bloomed together at Christmastime in those years that we were spared a hard freeze; other years the buds froze but the plants were not badly damaged. Herbaceous perennials were my favorites in the North, and after learning their Florida requirements, pleased me in the South, too. Here are my comments on some of the perennial flowering plants that I was — at last! — able to grow.

Achillea (A. filipendulina, **fern-leaf yarrow;** *A. millefolium*, **common yarrow)** Provide light shade and improved soil, and you should have a nice crop of yarrow for fresh or dried bouquets. Plant seeds in fall for spring bloom, and don't expect the plants to be especially long-lived.

Amaryllis **(all species)** This is Florida's answer to the daffodil, usually blooming in March. It grows well in all parts of the state but needs mulch in the northern third. Grow the bulbs in light shade in good soil, barely covering them. Let the foliage ripen before cutting it down. Your plants will thrive and multiply for years.

Aquilegia canadensis **(wild columbine)** Plant seeds in shady places in fall for flowers in spring. But don't expect the plants to survive the summer, except in the coolest parts of the state. I only tried this species but I suspect others would perform as well.

Asclepias tuberosa **(butterfly weed)** This hardy perennial grows practically anywhere, including Florida. It is so rugged that seeds sown in summer will grow, but it is safer to plant in early fall.

Campanula **(bellflower)** I liked to grow the biennial type (*C. medium* 'Calycanthema') because the perennials seemed too delicate to make it through the long, hot summer. Sow seeds in fall or buy plants in early spring. I read recently that *C. isophylla* 'Stella' is a hardy groundcover in hot areas, but didn't get the chance to try it.

Chrysanthemum (C. x morifolium, C. x superbum, **shasta daisy)** Florida gardeners have lots of choice. Late-blooming and florist cultivars have time to bloom, and the other types do well, too. Naturalized chrysanthemums bloom in spring and fall, and need extra fertilizer for this reason. Cuttings are easily rooted, even budded ones. If you grow chrysanthemums from seed, they will bloom the first year. Shasta daisies need rich soil and midday shade. Though they do best in full sun in the North, this is too harsh an exposure for them in Florida. Provide light shade. Divide them in late fall.

Coreopsis (**tickseed**) The different perennial types grow well enough in Florida, but prefer partial shade. They are not so long-lived here. I liked the annual *C. tinctoria*, planted in fall and grown as a biennial for spring flowers.

Crinum Crinum lilies are spectacular in Florida where heavy frost is no problem. These majestic lilies, similar to amaryllis, are up to eight feet tall with as many as 25 flowers per umbel. Bulbs are gigantic and very expensive. My bank's parking lot had a showy planting of them. I rescued some seedlike bulbils before the maintenance crew came along to deadhead the plants, and grew them at home for freebies. They were coming along well, but I had to move away before they bloomed.

Echinacea purpurea (**purple coneflower**) These daisies are tough and resilient. They are good in Florida, but may need extra protection against pests. They make good background plants in a border, and combine well with blue or yellow annuals.

Dietes vegeta (**African iris**) These plants are wonderfully graceful even though they are among the sturdiest, most heat- and insect-proof plants in the garden. The white blooms touched with speckles appear in spring and sporadically at other times. The two-and-a-half-foot swordlike foliage never droops or straggles. Partial shade is the best exposure, but full sun is tolerated.

Freesia x hybrida This was my greatest Florida surprise. The lovely, fragrant freesias which had never grown for me in the North did well in my Florida woodland garden, where I naturalized them. Without expecting much, I planted some and found that they multiplied and improved over the years, blooming in February. Plant them where corms will not be disturbed.

Gaillardia aristata (**blanket flower**) This is so well adapted that it grows wild in Florida sand dunes. It seems to be Florida-proof, and is a favorite of mine.

Gerbera jamesonii (**African or Transvaal daisy**) This is grown everywhere in Florida, and why not? These large, bright daisies grow effortlessly in the Florida climate. Plants like a neutral or slightly sweet soil. Don't try to purchase seed, for it doesn't keep well in storage, and it's very expensive. Buy plants in bloom, save ripened seed, and promptly plant.

Gladiolus Glads are effortless in Florida if your corms and soil are disease-free. Just leave them in the ground all year and divide them after they bloom (usually in mid to late spring) if they get too crowded. For bloom over a longer period of time, plant corms at intervals from February to June.

Hedychium coronarium **(butterfly ginger lily)** In sites with plenty of water and rich soil, butterfly ginger will flourish, like it does near a stream at Leu Botanical Gardens in Orlando. It blooms for months, spreading a marvelous fragrance from every white flower. Foliage is lush and resembles corn plants before they tassel. The plants are damaged by frost, but regrow quickly from underground rhizomes.

Hemerocallis **(daylily)** These wonderful plants are just as infallible in Florida as they are everywhere else. Give them light shade, though. Enough said.

Iris I had no luck with bearded iris. Dutch iris (*I. xiphium* hybrids) bloomed once but never bloomed again, though the foliage returned. Try out your favorite irises in a small way before making a big investment.

Narcissus Most daffodils won't grow here, so forget it. There's one exception, *N. tazetta*, the paperwhite narcissus that Northerners force indoors at Christmas time, which grows well outdoors in Florida, in partial shade. In most of the state it blooms in late winter.

Papaver (P. orientale, **oriental poppy;** *P. nudicaule,* **Iceland poppy)** I tried oriental poppies once but they dried up in the heat, though I heard rumors that they could be grown in Central Florida. I would expect *P. orientale* to be a better bet in North Florida in partial shade, and a lost cause in South Florida in any exposure.

Plant seeds of *P. nudicaule* in early to late fall for spring bloom. Iceland poppies won't be perennial here; you'll probably lose them during summer heat, but first they will bloom very well and everyone will be amazed. I had great results with them.

***Rudbeckia hirta* (black-eyed Susan)** Another heat-loving plant that does well in Florida, this is good but can look ragged after blooming awhile. If so, cut the stems (not the basal leaves) down near soil level to promote new growth at the base.

***Rumohra adiantiformis* (leather fern)** This grows very easily in shade in Central Florida, which is in the lower part of USDA zone 9. You'll recognize it as part of a typical florist's bouquet, but it makes a great groundcover where it is hardy. Mulch this well in upper zone 9, for it is sensitive to frost.

***Strelitzia reginae* (bird-of-paradise)** Both tall and short types are truly tropical in form and in their needs. They are easy to grow if protected from frost; in northern parts of the state grow them in containers so that the plants may be carried indoors when cold or freezing weather threatens. Give plants plenty of water and fertilizer, but let the soil drain well.

Viola Buy pansies and violets in fall for bloom all winter and spring. Being economy-minded, I got mine as rooted cuttings in soilless bundles of 25 at a favorite nursery. There are mail order places such as TyTy Plantation Bulb Company that sell them by the hundred, very cheaply. Pansies are great winter bedding plants because a light frost doesn't hurt either the flowers or the leaves. But they won't make it through the summer heat no matter what you do.

***Zingiber* species (true ginger)** I had two kinds of ginger in my yard, pinecone ginger (*Z. zerumbet*) and common or culinary ginger (*Z. officinale*), and I loved them both, even though they were invasive and needed watering. Actually, I left the state before learning how far my ginger was going to go, but was starting to feel alarmed.

The two types are closely related, but pinecone ginger is much larger and taller—over four feet tall and much like ordinary corn in appearance. It earned its keep by growing lushly in a difficult spot in very poor, sandy soil which I fertilized periodically. The magnificent, long-lasting blooms resemble fiery red six-inch pinecones on tall stems. The color comes from overlapping red bracts; the actual flowers are white and short-lived. Culinary ginger (mine was propagated from ginger root purchased at the grocery store) seemed the same as the pinecone type, but in miniature, growing about a foot and a half tall. The cones stayed green; or did I cut them before they could turn? Both species recovered well after spells of freezing weather, regrowing from the ever-creeping rhizomes.

I was sorry to leave Florida when my husband was transferred to Philadelphia. I was there only four years, but it was long enough to learn some key things about perennials, many of which have not been tested very fully in Florida conditions yet. There was much more information available when I left than when I came; quite a few books became available in that time, including my own (now out of print) *A Cutting Garden for Florida*, and I've seen several more that were published after I left in 1987. This is very gratifying because the problems of growing flowers in Florida, though real, are exaggerated. Alternative gardening methods and different plant choices permit the development of wonderful gardens in places where most people think nothing but marigolds will grow. It's truth in advertising; the rules *are* different here.

CENTRAL FLORIDA BOTANICAL GARDENS

Cypress Gardens
Cypress Gardens, FL 33880
(south of Orlando)

Leu Botanical Gardens
1730 N. Forest Avenue
Orlando, FL 32803

Marie Selby Botanical Gardens
811 South Palm Avenue
Sarasota, FL 33577

Walt Disney World
Magic Kingdom Horticulture
Lake Buena Vista, FL 32830
(near Orlando)

SOURCES
(See "Sources & Resources" appendix for complete addresses.)

Burpee

The Country Garden

Hastings (Seeds, bulbs, and plants for the South)

Mellinger's Inc. (Supplies for greenhouse and garden)

Park Seed

Smith & Hawken (Garden furniture, supplies, containers, and bulbs)

Thompson & Morgan, Inc.

TyTy Plantation Bulb Co. (Amaryllis, canna, calla, crinum lily, and other bulbs for the South. Bare-root pansies by the hundreds)

Van Bourgondien & Brothers, Inc. (Dutch bulbs, tender and hardy)

STEPHANIE SPENCER is an art historian who balances a teaching career with the practical demands of gardening. Like Betty Mackey, she found that gardening "rules" don't necessarily travel well. Her present garden, in Raleigh, North Carolina (USDA zone 7–8), may not contain her favorite bleeding hearts, but it does boast an ever-increasing number of perennials that are tolerant of her region's hot summer nights.

Gardening in the South
SURPRISES FOR THE NORTHERN GARDENER
Stephanie Spencer

I moved to Raleigh, North Carolina, five years ago, bought a house, and started a garden. As a transplanted Northerner, I had certain ideas about when things should be planted, when they bloomed, and what was easy to grow. I quickly learned that many of these ideas were not transferable and that gardening in the South is a very different proposition from gardening in the North.

To begin with, Raleigh is located on the line between USDA zones 7 and 8 on the standard temperature maps. As a result, plant selection based on heat and cold tolerance is not a simple matter. While some warm-climate plants will grow this far north, others will not. Similarly, some cold-climate plants will not accommodate cheerfully to the warmth of this end of their zone. The only way to find out is to experiment and typically, just when you think you can draw some reasonable conclusions, an unusually cold winter or abnormally hot summer comes along and kills the plants.

The climate of this part of North Carolina is in fact extremely variable. Long-time residents concede that there really is no such thing as a typical season. Summers are always long but they can be either very dry, very wet, or first one and then the other. This too makes plant selection something of a challenge.

Another factor in plant longevity that has recently been identified has to do with the high nighttime temperature during the summer.[1] Basically, nighttime temperatures are so high that plants continue to use the energy they produced during the day in the process of transpiration. Since they never have the opportunity to store energy, they eventually wither and die. This discovery may go a long way toward explaining the otherwise mysterious demise of plants that should be hardy according to the traditional temperature zones.

My garden ranges from deep to partial shade. While this too limits plant selection, it is actually a highly desirable situation for humans since no one can tolerate the full brunt of the North Carolina summer sun. I am fortunate in having reasonably good soil in my garden, since what is jokingly referred to as soil in this part of the country has all the characteristics of building brick. To call it clay is an understatement. While I did improve the soil with the addition of organic material, it was not actually necessary to chip planting beds out of solid clay.

I do it, it obviously works better, but its still does not feel right.

However, there is still enough clay in the soil that it can be quite waterlogged in spring and hard as a stone during dry summers. Irrigation is definitely necessary.

I encountered my first gardening shock in the spring. Since I had always set out new plants in May and June, I proceeded to do so here even though it was already much warmer than I was accustomed to for that time of year. The sun promptly fried all my little plants. Undaunted, I did the same thing the next year and got exactly the same results. Reluctantly, I had to admit that my system was not working; I now plant lettuce and peas in January and set out more tender plants in March and April. I do it, it obviously works better, but it still does not feel right.

I also discovered that certain plants I had always counted on in the North do not do well in the South. Tulips, for example, do bloom but they have to be treated as annuals since the temperature in the winter does not get cold enough for them. Grape hyacinth (*Muscari armeniacum*) seems to have much the same problem. Crocuses also bloom but if you view them as the first signs of spring at the end of a long hard winter, they seem rather pointless in the South because there is no such thing as a long hard winter here. Besides, many bulbs including daffodils bloom earlier, which rather spoils the symbolism. Spring bulbs are by no means a total loss, however; daffodils and narcissus do exuberantly well and hyacinths do as well as they do anywhere.

I had always considered bleeding hearts an essential ingredient in any garden. However, neither *Dicentra spectabilis* nor *Dicentra eximia* consent to live in my Raleigh garden. The former bloomed one year and then disappeared permanently, the latter struggled along for a month or two and then gave up. I think lack of moisture was the problem, even though I did irrigate. I have to admit that having my fox terrier dig up the *D. eximia* probably did not help.

Delphiniums and lupine (*Lupinus* Russell Hybrids) are out of the question, as they have failed uncounted times for me. However, foxglove (*Digitalis purpurea* and *D.* x *mertonensis*) can be used in their place. These, to my joy, not only survive but also reseed themselves. Peonies (*Paeonia lactiflora*) are not supposed to do well in the South and it is true that the young one I planted did not make it through midsummer. In contrast, I inherited a big 'Festiva Maxima' that has obviously been around for a long time and still blooms enthusiastically. It is true that it usually develops serious black leaf spots by August—a plague of nature for which I have found no successful organic cure—but this peony keeps returning nonetheless. Lady's mantle (*Alchemilla mollis*) is also not happy in the South. Everyone I know who has tried to grow it has ended up with crispy brown plants. Again, I think heat and lack of moisture are probably the culprits.

Of the staple fall perennials, I have had a great deal of difficulty getting chrysanthemums to grow. In this case, it is not the heat so much as predators that are the problem. Something that I have still been unable to identify eats them right down to the stem. The plants try valiantly to revive—I presently have a two-inch-tall chrysanthemum with two leaves and three buds—but it is clearly a struggle. The answer here may be to treat these as annuals, too, buying plants late in the summer and enjoying them while they last.

Two final notes about Southern gardening may be useful. Definitely do as much planting as possible in the fall; plants introduced to the garden when the weather is cooler do demonstrably better than those planted in the spring. Keep in mind that fall in the South extends well into November and sometimes even later so plants that are added in September still have at least a month or two to establish themselves before the weather turns cool. Local nurseries and garden centers still offer the bulk of their stock in the spring, but many of them also have fairly extensive offerings in the fall. Second, you need to recalculate bloom time as listed in the national seed and plant catalogs. These seem to be based on climates of the Northeast and Midwest and in no way relate to the realities of the Southeast. Generally speaking, everything blooms about a month earlier here. Most catalogs, for example, talk about June and July flowering lilies; mine bloom in late May and early June. When I am looking for other plants that will bloom at the same time, I just look for what the catalogs call June-flowering plants and adjust mentally.

Finally, I do not want to give the impression that gardening in the South is a matter of sacrifices and compromises. While I do miss some of my old favorites, I very much enjoy growing plants that would never survive in a colder climate. I think that the glory of Southern gardening probably lies in the extensive range of flowering trees and shrubs that flourish here. You have never really seen a dogwood or an azalea until you see it bloom in this climate! Spring goes on with wild abandon for at least a month, unlike the meager, though welcome, springs I had been accustomed to in the North. Once the transplanted northern gardener has come to terms with a few basic differences, gardening in a warmer southern climate can be every bit as enjoyable and rewarding.

NOTE

1. D. L. Deal and J. C. Raulston, "Plant High Night Temperature Tolerance Zones: Describing and Predicting Summer Night Temperature Patterns and the Southern Limits of Plant Adaptation," *Agricultural and Forest Meterology* 46 (3), May 1989, 211–226.

ALLAN ARMITAGE is a professor of horticulture who has written for numerous national publications and frequently leads international garden tours. He is also an avid and expert gardener whose recent book, *Herbaceous Perennial Plants* (Varsity Press, 1989), reflects experience gained both in his current garden in Athens, Georgia (USDA zone 8), and in his previous gardens in Montreal, Canada, and in Michigan. Though many things are different down South, Dr. Armitage finds pruning hellebores with his Lawn-Boy mower just as effective as it was up North.

Evolution of a Gardener
A LESSON IN ADAPTATION
Allan Armitage

I have learned a lot about plants since moving from the white snowfields of Montreal to the red clay fields of Georgia nine years ago. I was a fairly ordinary fellow who, through some guidance, divine or otherwise, found himself and his family on the long road to Georgia to accept a position at the University. Susan was eight months pregnant and the thought of a two-day trek in a U-Haul van with two small children and one large dog was not at all appealing. However, with her usual candor, she declared that we should look at this terrible deed as a "foreign assignment." "After all," she declared, "we will only be there for two or three years at the most." We departed in September as temperatures were cooling and the annual symphony of leaf color was beginning. After a long, eventful, and never quiet three-day excursion, we arrived in Athens to be greeted by hot, steamy air that made us feel like eggs poaching on the range. Our helpful neighbors tried to relieve our dismay by telling us that the days could be much hotter. That didn't help. Every now and then I would force myself out of the air-conditioned den to make a rapid reconnoiter of the barren area destined to be the flower garden. I could not believe that man, beast, or plant could survive such a summer. It was obvious to everyone that not only was I a wimp, but a northern one as well. Fortunately I was a foreigner and not a Yankee or I would have been run out of town.

The daunting task of making a garden loomed ahead. Advice was readily offered, but it was obvious that gardening in the South consisted mainly of green peppers, okra, and collard greens. Vegetable gardening was king; flowers were something that produced fruit. It was equally obvious that the light, black soils of Montreal had been replaced with heavy, red clay that broke shovels and spirits equally rapidly. When "winter hardy" perennials failed to reappear in the spring, it slowly dawned on me that plants were drowning, not freezing. Winter rains formed puddles in the clay around the dormant roots and crowns. After a dozen species had slowly suffered cold, miserable deaths, raised beds consisting of manures from various farm animals, pine bark, and whatever else I could find to enhance winter drainage were hastily formed. The results were like night and day; plants

After long and thoughtful study, I surgically removed the damaged foliage with my Lawn-Boy mower.

which had seemingly succumbed to heat and humidity in the "bog" stood tall in those woody droppings! As obvious as this problem was, the realization of its importance was slow in coming. I felt like Newton as he stared at the bruised apple. I have never forgotten the lesson that lack of winter drainage is the single most important reason plants die in Southeastern gardens. I now embarked on the job of learning to garden all over again.

While much of the country is denuded and snow-covered in the winter, some of my favorite plants put on their best Sunday dress during January and February in my garden. The foliage of American alumroot, *Heuchera americana*, and Italian arum, *Arum italicum* 'Pictum', provide immense pleasure on winter rambles through my Athenian garden. Although frost may cause them to cower, they rebound as the ice melts, and go on with their lives. They provide a contrast in height to the regal winter skeletons of *Miscanthus* flowers, the red fruit of the Gladwin iris, *Iris foetidissima*, and the blue-black berries of blackberry lily, *Belamcanda chinensis*. This "lily" (actually a member of Iridaceae) provides beauty and interest with its orange-scarlet flowers in mid-July and then outdoes itself with rows of berries in late summer, fall, and winter. Unfortunately, many birds also enjoy the fruit and the winter show may become a thrasher's meal. I often read about the winter beauty of the fruits of *Sedum* x 'Autumn Joy' but to me they simply look like

133

brown dead flowers and I discard them in the fall. One man's ceiling is another man's floor.

While spring is a wonderful time of year from Anchorage to Miami, there are fewer more beautiful springtimes than those in the Southeast. Spring brings a rainbow of color to the landscape. Wisteria, dogwood, Bradford pear, redbud, star magnolia, forsythia, quince, and the ubiquitous many-colored azalea annually compete in a four-week-long Olympics of color. Spring in northern Georgia is like the young man burning the candle at both ends. When warned it would burn too fast he replied, "Yes, but, oh what a glorious light it gives." To visit Athens in March, April, or May is to visit a little piece of Heaven, a place far different from the one encountered in August. Although trees and shrubs dominate the spring landscape, many perennials flex their flowers in victory after putting up with summer heat and winter puddles. Seasons in the Southeast do not follow calendar dates, obviously set out by the good people in Crivitz, Wisconsin, or Duluth, Minnesota. Spring in the Southeast may start as early as February and persist until June, although the heat usually camps in by mid–May, at which time the weather has turned decidedly summer-like.

Although often listed as a late-winter-blooming plant, I consider the flowering of Danford iris, *Iris danfordiae*, the beginning of spring in the garden. The Danfords reside at the front of a shaded garden pond but they flower so early that the foliage is almost totally gone before the oaks leaf out. I look forward to the bright yellow flowers atop the short shy foliage. The Danford is a member of one of the most satisfying genera of cultivated plants. The crested iris, *Iris cristata*, lights up the shadows of my garden path while the fat leaves and blue-streaked crested flowers of *Iris tectorum*, Japanese roof iris, thrive in the border. The cultivar 'Alba' is an even showier roof iris, with white flowers and a lovely yellow crest. I am a sucker for species plants; I would rather first grow the species than a cultivar, if the species still exists. That is why I am so taken with *Iris sibirica*, whose fine leaf lines and sophisticated flowers add a touch of class to the late spring garden. This iris has surely inhibited my zeal for collecting cultivars because, regardless of the beauty of her offspring, I always return to the mother. Nor can I neglect the toughest of the ladies, *Iris pseudacorus*, yellow flag iris. She stands four to five feet tall and from the rich green foliage emerge dozens of lemon-yellow flowers with brown crests. More stately plants can be found, but few are as tolerant of environmental conditions as this one. Plants grow in partial shade in the corner of the well-drained upper garden and also flower from roots submerged in the shaded pond, a range of tolerance envied even by native species. I also enjoy the rich blues of *Iris reticulata* in the spring. In my eclectic garden, a large clump has taken up residence by a planting of Lenten rose. I keep thinking the height difference between the two could be a disadvantage to both, but to my plantsman's eyes, they complement each other. I am not sure my design friends would agree.

Lenten rose, *Helleborus orientalis*, with large dark green leaves and white to purple chalices, provides months of carefree enjoyment. This plant is less persnickety than its cousin, Christmas rose, *H. niger*, which must be provided with the right site to flourish, and it fills in faster than *H. foetidus*, stinking hellebore, so named because of the pungent odor of the foliage and roots. The green-black foliage of stinking hellebore is darker and more deeply cut than Lenten rose and plants bear hundreds of small light green flowers from February through May. While not quite as tough as the Lenten rose, it is a favorite of mine and is being rediscovered by more and more gardeners. The hellebores are evergreen but can look forlorn after being tattered and bruised by cold windy days. After long and thoughtful study, I surgically remove the damaged foliage with my Lawn-Boy mower. Fast, painless, and effective. New foliage emerges readily and renewal is complete. Obviously I am not often asked to lecture on pruning techniques.

Other spring favorites are *Phlox* x *chattahoochee*, which flowers at the same time as foamflower, *Tiarella cordifolia*, and cheddar pinks, *Dianthus gratianopolitanus*. In my zeal for artistry, I planted them together and let them fight it out. The foamflower is a favorite; the creamy white flowers complement the rather vivid blues and pinks of its neighbors. Of the three, the cheddar pinks are winning the Golden Gloves award, although each is holding its own. Of the many spring-flowering plants that have found their way into the garden, one of the most persistent is Canadian columbine, *Aquilegia canadensis*. Plants arise from self-sown seed by magic, one year here and the next there. The clumps continue to multiply and I have run out of friends to whom to give them. The small scarlet-yellow nodding flowers provide a wonderful show in early spring, and the foliage is far less susceptible to leaf miner than many of the hybrids. Though not as showy as some of the hybrids, they always return, which cannot always be said of the hybrids. Another columbine that has been surprisingly persistent is Rocky Mountain columbine, *Aquilegia caerulea*. The same plants have flourished in the Horticulture Gardens at the University of Georgia for five years. The blue and white flowers are held upright and measure three inches across. Who would have thought that plants with names like "Rocky Mountain" and "Canadian" would find the Southeastern climate to their liking. I am sure there is a lesson here somewhere.

But before the reader is mesmerized into believing that the Southeast sounds like God's gift to gardening, let me assure you that the heat and humidity are not to be denied. When the sum of the temperature and humidity equals more than 160 for weeks on end, it always surprises me to find some plants actually thriving. *Achillea* x 'Coronation Gold' is the best large yellow-flowered form of yarrow and looks particularly outstanding beside balloon flower, *Platycodon grandiflorus*. A simple truth in gardening prevails: The more densely planted a garden, the taller will be the plants within. Since I dislike the job of staking, I plant densely so that tall plants can lean on each other. This lazy man's technique more often than not results in tangled stems and flowers but it works wonders with balloon flower. It is squeezed between *Iris pseudacorus*, lilies, and *Geranium thunbergii*, and attains the same height as the yarrow.

Like a good book, lilies hold my interest from the time they emerge until they flower. Every evening in mid-June, I walk through the garden and allow the fragrance of the regal lilies, *Lilium regale*, to caress my senses. Five-foot-tall spires of white trumpets with yellow centers are impressive in their own right, but the sweet fragrance on a still, quiet Georgia evening is impossible to ignore. They flower a little later than gold band lily, *Lilium auratum*, but earlier than *Lilium henryi*. The incurved dark orange petals of Henry's namesake bear flowers for four weeks in July and attract a myriad of butterflies. I can't find any perennials tall enough to support these six-foot giants so I use the straight branches of tulip poplar to bind them. I am glad I finally found a use for that tree. Many of the species lilies are marvelous and it is a shame that one has to hunt high and low to find them.

I use *Verbena bonariensis* every now and then and the small purple flowers atop four-foot-tall rigid stems renew my faith in plant tolerance. Many verbenas are naturalized in the Southeast, including *V. rigida* (rigid verbena), *V. canadensis* (clump verbana), and *V. tenuisecta* (moss verbena). They tolerate heat, drought, and stress far better than the bedding verbena, *Verbena* x *hybrida*, beloved of spider mites. In late summer, the daisies take over. Purple coneflowers, *Echinacea purpurea*, give way to yellow coneflowers. Cutleaf coneflower, *Rudbeckia laciniata*, and black-eyed Susans, *Rudbeckia hirta*, flirt with the echinaceas and, just as they reach their peak, the flowers of *Rudbeckia fulgida* var. *sullivantii* 'Goldsturm' and *Rudbeckia triloba* begin to take center stage. The rudbeckias provide a show from June to late August and although yellow blahs may set in, other plants come to the rescue. In my garden, I could not do without *Boltonia asteroides* 'Snowbank' and Russian sage, *Perovskia atriplicifolia*. The flowers of Russian sage are nothing to write home about but the foliage provides season-long fragrance (some say stink). The gray-green finely cut leaves provide contrast to the coarser leaves of the daisies and no self-respecting pest would touch it. *Boltonia* lights up the late summer and fall garden; leaves of gray-green are set off by creamy white flowers with yellow centers.

While some plants come and go, sometimes seemingly out of nowhere, one plant has held its foliage high all season and parades its flowers in late summer. The foliage of grape leaf anemone, *Anemone tomentosa* 'Robustissima' (syn. *A. vitifolia*), always looks fresh and crisp. Even when daylilies are wilting, the anemone foliage never lets me down. The stout flower stalks finally rise above the plant in late July, and by the beginning of August and for three weeks thereafter, the rosy flowers turn their faces to the sun. Plants tolerate conditions of full sun as well as partial shade. The only drawback is that they are invasive, but if a single clump is all I need, I make many new friends by giving away the offspring. Flowers are not as showy as the Japanese anemones, *Anemone* x *hybrida*, but the plants are more robust and the foliage more ornamental. And as the anemones and daisies take me to autumn, I revel in the number of summer flowers that thrive in the heat and humidity and I am humbled by the abundance of plants that put up with it to strut their stuff in the fall.

Fall is a long season in the South and is full of wonders. By the calendar, fall starts in September, but it's often as steamy in September as in July. However, red spider lily, *Lycoris radiata*, magically reappears in mid-September, but if you blink, you might miss it. Although flowers persist for such a short time, I look forward with anticipation to its resurrection. Cool weather meanders along sometime in October and sneaks in while no one is looking. Along with the cool weather come the flowers of velvet sage, *Salvia leucantha*, and pineapple sage, *Salvia elegans*. The former produces four-foot-tall and four-foot-wide shrubs of velvet blue flowers with white centers while the latter really does smell like pineapples (or carrot cake, according to my wife Susan). *Sedum* x 'Autumn Joy' is in marvelous form and the flowers of the *Miscanthus* grasses reach to the sky. *Vernonia glauca*, ironweed, will grow eight feet tall unless pinched at least once in mid-summer, but if handled well it puts on a marvelous display in late summer and fall. *Aster tataricus*, tatarian daisy, stuck over with the tuberose, *Polianthes tuberosa*, patiently waits until late October and November to show off its large blue flowers. The asters, chrysanthemums, and miscanthus lead me into winter. All in all, the garden has performed well and I have little to complain about. As I look out the window in January, the children are bundling up and mumbling something about being too cold. However, as others are shivering, I nonchalantly stroll through the garden to peel the frost from the heuchera and arum.

I have learned a great deal about plants and their ability to adapt to harsh conditions. However, it is me who has adapted the most. I no longer worry about snow-in-summer, lady's mantle, ligularia, or gentians. I don't give a flip if I can't grow dahlias or stocks to compete with northern gardens. I have had many opportunities to leave the South but I am still here. My garden grows a little each year and as the memories of aconitum and delphinium fade, the pleasures of verbena and boltonia are that much more appreciated.

Part 4. SPECIALISTS

Partiality is the very essence of garden making. Our gardens are built out of love, our plant choices perhaps reckless, but rarely perfunctory. As we gain experience, most of us develop a particular fondness, perhaps for iris or lilies or plants with green flowers. The worst-hit become collectors; these gardeners tend to suffer multiple passions, their gardens packed with category plants. This may mean Japanese woodlanders, species roses, or any plant named after E.A. Bowles! Of course there's room for a few dozen new daylilies each year. It won't be hard to find just the right spots for ten more clematis, even though there is already at least one crawling up every tree and shrub in the yard. Naturally, we can squeeze in every eryngium known to man; why not? For collectors and specialists, design concerns are not entirely absent, and may indeed be of great importance; yet, the well-being of our plants comes first, while the plants themselves just keep coming, first, last, and always. Not for us those stiff green spaces, dispassionately assembled according to a safely tasteful design theory and involving but a small number of reliable if unthrilling plants. Ours is a demanding passion, always pushing us forward. If our gardens are sometimes rather muddled, they are magnificent muddles, and never boring.

Garden specialists may focus on one family, perhaps aroids, or grasses, or they may embrace wider fields, such as monocots, Chinese plants, or herbs grown in Elizabethan gardens. While there are a few whose zeal for the chosen precludes other plants from their gardens, most specialists are plant lovers with significant but not exclusive predilections. Judith Jones does indeed grow a staggering number of ferns, but they are joined at every turn by perennials of other persuasions. John Kenneth Elliott's main interest may well be conifers and dwarf shrubs, yet his peaceful garden retreat is a sanctuary for chrysanthemums and hellebores, phlox and dianthus, irises and lupines, as well as a host of rock plants.

Plant enthusiasts, who appreciate the sometimes minute differences between related species, teach us both to see our plants and to study their specific cultural needs. In sharing their excitement about their own favorite plants, they encourage us to explore a little

140

further down the garden path. Carole Ottesen writes persuasively of ornamental grasses as border candidates. Joined with more conventional perennials, they add lovely texture, both in blade and blossom, elevating the border beyond the ordinary. Tom Woodham leads us past the matronly ruffles of the familiar bearded border iris to admire the subtle and varied beauties of species iris. Peter Ray and Mike Shoup are professional growers, better aquainted with the long-term needs, strengths, and weaknesses of their plants than are most hobby gardeners. Their perspectives and insights provide invaluable leads for those seeking willing yet uncommon perennials, or perennial partners for roses and other flowering shrubs. Varied, individual, even quirky, the following are tales from the smitten, lovers who want to parade the particular beauties of their plant passions before the rest of us.

JUDITH JONES is the proprietor of the Fancy Fronds fern nursery and a frequent lecturer on ferns in the garden setting. In her Seattle garden (USDA zone 8), she pairs these intricate, feathery plants with other perennials, placing the tolerant in full sun. The result is a series of eye-opening combinations that encourages visitors to rethink their assumptions about the role of ferns in their own gardens.

The Place of Ferns
Judith Jones

The place of perennials in the garden, then, is *everywhere*, to act as complements to the greater or lesser things around them.

Graham Stuart Thomas,
Perennial Garden Plants or
The Modern Florilegium

I f these words evoke images of successful or daring innovations masterfully set in place in your garden then perhaps I can interest you in further untraditional placement concepts. I'd like to present to you a few members of an ancient and honorable family who made their first terrestrial debut over 400 million years ago. Although their living descendants are relatively few in number and small in stature, it may be said that what they lack in size and number they make up for in the will to live. You will find them wallowing in water and wetlands, flourishing in forests and fields, tightly clutching and climbing tree trunks and limbs, and nestling in rock crevices in arid environments. One incorrigible family member is found on every continent except Antarctica. With such diverse and versatile natural life styles, why have they been relegated to subordinate use only in the woodland garden? I fail to comprehend the low status now accorded to a plant family that was eaten by dinosaurs yet survived the cataclysmic forces that rendered dinosaurs extinct.

You are no doubt wondering where this raving is leading you, and perhaps a faint glimmer of recognition is occurring as to the identity of this mystery family. You are in the hands of an avowed pteridomaniac, so grab your favorite spade or fork and traipse with me out of the woodland to the herbaceous border, because it is

142

about time that that grand garden area was properly integrated with ferns. This is not such a radical idea; ferns have cohabited with other herbaceous plants on their own. Of course they are quite fond of intermingling with the traditional woodsy folk, accenting the anemones or vitalizing the violas, but picture them mingling with musk mallows or meadow-rues. The results of this migration of ferns into the heart of the floral bed are astonishingly effective, both visually and functionally.

I must confess that I was forced to try this concept because, as a professional grower, it is my goal to increase the number of temperate species and varieties available to gardeners. With more than two hundred fern species and varieties to accommodate in my own finite gardening plot, I had no choice but to invade my only sunny border with those ferns that I considered capable of the challenge. This necessity has had some fortuitous benefits such as using the ferns as support systems for plants that lean or trail, and extending interest into the fall and winter months.

I fail to comprehend the low status now accorded to a plant family that was eaten by dinosaurs yet survived the cataclysmic forces that rendered dinosaurs extinct.

The temperate species of the genus *Dryopteris* have been most rewarding since these ferns are robust growers able to adapt to a fair degree of sun and they hold their foliage long after most herbaceous plants resemble dried stubble. I have used a great number of British Victorian fern varieties, since they are one of my special interests, and because they dependably provide a wide range of intriguing form and size.[1]

Beginning with *Dryopteris filix-mas*, the common male fern, you can choose varieties ranging from a twelve-inch crisped* and crested* dwarf, *D. f.-m.* 'Crispa cristata', to a slender but towering four-foot high fern, *D. f.-m.* 'Barnesii'. Described as "moderately evergreen in sheltered areas" in England, the male fern is often deciduous in North America's cooler climates. A handsome and large fern, *D. filix-mas* has pinnate-pinnatifid*, lance-shaped fronds* arising from an upright crown in vertical clusters. It is a very fast and easy grower capable of producing substantial clumps in just a few short years and is particularly likely to self-sow in suitable conditions.

The most common cultivar[2] is *D. f.-m.* 'Cristata', in which the pinnae* tips and frond apex are forked in a fan-like fashion. I prefer the cultivar called *D. f.-m.* (Cristatum) 'Jackson' (or 'Cristata Jackson'[3]), on which the pinnules* are wider and more leafy than normal, billowing out in expanded exaggeration. Its frond apex and pinnule tips are amply carved into crests. At a mature height of three feet, this well-bodied fern is stout enough to help support a neighboring, waywardly leaning white musk mallow, *Malva moschata* 'Alba'. Of a more restrained appearance is the finely-tasseled *D. f.-m.* 'Digitata Dadds' with elegant long-fingered extensions on the pinnae and apex. *D. f.-m.* 'Barnesii' is a tall narrow stately form with slightly ruffled egg-shaped pinnules. It is well suited to support weak-stemmed neighbors or to provide a vertical accent within or at the back of a herbaceous border. For a light airy backdrop or mixer, try the skeletal *D. f.-m.* 'Linearis polydactyla'. The slender reduced pinnules of this fern are finely tasseled with delicate long-fingered crests on all the final tips. Even the clusters of spore cases (or the sori*) add to its visual interest. The pinnules develop beaded edges where the large sori overlap the sides, creating a hard frizzled texture. Hardy geraniums are decorous companions for this fern. The foliage of each enhances that of the other and you will discover an interesting similarity between geranium seedheads and the beaded pinnules of *D. f.-m.* 'Linearis polydactyla'.

Moving toward the front of my border, there are two particularly nice mid-sized varieties I find indispensable. Here I use *D. f.-m.* 'Cristata nana' to support and defend a planting of the *Diascia rigescens*. Without being gently uplifted by the fern, the twinspur would almost surely meet decapitation in the mower's maw. This mid-sized crested male fern, two feet in height, has narrowly fanned tips, lending an air of finesse that would please even the purists, those who eschew all fern cultivars in favor of species. But for those not averse to flamboyance, the crested male fern for the front of the border is *D. f.-m.* 'Cristata Martindale'. It is 18 inches of swirling, fishtail-like crests on sickle-shaped ascending pinnae. And the grand finale is the "koi-ish" fillip at the tip of the frond. You may even want to keep surrounding flora from leaning on it so as to more fully appreciate its novelty. Luckily this piscatorial allure is only visually stimulating to humans; feline interests are not stimulated or else the border would surely be plundered.

The golden-scaled male fern, *Dryopteris affinis* (formerly known as *Dryopteris pseudomas* or *D. borreri*), is the male fern honed to classic perfection. Imagine amber-hued fronds, leathery in texture, grouped in graceful shuttlecock clusters held aloft by stout stipes* covered in parchment-like orange-brown scales*. Imposing symmetrical lances of pinnate-pinnatifid fronds appear purposely tailored. Each secondary division of the frond (pinnule) is square-edged and aligned with the next as if shoulder to shoulder. In the spring, brilliant golden fiddleheads or croziers*, are splendidly attired in apricot-gold scales.

D. affinis 'Crispa' (in reality a hybrid of two English species, *affinis* x *oreades*) is one of my absolute delights, with its upwardly crinkled pinnules. This fern blends well with such companion plants as yellow-blooming *Corydalis lutea* or the less common, parchment-white-blooming *C. ochroleuca*. Flank this ensemble with *Meconopsis betonicifolia* (Himalayan blue poppy) or the somewhat larger *M. grandis*.

Other cultivars of *Dryopteris affinis* demand acclaim. Mature specimens of 'Cristata The King' invite cries of rapture from garden patrons at its sumptuousness. This splendidly symmetrical fern has large shapely crests that cause the fronds to bend in sinuous four-foot arches. 'Angustata cristata' mimics this grand monarch on a smaller scale. 'Angustata cristata' seldom grows higher than 18 inches and the frond width is a mere three inches instead of eight inches. Its upward-lifting pinnae, surmounted by sculptured crests, give each frond a three-dimensional appearance, as if a valley had been chiseled down the center of the frond. Similarly narrow in form but reaching a height of three to four feet is 'Stableri'. Its pinnules are more rounded with slightly undulated edges.

Once you have grown these two garden workhorses, *D. filix-mas* and *D. affinis*, you'll be able to differentiate one from the other. But if doubt prevails, poke your nose down into a frond. If a blackish patch is visible where each pinna joins the main axis or rachis*, it is *D. affinis*.

Dryopteris dilatata (broad buckler fern) is a fern of finer detail with bipinnate* or twice-divided broad arching fronds. The broad buckler fern is a vigorous grower for intermingling in the border;

however, its stipe or stem is not as sturdy as that of the other *Dryopteris* discussed above. Yet its lacelike quality and deep bluish green color can add interest when placed among bolder plants. The flared vase-like arch of the downwardly curved (or recurved) pinnae of *D. d.* (Linearum section) 'Recurved' imparts a unique weeping appearance to this fern. Formerly listed as 'Recurvata', it is a gauzy two-foot umbrella ideal to suspend over *Hosta* 'Kabitan' and entwine with *Viola* 'White Czar'. The broadly triangular three-foot fronds of *D. d.* (Crispatum) 'Whiteside' ('Crispa Whiteside') begin in an upstanding V-shaped cluster. However, the weight of the mature crisped pinnules soon causes the fronds to sway outward. The frond color is lighter — somewhat more yellowish — than the usual muted dark green of the species. *D. d.* 'Lepidota cristata' is like a low urn of tatted lace with minute scalloped tips. Interplant this lovely fern in an embrace with the spires of *Astilbe chinensis* 'Pumila'.

The Far East has a wealth of *Dryopteris* suitable for placing in sunny sites for display or support. The most glamorous is *D. erythrosora* which more than lives up to its common name, autumn fern. Its color display is sensational. Exotic coppery-peach croziers unroll into rose-tinged, peachy-green fleshy fronds. With maturity, the three-foot fronds take on a rich leathery green while cold weather will bring a hint of russet to this peerless evergreen. As if this display were not enough, in midsummer the autumn fern produces cherry-red spore mounds on the underside of its fronds.

Much less resplendent is the shaggy shield fern, *Dryopteris cycadina* (sometimes mislabeled as *D. atrata*). Its three-foot frond is a simple pinnate blade*; the subdued olive green pinnae are marked by a darker green prominent mid-vein. Dense black scales adorn the rhizome*, stipe, and underside of the rachis, so that the unfurling fiddleheads look like menacing black caterpillars. The uncoiling of the octopus-like croziers of that imposing Goliath, *D. wallichiana*, is a breathtaking vision not to be missed. The young willowy-green fronds shine against the shaggy black stipe and rachis. Raised veining on the pinnules lends an intricately etched appearance to the mature emerald fronds, which are stout enough to act as a trellis for a leggy delphinium or foxglove. Although superficially this fern resembles *D. affinis*, it is slow to mature and shy with offsets.

For sheer impressive wonder the European royal fern, *Osmunda*

146

regalis var. *regalis*, has no peer.[4] This colossal phenomenon can attain a height of up to six feet, and a breadth of more than that, if situated near a natural pond or stream. Thick woody rhizomes overlap and interlace to form a matted spongy mass which, when given ample moisture, will sustain this fern in very exposed situations. But don't let the lack of a water feature in your garden keep you from growing this statuesque plant; it's an ancient survivor that can abide with plain garden culture. This is a fern of unparalleled mimicry; its sterile fronds copy locust tree leaves (*Robinia*) and its clusters of spore cases or panicles* resemble astilbe seedheads. In the spring, the pale pinkish-green croziers are covered at first with pale tan woolly caps that are later pushed off as the fronds develop. As the fronds grow, the color changes further from a roseate mustard to a shimmery yellow-green. The sterile fronds brown and wither with successive frosts. The fertile panicles are a vibrant green, changing to a burnished gold as the spores disperse and the fertile fronds age.

A striking variation of *O. regalis* var. *regalis* is 'Purpurascens'. The purple-stem royal fern maintains into maturity its vibrant claret-colored stipe and rachis, a pleasing color contrast against the fronds' pea-green, slightly golden hues. In England during the Victorian Fern Craze, a street vendor unknowingly collected a crested form of *Osmunda regalis* var. *regalis* that was sold while dormant to a nurseryman. The astute nurseryman refused a handsome offer for it from a famous Victorian fern specialist, E. J. Lowe. Mr. Lowe did eventually obtain this fern; he exhibited a specimen 14 feet in diameter in a flower show where he won first prize for the best fern in the show. The tips of each pinnae of the crested royal fern are beautifully fanned out like a peacock's tail; when mature, this fern is percristate*, bearing enlarged crests on the frond tip and on the pinnules as well as on the pinnae. Although this form generally will not attain the height of the species, it becomes a sizeable three to four feet. A planting of any of these royal ferns with *Anemone* x *hybrida* (the hybrid or Japanese anemone) is grand pageantry.

As I slip back into the shaded bowers of the garden where most of the larger ferns reside, I must share one last spectacular selection with you. An Asian import that is little known as yet, *Athyrium otophorum* has some of the appealing coloration of its cousin *A. niponicum* 'Pictum', the Japanese painted fern. My first experience with this fern was seeing a young plant in an English garden.

SPECIALISTS

Muted taupe-green fronds played against the shimmery purple stipes and rachises. I begged for spores. The midsummer foliage I saw did not prepare me for the ghostly lime-green unfolding immature fronds of year-old offspring. Another surprise was the more winter-hardy character of this fern compared to the Japanese painted fern. Although deciduous, A. *otophorum* holds its foliage well into winter, whereas A. *niponicum* 'Pictum' will collapse with the first frost. Imagine this companion planting of perennial and fern: two feet of dramatically arched, burgundy-stemmed, spearhead-shaped fronds interwoven with the wiry stems and tiny plum-colored florets of the great masterwort, *Astrantia major* 'Rubra'.

What I have to share about to the pteridophytes I have sown and grown, loved and sometimes mourned, would be a volume in itself, but I hope the handful of ferns paraded here for your appraisal may fill a niche in your garden. For as Graham Stuart Thomas so wisely advises us in *Perennial Garden Plants*:

> Plants in the garden must fulfil an object — to make it beautiful of course, but at the same time to augment the quality of the neighbouring plants, or to act as a contrast to them.

NOTES

1. Throughout this article, terms will be used that may be new to the reader; therefore, the following Glossary has been provided. Terms that appear in the Glossary are marked in the text with an asterisk (*) after first appearance.

GLOSSARY

Blade	the expanded portion of a frond, not including the stipe.
Crested	having the tip divided into one or more divisions or crests.
Crisped	margins finely waved or curled.
Cristate	see crested.
Crozier	fiddlehead; coiled young frond of a fern.
Frond	a fern leaf including the stipe and blade.
Panicle	a many-branched, loosely arranged cluster of spore cases.
Percristate	all tips crested including the pinnules.

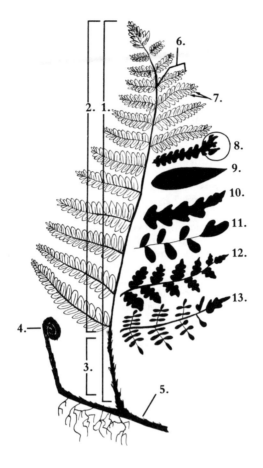

1. Frond   2. Blade   3. Stipe   4. Crosier   5. Rhizome   6. Pinna
7. Pinnules (segments)   8. Crest   9. Pinnate   10. Bipinnatifid
11. Bipinnate   12. Tripinnatifid   13. Tripinnate

Pinna	(plural-pinnae) primary division of a compound blade.
Pinnate	divided simply with pinnae arranged along either side of the rachis.
	Bipinnate: twice divided pinnately.
Pinnatifid	divided into lobes, with the clefts reaching halfway to the rachis.
Pinnule	a division of a pinna, the ultimate segment other than a pinna.
Rachis	(plural-rachises) midrib of a blade, a continuation of the stipe through the blade.

Rhizome	a thickened root stock that produces fronds above and roots below, usually creeping, although in some ferns it forms a clump holding the fronds closely together, and in others it is short, thick, and upright.
Scale	a membranous chaffy hair, found on rhizome, stipe, and occasionally the back of a frond.
Sorus	(plural-sori) arrangement or cluster of spore cases.
Stipe	leaf stalk or stem of a fern.

2. A cultivar is a horticultural variation of a species that differs from the usual form of that species by some significant growth feature. This difference is not substantial enough in terms of naturally occurring populations for a botanist to classify the variation at a proper varietal or subspecies level. There may be some overlap with the botanical division of "form," which covers naturally occurring botanical variations. Unless described as a form, minor variations or "monstrosities" may best be regarded as cultivars. When they become well established in cultivation they are certainly regarded as such. Cultivar names are indicated by the term "cv." before the name, which is capitalized if it is a proper name and lower case if it is a descriptive term, such as *Dryopteris filix-mas* cv. linearis polydactyla. Cultivar status may also be denoted by using single quotes. Capitalization is used for proper names and for the first Latinized term but not the second (if there is one); for example, *Dryopteris filix-mas* 'Linearis polydactyla'. The Victorian Latinized terms also agree with the gender of the genus to which it is applied; for example, *Athyrium* is a neuter, so a crested lady fern becomes *A. filix-femina* 'Cristatum', whereas *Dryopteris* is feminine, so the common crested male fern becomes *D. filix-mas* 'Cristata'. This concept is discussed thoroughly in J. W. Dyce's volume, *Fern Names and Their Meanings*.

3. The cultivar names of those ferns selected after 1959 will be denominated in accordance with the International Code of Nomenclature for Cultivated Plants (ICNCP). New cultivar names may not be in Latin or part-Latin but a little-used rule may be applied that allows fern growers to specify the cultivar group, so that the historical scheme of the English Victorian fern classification is not totally lost. In such a case, the cultivar group is placed in parentheses between the species designation and the given cultivar name; for example, *Dryopteris filix-mas* 'Cristata Jackson' becomes *D. f.-m.* (Cristatum) 'Jackson'.

4. The North American royal fern has been referred to as *Osmunda regalis* var. *spectabilis* in numerous botanical works since the last century. There are discernible physical differences that distinguish the North American populations from the British populations. *O. r.* var. *spectabilis* has a more willowy, habit with its pinnae pairs more widely spaced than the typical *O. r.* var. *regalis*. Most U.S. nurseries offer collected Eastern North American material and have obviously not done enough research to realize that there are botanically recognized differences between these populations. See Lellinger, Mickel, and Wherry.

BIBLIOGRAPHY

Druery, Charles. *British Ferns and Their Varieties*. London: G. Routledge & Sons, 1910.

Dyce, J. W. *Fern Names and Their Meanings*. London: British Pteridological Society, 1988.

Jones, Judith. *Fancy Fronds* (catalog). 1989.

Kaye, Reginald. *Hardy Ferns*. London: Faber & Faber, 1968.

Lellinger, David. *A Field Manual of the Ferns & Fern Allies of the United States & Canada*. Washington, D.C.: Smithsonian Institution Press, 1985.

Mickel, J. T. *How to Know the Ferns and Fern Allies*. Dubuque: W. C. Brown & Co., 1979.

Moore, Thomas. *The Nature Printed British Ferns*. 2 vols. London: Bradbury and Evans, 1859.

Ohwi, Jisaburo. *Flora of Japan*. Washington, D.C.: Smithsonian Institution Press, 1984.

Olson, Wilbur. *The Fern Dictionary*. Los Angeles: Los Angeles International Fern Society, 1977.

Page, C. N. *The Ferns of Britain and Ireland*. Cambridge: Cambridge University Press, 1982.

Thomas, Graham Stuart. *Perennial Garden Plants or The Modern Florilegium*. 2d ed. London: J. M. Dent & Sons, 1986.

Stearn, William T. *Botanical Latin*. 3d ed. London: David & Charles, 1983.

Wherry, Edgar T. *The Fern Guide: Northeastern and Midland United States and Adjacent Canada*. New York: Doubleday & Co., Inc. 1961.

CAROLE OTTESEN, a free-lance writer and photographer, has chronicled her plant loves in a number of articles and books, most recently in *Ornamental Grasses: The Amber Wave* (McGraw-Hill Publishing Company, 1989). Along with a good assortment of other perennials, ornamental grasses now fill two of the five acres that comprise her Maryland (USDA zone 7) garden. Her present interests include garden history, making outdoor rooms, and meadow gardening.

Ten Reasons to Love Ornamental Grasses
Carole Ottesen

We gardeners are susceptible to affairs of the heart. They usually begin this way: we see a gorgeous plant — always in someone else's garden — and, utterly captivated, we soon find we can think of nothing else. We may go to unbelievable lengths to acquire it. Sometimes, if we fall hard enough, the infatuation with a certain plant can become a sort of monomania in which we spend several years growing only that sort of plant and pretty much ignoring everything else.

My first big plant-crush was on tiny miniatures like pearlwort (*Sagina subulata*). That was followed by a fascination with creeping junipers. (Love is blind!) Thereafter came a long dalliance with edible landscape plants like Alpine strawberries and ostrich ferns. And of course, the unattainable stars of the traditional English perennial border first captured and then broke my heart. Nothing, however, has hit me as hard or lasted as long as my fascination with ornamental grasses.

There are reasons for this. Unlike the splendid delphiniums (which rot in our steamy Maryland summers), or minuscule plants (which are virtually invisible on the landscape scale), or junipers (!), ornamental grasses have real staying power. Their solid, enduring virtues are manifold, but the following ten qualities of ornamental grasses were what eventually turned my infatuation into an abiding love.

1. Ornamental grasses remind me of country fields. They are spontaneous, flowing, blowing subjects that soften hard lines in the garden. Not surprisingly, some of them — switch grass (*Panicum virgatum*), Indian grass (*Sorghastrum*), bluestem (*Andropogon*), and prairie cord grass (*Spartina*) — are prairie natives.

2. Ornamental grasses gratify not instantly, but very soon. A well-grown container plant, placed in the garden in spring, will very nearly have reached its maximum height and effect by the fall of its first year in the garden.

3. Ornamental grasses are easy to grow and maintain. Insects don't bother them and they are generally free from disease. Once planted, they can stay in one place for a decade. Herbaceous grasses require a trimming only once each year.

Of what other group of plants can it be said that gardeners plant them for the way they look in their dormant state when their foliage is dead?

4. Not just native grasses but others— Eulalia grass (*Miscanthus sinensis*), feather reed grass (*Calamagrostis acutiflora stricta*), and fountain grass (*Pennisetum alopecuroides*)—can take the heat of the American summer. Better yet, many (the *Miscanthus* tribe, *Arundo*, *Panicum*, *Elymus*, *Chasmanthium*) are at their peak during the dog days. Some are drought as well as heat tolerant: spangle grass or *Chasmanthium*, *Miscanthus*, *Panicum*, *Spartina*, and wild rye or *Elymus*.

5. In summer, ornamental grasses are peacemakers that blend well with other garden subjects. Place a few fountain grasses (*Pennisetum alopecuroides*) between a block of black-eyed Susans (*Rudbeckia hirta*) or orange coneflower varieties (such as *R. fulgida* var. *sullivantii* 'Goldsturm') and a field of scarlet bee balm (*Monarda didyma*). The cool green of the fountain grass establishes a calm, neutral neighborhood between clashing colors that somehow makes it all work. Soft, full grasses are also good companions to angular plants like roses.

6. Some ornamental grasses have colored or variegated foliage. Especially where hot summers shorten the blooming period of other perennials (nearly everywhere in the country), these grasses provide dependable color all summer long. Japanese blood grass (*Imperata cylindrica* 'Red Baron') is a clear red that is spectacular when backlighted. Porcupine grass (*Miscanthus sinensis strictus*) is a bright green with horizontal yellow bands. Velvet grass (*Holcus*), variegated miscanthus (*M. sinensis variegatus*), and bulbous oat grass (*Ar-*

rhenatherum elatius bulbosum variegatum) are striped white and green, while Bowles golden grass (*Carex stricta* 'Bowles Golden') and golden grass (*Milium effusum aureum*) are both a bright yellow-green.

7. Not only do ornamental grasses work hard in the summer heat, many provide a show in the fall when little else is happening. Flame grass (*Miscanthus sinensis purpurascens*) turns from quiet green to bright orange-red while prairie cord grass (*Spartina pectinata* 'Aureo-marginata') becomes a clear yellow. Others come into magnificent bloom when other perennials have already begun to shrivel into winter. Their flowers are wonderfully exotic—silken fans that resemble shimmering magenta satin and turn to bright cornsilk white. Late bloomers include foxtail or Korean reed grass (*Calamagrostis arundinacea brachytricha*), Eulalia grass (*Miscanthus sinensis*), giant miscanthus (*M. floridulus*) and giant reed (*Arundo donax*).

8. After serving in the garden colorfully and diplomatically throughout the long, hot summer, and splendidly in the fall, some grasses have spectacular winter presence. Some people actually plant fountain grass (*Pennisetum alopecuroides*), switch grass (*Panicum virgatum*), and Eulalia grass (*Miscanthus sinensis*) for the way that they look in the winter when repeated frosts have blanched them to shades of wheat and almond. Of what other group of plants can it be said that gardeners plant them for the way they look in their dormant state when their foliage is dead?

9. Ornamental grasses can take the cold of winter in the northern states. Gardeners in USDA zone 3 can enjoy wild rye (*Elymus glaucus*), switch grass (*Panicum virgatum*), and prairie cord grass (*Spartina pectinata* 'Aureo-marginata'). Northern sea oats (*Chasmanthium latifolium*), flame grass (*Miscanthus sinensis purpurascens*), and prairie dropseed (*Sporobolus heterolepsis*) are extremely cold-hardy plants (USDA zone 4). Northern gardeners should experiment; other grasses do well with winter protection.

10. Finally, ornamental grasses are nothing if not adaptable. Chameleon plants, they seem to belong in every garden and to suit every garden style. They are at home and as appropriate next to rock outcroppings or beside ponds in naturalistic gardens as they are in Victorian carpet beds. Place grasses in the perennial border and they will provide softness, body, and flowers in October. Use them in a sophisticated stylized meadow and they become the signature plants of a new American garden.

SOURCES
(See "Sources & Resources" appendix for complete addresses.)

Kurt Bluemel, Inc.
Limerock Ornamental Grasses, Inc.
Andre Viette Farm & Nursery

PETER RAY runs Puget Garden Resources, a specialty nursery on Vashon Island in Washington's Puget Sound (USDA zone 8). His display gardens are a showcase for his current favorite plants, which tend to be magnificent, if not outrageous. Photography is an abiding interest for Ray, who finds refreshment and new perspectives through the camera lens. Drought-tolerant plants, eucalypts, and uncommon border perennials are among his particular garden interests.

ISLAND
Peter Ray

When I was asked to write about my favorite perennials, I was reminded of a discussion from college days: which record collection of a musical group or composer would you most like to be stranded with on a desert island? Whether it would be the Beatles or Beethoven, Dylan or Mozart provided for some interesting conversation, but the point seemed somewhat moot because I would be looking for a way out of there, long before the sand clogged up the record grooves.

Fifteen years later I find myself living on an island with an eclectic stack of albums and an expanding collection of plants, a significant number of which are perennials. Because I am a grower as well as a designer and builder of landscapes, the search for and discovery of new plants seems endless. But soon you begin to realize that the limitations of space and various realities tend to force you into choices where the favorites usually win out.

The plants selected here are not necessarily boffo box office hits. Some are considered invasive while others are a bit too bold for those with delicate tastes or gardens of limited size. While tastes and interests change as you mature as a gardener, these plants have certain qualities that should always earn them a place in the garden.

The first of these is *Linaria purpurea*, the purple or pink toadflax, which seems to walk the line between annual and perennial. An established clump unfolds its multiple gray-green whorled spikes in the spring, climbing to an ultimate height of two to four feet and supporting sprays of miniature snapdragon-like flowers, pink ('Canon J. Went') or purple (species). The blooms last from June till August and are set in constant motion by wind or frenzied bee activity. If the plant is allowed to go to seed in an average soil, some seedlings will appear in the spring. A compost- or manure-enriched soil and a full-sun location will produce a sea of seedlings, dramatic in some areas though probably too much of a good thing in others. This tendency can be checked by removing the seedheads before they mature, and perhaps giving them to friends to unleash upon their gardens.

Erigeron karvinskianus also suffers from an unfortunate common name, bonytip fleabane. I suppose if the ranks of names like viper's bugloss, mugwort, and toadflax were much greater, true botanical names would be more readily accepted in the language of plant commerce. While I don't know if fleas give a wide berth to this creeper, it certainly flows over rocks and soil just as its true name rolls off the tongue, ("air-ridge-air-on").

Although sometimes referred to as the Massachusetts highway rose, *Rosa rugosa* does not deserve a plebeian status. . . .

Beginning its bloomfest in May, the erigeron starts with a small, single white daisy that fades to varying shades of pink over the next few days as more new ones are opening white, providing a consistent show until the first hard frost. It flowers well in both partially shaded borders and sunny rockeries. In the shade the foliage stays a middle green while adding a bronze-purple to its palette in full sun. Being another moderate self-sower, this is one plant I'm always happy to see pop up around the garden.

A plant that shouldn't make surprise visits, especially in small gardens where you are worried about scale, is the giant *Gunnera manicata*. Looking a bit like a prop from the movie *Lost Worlds*, *Gunnera*'s five-foot-wide leaves supported by thick, spiny stalks provide an excellent setting for playing with those trendy dinosaur toys, or just a place to hide from the sun, rain, or nosy neighbors. On a recent trip to England, three of us big kids were able to stand upright beneath the spreading leaves of a grove of gunnera plants while wondering if this was indeed the true garden room to which Vita Sackville-West was alluding. Being in the shadier part of Savill Garden, the stalks appeared to be stretching for light, while the plants in full sun stayed more compact, if that's what you can call it. In either sun or shade, give this plant wet feet, use a little imagination, and have a lot of fun.

While we are in the realm of big fun, we need to talk about *Inula helenium*. Starting out as a ring of purple-green shoots in the spring, this plant soon unfolds to a massive foliar display somewhat resembling a hosta, with its dark green leaves spilling in all directions. A plant from seed will only produce foliage the first and sometimes even the second year in the garden. But when the plant is mature, the foliage show is just the appetizer. By mid-July, what was once a solid leaf mass three feet tall now opens into a translucent sheaf as the flower stalks stretch skyward. Having reached its ultimate height of six to eight feet by mid-August, *Inula* holds its clusters of three-inch-wide yellow-orange flowers against the blue skies of late summer. Who needs fireworks with this plant around the garden?

Actually I enjoy pyrotechnic display, so a botanical simile or metaphor is always welcome in the garden. *Allium christophii* (star of Persia) reminds me of a July Fourth starburst shower that has been frozen in space and time, and its spent bloom remains in my garden as I wish those gold and silver streamers would hang in the July night sky. But while the *Allium* bloom fades away, various species of *Agapanthus* and the feather grass, *Stipa gigantea*, carry on an aerial display late into the summer.

Three *Agapanthus* varieties have proved hardy here. Even after our unexpected zone 7 plunge last winter, all African lily plantings reported in healthy this spring. The British Headbourne hybrids are supposed to be the hardiest of the lot; while I'm not looking forward to a winter like the last, it would nonetheless be interesting to see how the different agapanthus fare in a similarly cold winter without snow cover. But let's get back to summer. *Agapanthus* starts as a clump of dark green, strap-like leaves, somewhat like *Liriope* (lily-turf) on steroids. Then in mid-July, flower stalks shoot up out of the foliage to support umbels of blue or white (and in the case of one of my seedlings, white fading to pale blue) trumpet-shaped flowers. These are fairly long-lived in the garden and, as florists will tell you, they do quite well as cut flowers. The highly ornate blooms and lush foliage belie the fact that *Agapanthus* is tolerant of a fair amount of drought, which makes it an excellent plant for the water-conscious gardener as well.

Stipa gigantea (giant feather grass) is also drought tolerant, unlike its emerald carpet relatives. But this is a grass that should never see a scythe during the summer, let alone the underside of a Lawn-Boy mower. As the third part of the garden fireworks trio, it is the longest blooming and most delicate of the three. This *Stipa* is a clumping grass with its blades reaching to two feet and remaining mostly evergreen. The bloom stalk appears in May with the flowers — or what the botanists call spikelets and glumes — coming on not long thereafter, but before the stalk has reached its full height of six to seven feet. As the flowers fade and the seed drops, the amber-colored chaff hangs on in a delicate display that lasts the rest of the summer. I have yet to find any seedlings, for plants in this area seldom if ever set viable seed.

Nothing has been mentioned so far about fragrance as a garden attribute. Some may see this as a gross oversight on my part, but it is truly not intended. As I write this, the fragrance of fresh carnations is wafting across the kitchen counter, the *media res* of this household. As I wander about the nursery, which I tend to do quite a lot, the boldly aromatic *Spartium junceum*, or Spanish broom, sweetly scents the air all summer. So perhaps fragrance is just taken for granted around here and the visual qualities most often define plant favorites. Two plants did, however, make the list that have fragrance as a major attribute: *Rosa rugosa* and *Romneya coulteri*.

Although sometimes referred to as the Massachusetts highway rose, *Rosa rugosa* does not deserve a plebeian status, nor the trashing it received at a rose symposium I recently attended. Taken out of that rarefied conference context and placed in the nursery demonstration bed, the Rugosa receives summer-long compliments for its clarity of bloom, clean foliage, strong fragrance, and the spectacular display of hips it puts on throughout the waning days of summer and into the fall. And this is not the highly touted 'Fru Dagmar Hastrup', but rather a random group of now mature seedlings that were planted before they had bloomed a first time. Three more marks in the plus column for this general factotum of Plantland are that, once established, it needs no irrigation; it doesn't need pruning; and its hips are a great source of vitamin C. About the only thing *R. rugosa* doesn't do is provide a shady spot to read a book on a hot afternoon, but that is a tree's job.

Romneya coulteri, the Matilija poppy, is also located in the dry garden demonstration bed and seems to thrive on neglect. About the time the last blooms are fading from *Rosa rugosa*, the first tissue-paper-thin white blooms with raised, egg-yoke-orange centers (hence the name "fried egg plant") begin to open. With the flowers borne on sparsely foliated gray-green stalks up to five feet tall, this plant comes back from its winter pruning to form an impressive mound of foliage, and blooms with a mild fragrance reminiscent of *Rosa rugosa*'s. It is also an underground runner, but is easily controlled by selective root pruning. Although the Matilija has a reputation for being a difficult plant to start, given a well-drained, sunny location and a moderate amount of initial attention, it should grow to be a prominent attraction in the garden.

So, too, should the last plant on my list. *Verbena bonariensis* (Brazilian verbena) looks like it comes straight out of some sci-fi metallurgy lab, constructed with superlight, superstrong alloys. But it's just a collection of cells and chlorophyll, put together to defy gravity, with a hint of alien mysticism. Its lavender-purple four-inch-wide clusters of tiny flowers are held four feet off the ground by pencil-thin (a gardener friend calls them pencil plants), nearly leafless stalks. While it can go anywhere in the garden, I like to put it in front of shorter plants. Viewed through its blooms, those plants' blossoms blend with the color of the verbena. This *Verbena* can mix with *Platycodon* (balloon flower) or *Liatris* (gayfeather) and contrast with *Asclepias* (milkweed) or *Kniphofia* (torch lily) and still not be in the way. *Verbena bonariensis* belongs in almost any garden. Invite one home, if for no other reason than to amaze your friends with its cosmic balancing act.

Now it is time to get off the page and back to the soil. Seed is waiting to be collected and sown while cuttings need to callus and root. I will sit and listen to Mozart and the Dead Milkmen, as I will continue to grow *Codonopsis* (bonnet bellflower) and *Nigella* (love-in-a-mist). Perhaps next year's favorite plant will come from a substitute seed packet in an overseas order or as a discarded plant from a friend's garden. When dealing with one's own garden, it is easy to see how once-favored plants can fall into disfavor because of habit or scale or change in taste. But when creating gardens for others, certain plants become like favored old craftsmen, always ready to work their magic on a given area of the garden. Still, even favorites can change; ask me in ten years which ones are still around the garden.

LIZ DRUITT and **MIKE SHOUP** are united in their appreciation for roses. Druitt, a free-lance writer, heads the research department of the Antique Rose Emporium in Brenham, Texas (USDA zone 8). The nursery, which specializes in own-root heritage roses that take the Texas climate with aplomb, is owned by Shoup. The two have collaborated on numerous articles for national publication, and are working on a book about old roses in garden design.

A Garden Wedding
Liz Druitt and Mike Shoup

S omething old, something new, something borrowed. . . . " That old lucky charm that is supposed to start a marriage off right has a great deal of application in the modern garden. Now that gardeners are beginning to regret their dull and tidy privet hedges and to yearn for a garden like their grandmother's, full of a soft riot of changing colors, there's a lot to be said for combining old and new, creating a modern garden that uses the best of the past.

One very popular form of old-fashioned garden that has been taken out of mothballs is the herbaceous border. This style of planting along a wall or pathway offers multi-season color, plus a layered beauty of contrasting form and texture in a mixture of perennials and lush old roses. Since it can be planned to fit any size yard, whether the space is a ten-foot cottage flower bed or a 200-foot formal border, the herbaceous border is a fine "something old" idea to bring forward into today's gardens.

"Something borrowed," in order to create this beautiful effect, is a plant list from Grandmother herself. With color coming back into the American yard there is a reawakening to the value of old and beautiful plants. Many of the desirable plants that Grandmother grew were colorful, delightfully fragrant, and very hardy. This last is fortunate, because otherwise many of them would not have tolerated the last 50 or 80 years of neglect, hanging on in forgotten places like cemeteries (that do not have "perpetual care" service) and abandoned homesteads. True, many of the old perennials were native American plants such as the salvias, purple coneflowers, lantanas and others that can still be collected in the wild and brought back into the garden. European introductions, though, have also managed to prove themselves by surviving and naturalizing: yarrow, for example, or the beautiful, but in some climates invasive, purple loosestrife (*Lythrum salicaria*).

These old-fashioned perennials are not the only valuable remnants from bygone gardens. Some of the most wonderful survivors from the past are the forgotten varieties of garden roses. Indispensable as the backbone of the old herbaceous border, a multitude of neglected classes is being rediscovered with amazement by gardeners who thought roses only came in "large-flowered" (Hybrid Tea) and "cluster-flowered" (Floribunda and Grandiflora) types.

Place a prickly, shaggy-budded Moss rose such as the three-foot-high 'Little Gem' (1880) next to á six-foot-tall 'Mutabilis' (1896), a China rose with red-tipped, neatly pointed foliage and flowers whose five silky petals change from peach to pink to dark rose under the strong Southern sun, and any normal gardener will begin to get interested. Or juxtapose the full sleek bush of an old Tea rose, such as Teddy Roosevelt's favorite, the robust-flowering pink 'Duchesse de Brabant' (1857), with the squat rough-leaved form of the rich crimson Rugosa hybrid 'Mrs. Anthony Waterer' (1898). "Is that a rose?" the gardener can't help asking. "And that? And that, *too*?" It soon becomes obvious that the Hybrid Tea class is just the tip of an immense iceberg of beautiful varieties.

There is, in fact, enough variety of form among the classes of roses that a gardener wishing to try "something new" with the old varieties could have a field day. Instead of a lush and varied herbaceous border created primarily of perennials, accented by a few choice rosebushes, a similar border can be imagined using contrasting forms of roses with a few choice perennials that complement and heighten the effect. After all, one can grow tired of daisies, bored to tears with evergreens, sick even of the penetrating scent of jasmine or gardenias, but of roses, in their delightful diversity, where even the fragrance varies wildly from class to class, there can never be too many.

From a practical standpoint, a border dominated by a mixture of old roses would be much simpler to maintain than a full bed of herbaceous plants. Many varieties of old garden roses will bloom repeatedly through the entire growing season, and will stay lush and green even when not performing. This eliminates some of the difficulty of planning for potential bare spots as different perennials stretch up to bloom and then sink back down to their display of uninteresting foliage or disappear below the soil line. Unlike their modern cousins, old roses are generally more resistant to disease, so planting masses of them wouldn't require an exhaustive spraying program or frequent replacement of plants. Why not then be selfish in the garden, and at the same time generous with the beauty of roses?

It's easy to picture a beautiful, unique border featuring a back row of leggy, upright Hybrid Perpetual roses such as 'Paul Neyron' (1869), 'Souvenir du Dr. Jamain' (1865), 'American Beauty' (1875), and 'Frau Karl Druschki'(1901) in the six- to eight-foot range, broken now and then by a large mound of the old Rambler 'Russelliana' (pre-1837) to bloom crimson in the spring, or *Rosa moschata* to bloom pure white in the summer and fall.

Some of the most wonderful survivors from the past are the forgotten varieties of garden roses.

In the three- to five-foot middle ground, full bushes of constantly blooming Teas, Chinas, and Rugosas could be planted in drifts of like colors: shades of pink or crimson, or apricot and white. The strong differences in their leaves, prickles, and branching habits would keep the eye quite easily entertained, while the diversity of rich fragrance would be a delight to the nose.

Space in the foreground could be filled with the smallest (one- to three-foot tall) Chinas like 'Hermosa' (1840) or 'Roulettii' (pre-1818) and with the bushy little Polyanthas like pale pink 'The Fairy' (1932), white 'Katharina Zeimet' (1901), or apricot 'Perle d'Or' (1884). The short, upright Hybrid Perpetual 'Marquise Boccella' (1842), or some of the once-blooming but charming little Moss roses, would provide a spiky contrast at this front level.

To enhance the roses, silver-foliage plants like the large short-lived dusty miller (*Centaurea cineraria*), which makes a three-foot lacy mound that blooms with purple thistle-like flowers in summer, could be placed towards the back, with downy gray lamb's ears (*Stachys byzantina*) in soft, thick mounds planted in patches at the front of the border. Forming compact one-foot masses, 'Sheila McQueen' is an ideal lamb's ear for fronting rose beds. These pale foliage colors bring light and calm into a vivid, richly colored garden.

For the requisite "something blue", the cultivars of mealy-cup sage (*Salvia farinacea*) are excellent, from the huge, four-foot broad display of 'Indigo Spires' (an exciting modern *S. farinacea* cross) to the more compact dusty-blue mealy-cup sage cultivars such as 'Victoria' and 'Blue Bedder'. The blossoms of 'Indigo Spires' are a rich, dark color and the other cultivars offer a pale, sophisticated gray-blue. The salvias are in bloom throughout the growing season with long blue spikes that are splendid to include in cut arrangements with old roses.

Poppies and columbines in delicate jewel tones, pinks and daylilies with old-fashioned fragrance and reliability, and bearded irises with handsome flowers and erect evergreen foliage could all be tucked in clumps between rose bushes for the pleasure of it, as could scented violets (*Viola odorata*). Lavender-flowered bouncing bet (*Saponaria officinalis* 'Rosea Plena') might be planted as a hardy groundcover.

These tried and true perennials would make an effective court to support the Queen of Flowers, and would offer the additional benefit of filling in any dull spaces as the rose bushes came in and out of bloom, as well as adding visual spice to the changing seasons. The final effect would be enough blooming beauty to give gardeners in the neighboring yards knotted stomachs from jealousy and should provide almost (perhaps) enough roses to satisfy anyone.

If this sort of border seems like a daring step away from known ground, it is really no different than any other marriage. Built solidly on the foundation of past styles and plant choices, with a few innovative ideas for a promising future, it is a combination that even Grandmother would understand. Now that gardens are moving away from the green shrub look, as boring as lime-colored Jello gelatin, and toward the exciting possibilities of color, remember those plants that have stood the test of time in all their beauty and dare to use them in new ways. Gather your roots and move forward.

SOURCES
(See "Sources & Resources" appendix for complete addresses.)

Antique Rose Emporium
Heritage Rose Gardens
Historical Roses
Pickering Nurseries, Inc.
Roses of Yesterday & Today

JOHN KENNETH ELLIOTT has lived through many plant passions, and his garden, on Massachusetts' Cape Cod (USDA zone 5), bears witness to his ability to combine his collections artistically. Each plant is grown as well as possible and all are woven into a harmonious whole. The garden itself is not intended to be a showplace but a soothing retreat in which visitors are offered "freedom from worldly thoughts."

Perennials at San Mai An
John Kenneth Elliott

B ut everything is GREEN!"
The speaker, a visiting gardener, had just walked with me through my gardens, and in response to my casual, "Well, what do you think?" offered her incredible statement. Incredible to me because I saw color!

My thuja-hedged garden is dominated by a collection of dwarf and pygmy conifers, small and unique rhododendrons, compact evergreen azaleas, choice heaths and heathers, distinctive hollies, delightful ornamental grasses, and rare dwarf Japanese maples. Mostly green. But green *is* a color—one of quiet, peace, and serenity. As William Cullen Bryant observed, "The groves were God's first temples."[1] And so green is what I have.

Had my wits been a bit quicker at that moment, I might have expanded my visitor's vision. Everything isn't green! I have the breath-taking red and orange brilliance of the first maple leaves, the burnished bronze and the soft mauve winter foliage of various dwarf conifers as well as that of certain calluna cultivars, whose off-season foliage colors match the excitement of their late summer bloom. And berries—red—of the bearberry cotoneaster (*Cotoneaster dammeri*); of American holly (*Ilex opaca*); of English hollies (*I. aquifolium*) 'Boulder Creek', 'Balkans', 'San Jose'; berries that are irresistible to the mockingbirds, catbirds, robins, and blue jays that leave the garden devoid of all berries by early March! And, here, too, are the reds, blues, and shining blacks of such ornamental grasses as the Japanese blood grass (*Imperata cylindrica* 'Red Baron'), blue sheep's fescue (*Festuca amethystina* 'Superba'), and black mondo grass (*Ophiopogon planiscapus* 'Nigrescens')! Incredible, indeed!

Still, her comment lingered in my mind, and I began to realize

166

that to many gardeners the seasonal colors of flowering woody perennials might not compare with those of herbaceous perennials. Should perennials have been my quest instead of conifers? Should I, Iago-like, have said to myself, "Put perennials in thy garden. When you are sated with heathers and conifers, you will rue the error of your choice. Therefore, put perennials in your garden"?

No. I had made my choice and followed where it led me, and so while remaining faithful to my little trees, I moved toward using herbaceous perennials as adjuncts, companion plants, colorful accents that contrast with the serenity of green conifers. I would try perennials as marginal blendings, as sudden surprises, appearing in pots,

For whatever reason, whiteness *does* appeal and gardeners create white gardens.

beds, groups, as low hedges, borders, and contoured dividers between larger areas. Perennials would be secondary plants to be sure, but treated always with sensitivity and respect for their varietal uniqueness, their unusual forms—all in keeping with my interest in specialty plants of distinction. Such discriminating usage produces subtle but satisfying growth patterns that enhance each other "like the superimposed themes of contrapuntal music".[2]

If you will let me lead you along my grassy paths, I will show you how perennials have enriched my Cape Cod garden, San Mai An. Entering through the Crane Gate, we see a contoured prospect that is representative of the entire garden: small plants, a small world, a forest of lilliput. A dense eight-foot-high thuja hedge quite effectively conceals the outside from us, thereby granting us "freedom from worldly thoughts" or San Mai An, a Japanese phrase that I have taken as an appropriate name for my peaceful green microcosm.

The tall thuja hedge to our right is there not because the dwarf conifers need its protection, but because it helps to unify the entire scene and to emphasize the concept of a small world that is not intruded upon by outside thoughts. Hedging was a practice advocated by an Old Testament writer who cautioned, "Look that thou hedge thy possessions about . . . for where no hedge is, there the possession is spoiled."[3] On behalf of the plants less hardy than the conifers, this warning sounds anew, for winter on Cape Cod brings killing northwest winds and sudden, drastic temperature drops. Without adequate or lasting snow cover, without the hedge, this coastal climate would play havoc with tender perennials.

The grassy sward before us separates a heath and heather garden from a dwarf conifer planting; I call it the "approach." Just as the approach to ancient Shinto shrines prepared the visitor for the quiet within — the long pathway from the outer gate enabling one to shed the distractions of the world, to clear the mind so that one could meet the serenity of the inner compound with a quiet spirit — so this short walk from the Crane Gate past these dwarf conifers prepares us for a world of small, irregular, continent-like beds held together by sinuous grass paths.

On one hand, we see a choice Canadian hemlock (*Tsuga canadensis* 'Curley') and a graceful Norway spruce (*Picea abies* 'Inversa') in the colorful company of assorted callunas and ericas. On the other hand, there is a dwarf weeping *Ginkgo biloba*; a feathery, ivoried Japanese cedar 'Sekkan-sugi' (*Cryptomeria japonica*); even a tiny 15-year-old, six-inch English yew 'Standishii' (*Taxus baccata*) surrounding a low but sedate Japanese maple (*Acer palmatum* 'Shishigashira' or "mane of a lion"); all of them lead to the diminutive mound where a lovely specimen of Japan's sacred tanyosho pine, *Pinus densiflora* 'Umbraculifera', has held court since its youth 12 years ago.

After leaving the evergreen approach, we pass the White Garden. This garden, the foremost of several perennial surprises, appears at our first turning; it is a small rectangular bed between two 20-year-old American hollies (*Ilex opaca* 'Jersey Princess') and two Eastern white pines (*Pinus strobus*) whose candles have been cut each spring for 20 years so that they are now like two clouds of blue-green softness. I call them my "powder-puff" trees.

This is the White Garden. "Whiteness," wrote Herman Melville, "enhances beauty, as if imparting some special virtue of its own, as in marbles, japonicas, and pearls," to which ponderous thought he adds, "We have not yet learned why whiteness appeals with such power to the soul."[4] To Melville's list of white allurements, I add this garden's inventory: white *Stachys byzantina* (lamb's ears); white *Dicentra eximia* 'Alba' (fringed bleeding heart); white *Phlox paniculata* 'Mt. Fuji' (garden phlox); white *Chrysanthemum* x *superbum* 'Alaska' (Shasta daisy); white *Helleborus niger* (Christmas rose); white *Anem-*

one x *hybrida* 'Honorine Jobert' (Japanese anemone); white *Chrysanthemum weyrichii* 'White Bomb' (Miyabe); white *Delphinium* x *belladonna* 'Casa Blanca'; white *Arabis caucasica* 'Snow Cap'(wall rock cress); white *Iris cristata* 'Alba' (crested iris) and *I. sibirica* 'Fourfold White' (Siberian iris); white *Iberis sempervirens* 'Little Gem' (evergreen candytuft); and others. White, all white. Whiteness *does* enhance beauty. These plants are more than just lovely perennials. They are *white* perennials.

For whatever reason, whiteness *does* appeal and gardeners create white gardens. They also create blue, pink, or yellow ones, "name gardens" Gertrude Jekyll called them. In one of her inimitable observations about such gardens, her exasperation is evident:

> It is a curious thing that people will sometimes spoil some garden project for the sake of a word. For instance, a blue garden, for beauty's sake, may be hungering for a group of white lilies, or for something of palest lemon-yellow, but it is not allowed to have it because it is called the blue garden, and there must be no flowers in it but blue flowers . . . Surely the business of the blue garden is to be beautiful as well as to be blue. My own idea is that it should be beautiful first, and then just as blue.[5]

My agreement with that lovely rebuke is perhaps the reason why there is a pink lenten rose, *Helleborus orientalis*, growing alongside of the white garden!

Just beyond the White Garden is the Wall Garden, a small flat area that features a lotus pool, several dwarf conifers, and a magnificent 20-year-old specimen of *Picea pungens* 'Glauca Pendula'. The drooping horizontal main branches of this unique Colorado blue spruce tumble over a low brick wall to a short pathway that is bordered by evergreen azaleas of the 'Satsuki' strain. We have returned to the green world unless we pass here in June. Then, the salmon or orange blossoms of the azaleas blend nicely with the orange-red of the wall.

From the patio adjacent to the Wall Garden, we look back across a very gentle grassy slope to the contoured perennial garden dividing the scene from left to right. In this long, free-form perennial bed (as close as we have come to the traditional treatment of perennials), I strove for a balance of color, texture, form, winter hardiness, soil compatibility, durability in and out of the bed ("and," quietly added my wife and gardening partner, "just plain old favorites!"). So many instrumental qualities must be balanced in the garden's visual symphony. Each quality must be allowed to express itself to the utmost, yet great care must be exercised. Allow any one to these to cancel out the others and a cacophony would result.

Here in full sun, where the color intensity of bloom and foliage is highest, the clear light works its magic over leaf size, texture, plant height, and blossom. Variety and color abound. For the perennial contour we chose blues such as billowy *Linum perenne* (perennial flax); startling *Eryngium maritimum* (sea holly); *Platycodon grandiflorus* (balloon flower); *Iris sibirica*; *Polemonium caeruleum* 'Blue Pearl' (Jacob's ladder); *Tradescantia* x *andersoniana* (spiderwort); pinks such as *Platycodon grandiflorus* 'Shell Pink'; *Dianthus gratianopolitanus* 'Tiny Rubies'; *Phlox paniculata* 'Bright Eyes'; raspberry-hued *Astilbe chinensis* 'Pumila'; *Heuchera sanguinea* 'Rosea'; yellows such as *Oenothera tetragona* 'Highlight' (sundrops); lemony *Lilium*; *Lupinus*; buttery *Hypericum calycinum* (Aaron's beard); lavenders such as *Iris ensata* (Japanese iris); royal purple *Lupinus*; oranges including *Lilium*; *Trollius* x *cultorum* 'Empire Day' (hybrid globeflower); and whites such as pristine *Phlox paniculata* 'Mt. Fuji' and creamy *Narcissus*. In addition, there are mixes elsewhere of yellow, bronze, and pink chrysanthemums; dahlias in three color groups (red and pink, orange and yellow, and lavender); a potpourri of primula, delphinium, and clematis; and a long narrow border of perennial tulips.

Superimposing color choices on the seasons revealed some interesting perspectives. Autumn's Japanese exhibition chrysanthemums (sprayed with growth retardant and carefully pinched on schedule) are perennial excitement to a high degree. The chrysanthemums are challenged only by the dahlias bravely pushing forward with the last of their seasonal reserve, while quietly, nearby, the soft, subdued foliage of sundrops, *Oenothera tetragona* 'Highlight', elicits appreciation. Elsewhere in San Mai An, winter is graced by the yellow, orange, red, and plum hues of heather foliage and the January-February blossoms of spring heath; here in the perennial garden, winter would be bleak indeed without the tiny, intense pink and lavender clusters of hardy cyclamen from September to March.

Spring, however, is a strong perennial season for us. There are crocuses, daffodils, primulas, poppies (which have been called "the extreme of beauty" by an ancient Haiku poet[6]), tulips, violets, wildflowers, hardy cyclamen, and peonies—herbaceous and tree. With the exception of the *Oenothera* and tuberous-rooted begonias (*Begonia* x *tuberhybrida*, Blackmore & Langdon strain), summer colors are more soft than vivid. Summer is marked by the blossoms of phlox, lupines, balloon flowers, irises, dahlias, coral bells (blooming beautifully at the same time as the tree wisteria directly behind it), clematis, lilies, and daylilies. The daylilies are a poignant reminder of life's transience; the Japanese call them the "forget me" flower.

While there is, in this perennial contour, a careful arrangement of plants (my subconsious response, perhaps, to the influence of those ancient Chinese who cultivated a sense of where things belong), for me their place reaches far beyond this bed, and far beyond my garden. I see the placement of each particular species as a visual echo of that species' color, shape, and texture in all other times and all other places. At which mystical thought, I suspect, that wonderfully practical Gertrude Jekyll might smile indulgently, and softly (but firmly) add:

> The correct placement of plants is a reflection of one's aesthetic nature; if good forms and color groupings are realized, the result will be years of enjoyment. It is absolutely necessary that a plant group relate to what is near [and] to the overall nature of the garden as a whole.[7]

While rich and brilliant colors are to be relished, most of the hues in this bed are soft, making it yet another form of "approach," this time to the gardens farther back. The loose, airy forms of the perennials play in concert with the dappled patterns of sunlight filtering down among the pines in the grove beyond the contour bed.

Turn to the left and we walk through the Japanese Garden bounded on one side by a 20-year-old Atlas cedar (*Cedrus atlantica* 'Glauca Pendula'), and at one end by the *tsukubai* (the ritual water basin of the Japanese tea garden); the mid-point is marked by an *Acer palmatum dissectum* 'Crimson Queen'. The red branches of this threadleaf Japanese maple fall gently to the pine needle mulch while the soft gray-blue boughs of the cedar touch the ground and move over it.

It is here, in a quiet corner near the *tsukubai*, that we see the first of the ornamental grasses, an unobtrusive blue-green clump of *Festuca ovina glauca* that is often less noticed than the nearby variegated bamboo, *Arundinaria viridistriata*. The *Arundinaria* is placed behind a bamboo flume from which a steady trickle of water dances into the basin below; here, its gold and green leaves present a sharp contrast to the surrounding green of the woody plants. While visitors do not often comment on this subtle contrast, they will say the bamboo appears more "Oriental" or that it "seems to belong" where it is. This last observation is true both symbolically and traditionally.

I have always associated grasses with three specific settings that enhance their beauty: wide and open spaces in which an endless vista of glistening grass rolls wave-like toward an indistinct horizon; an open plaza of a great building before whose hard, flat surface the tall supple grasses arch over gracefully; a public garden in which clumps of showy grasses exhibit feathery plumes in a flamboyant display. But San Mai An is devoid of open space and tall, flat surfaces, and its resident gardener has a strong aversion to flamboyance. So the ornamental grasses, like the flowering perennials, appear as supporting players in the garden drama, discreetly visible beside a pond, around a jardiniere, within a circle of heath and heather, next to a bog. Their quiet presence, their reserved demeanor, charms the visitor whose pleasure is heightened by the discovery of them. Among our favorites: *Briza media* (quaking grass); *Imperata cylindrica* 'Red Baron' (Japanese blood grass); *Carex morrowii variegata* (silver variegated Japanese sedge); *Arrhenatherum elatius bulbosum variegatum* (bulbous oat grass); *Festuca amethystina* 'April Gruen' (olive-green sheep's fescue), 'Bronzeglanz' (bronze-color sheep's fescue); *Festuca amethystina* 'Superba' (blue sheep's fescue); *Phalaris arundinacea* 'Picta' (ribbon grass); *Equisetum scirpoides* (dwarf horse tail). Favorite bamboos and grass-like plants are *Ophiopogon planiscapus* 'Nigrescens' (black mondo grass); *Arundinaria disticha* (dwarf fern-leaf bamboo), and *A. pygmaea* (pygmy bamboo); and *Bambusa glaucescens* 'Alphonse Karr' (syn. *B. multiplex*).

Moving ahead, we reluctantly leave the Japanese garden with its playful trickle of water falling from the bamboo spouts over a "sea of stones," but soon we will again hear the soft sound of falling water. Our attention is drawn past two weeping cherries above dwarf conifers, past a primrose circle and the chrysanthemum bed, to Medake Pond ("Medake" means female or gentle cascade). If we rest for a moment at the pond house patio during spring, we are completely captivated by the herbaceous peony border. ("When the Peonies bloomed, it seemed as though there were no flowers around them."[8]) Blossoming here are 'Emma Klehm', 'Sarah Bernhardt', 'Miss America', 'Scarlet O'Hara', 'Mrs. Franklin D. Roosevelt' as well as 'Best Man', 'Sweet 16', 'Pink Parfait', 'Charlie's White', 'Festiva Maxima', and others.

Along the edge and to one side of this patio is a judicious grouping of potted tuberous-rooted begonias. Their display of brilliant colors—bright pink, deep crimson, pure white, and vibrant orange—stands out from the conifer backdrop and makes a bold statement, much like that of the doomed but defiant Antigone uttering her impassioned plea before the dignified chorus. Such surprises demand that we attend their stimulating effect. This use of a single plant type as an accent, which I have done in several places and in a variety of ways at San Mai An, is a statement not only of beauty but also of practicality. It serves to further unify the overall design.

As every serious gardener knows, perennials are not purchased as groceries are, by the bagful. Nor are they placed all together any more than all foodstuffs would be stored in one cupboard. The placement of perennials requires a discriminating mix; perennial selection and arrangement are concomitant to me. The overall garden design—not of one single area such as the White Garden or the Japanese garden, but of the whole—peers over my shoulder, watches critically, and never hesitates to express itself forcefully.

The design procedure is long and demanding. Constant attention, increased knowledge, and experience result not only in more and different plans, but also in renewed determination to alter (often drastically) an established design. In the case of San Mai An, this procedure led me to add the seasonal color of herbaceous plants to the garden's tranquil groves of green.

Selectivity evolves from steadfast research, and results in a multitude of "rejections" (a word used to ease the pain of "failure"). A gardener must be able to pull up a plant that is not living up to high standards, even to say "To hell with it," and throw it on the rubbish heap. If one has a commitment to the pursuit of excellence in the art of gardening, then compromises are not acceptable.

We are very like Vergil's gardener: "animated by [a] belief in life, impelled by [an] appreciation of earth's bounty, governed by intelligence, inspired by purpose."[9] It is this that motivates us to produce, in cooperation with our environment, results that will evoke within our gardens' visitors a sense of fulfillment and an appreciation that is more for nature than for our poor handiwork. Our reward lies deep within our covenant with the natural world and might well be expressed as a Wordsworthian echo:

> . . . Nature never did betray
> the heart that loved her; 'tis her privilege,
> Through all the years of this our life, to lead
> From joy to joy.[10]

Visitors to San Mai An today continue to experience the garden's green quiet. While San Mai An was never conceived as a perennial garden in terms of perennial design, plant lists, color schemes, or favorites, and while it has not evolved into a perennial garden, its grassy paths, which meander through patterns of evergreen and flowering woody plants, do bring the visitor frequently before the hardy perennial. My perennials are like a line of onlookers that stretches for miles at a giant parade, with each individual waving, having already waved, or preparing to wave a small colorful flag. Each is eager to express itself in a banner of beauty, and each is cherished for itself. So do my perennials stand. Some are at the beginning of a seasonal line, others at the end. Together, they lead visitors from joy to joy.

NOTES

1. William C. Bryant, *The American Tradition in Literature*, Vol. 1, Revised Edition (New York: W.W. Norton & Co., Inc., 1961), p. 438.

2. William R. Nelson, *Planting Design* (Champaign: Stipes Publishing Co., 1985), p. 10.

3. Frank C. Thompson, Ed., *The New Chain-Reference Bible*, 3rd Improved Edition (Indianapolis: B.B. Kirkbride Bible Co., 1934), p. 647.

4. Herman Melville, *Moby Dick* (New York: Bobbs-Merrill Co., Inc., 1964), pp. 253, 263.

5. Gertrude Jekyll, *Colour Schemes For The Flower Garden* (Woodbridge, Suffolk: Antique Collectors' Club, 1982), Frontispiece.

6. R. H. Blyth, *Haiku*, Vol. 3 (Tokyo: Hokuseido Press, 1968), p. 317.

7. Jekyll, p. 296.

8. Blyth, p. 285.

9. Smith Palmer Bovie, trans., *Vergil's Georgics* (Chicago: University of Chicago Press, 1966), p. xxx.

10. Alexander M. Witherspoon, *The College Survey of English Literature* (New York: Harcourt, Brace, & World, Inc., 1951), p. 719.

TOM WOODHAM is the co-owner of The Potted Plant, The Cottage Garden and The Connoisseur's Garden, all garden shops in Atlanta, Georgia, and has written a number of garden articles and columns. Though his garden (USDA zone 7–8) holds various species iris, along with significant collections of many other plants, he reckons that his greatest horticultural pleasure lies in designing and making gardens.

The Stately Iris
PERENNIAL ELEGANCE IN THE GARDEN
Tom Woodham

T he winds will be coming soon," she said gravely. "Whenever the purple iris starts to bloom, sand blows from the fields and tears them apart." The next day the winds swept across the countryside on cue, bearing the sharp, destructive bits of sand that shredded every single bud and tender blossom as my mother had predicted. As a child I was touched by the fate of the fragile iris, awed by the barbaric winds, and amazed to learn that my mother was apparently clairvoyant. What appeared to be insight into the future, however, was actually knowledge gained from years of careful observation in the garden.

The old purple "flags" (*Iris germanica*) that grew in profusion along our front path and that harken back to Colonial times, can be found in older gardens throughout the South, and especially in the countryside where, along with the old-fashioned white iris, they often appear to have escaped from abandoned gardens and old homesites. Shorter than the modern hybrids, sturdy and tenacious, these early types are the first to bloom in the spring after the daffodils have quieted down, introducing a succession of iris that bloom into June.

The popular tall bearded irises are widely cultivated today just as their ancestors were in the Old World north of the Mediterranean. These hybrid flowers are as wondrous as the terminology used by specialists to describe them. The word "falls" describes the outer three parts, or sepals, that usually curve downwards and that perhaps do resemble water pouring over a spillway. The inner, erect petals are "standards"—upright and principled. And the other descriptive terms, "blades," "hafts," "selfs," and "beards," sound like words overheard in a hand-to-hand combat exercise. Equally intriguing are variety names such as 'Superstition', 'Latin Lover', 'Pacific Panorama', and 'Gypsy Caravan'.

And they live up to their names in person. For instance, the deep red coloring of 'Superstition' is rich and seething and seems to conjure suspect imaginings and otherworldly turns, while the medium blue of 'Pacific Panorama' has as calming an influence as the waters of its oceanic namesake. The stately, elegant stalks of these typical modern hybrids bear their bloom aloft over pansies (*Viola* x *wittrockiana*), Johnny-jump-ups (*Viola tricolor*), forget-me-nots (*Myosotis sylvatica*), and yarrow (*Achillea*) in the mixed flower border. There, planted in groups of three or so along

Each year the clump grows larger . . . all concern for potential disaster is lulled away by beauty.

with Shirley poppies (*Papaver rhoeas*), foxgloves (*Digitalis*), bellflowers (*Campanula*), wild indigo (*Baptisia*), and sweet rocket (*Hesperis matronalis*; the white form, *alba-plena*, is especially good) they seem to float like bits of colored clouds in this picturesque vignette, inspiring gardeners, artists, and poets alike.

Iris culture is remarkably simple. A few years ago while sifting though stacks of old papers in a storage room at my Grandmother's farmhouse, I came across an old paper, brown with age, on which was written the following advice on planting bearded iris:

"How to plant Iris quickly and well"
Choose a location with good natural drainage and sun at least half of the day. Fork the soil thoroughly and relevel the bed. Slant two cuts into the prepared soil, leaving a ridge between them. Set the plants astride ridge. Spread anchor roots into the two depressions. Press rhizome firmly in soil so leaf fan remains upright. When resetting the plant, trim the foliage to 7-inch fans. Mound 1 inch of soil around base. Iris absorbs moisture through the rhizome roots.

This advice, to be followed here in the South from mid- to late summer, serves the flower gardener well, and the framed paper now hangs near my gardening books as a reminder of my horticultural heritage.

The rhizomes of the "flags" do indeed need to be hard and up

177

against the sun. If they are buried too deeply, covered with too much mulch, manure, or fertilizer, or if they stay too wet, they will rot hideously and completely.

The rampaging popularity of the bearded iris caused other interesting irises to practically disappear from many gardens. The Japanese iris (*I. ensata*), the yellow water iris (*I. pseudacorus*), Siberian iris (*I. sibirica*), and the roof iris (*Iris tectorum*) now, happily, are making a strong comeback and are attracting a new generation of admirers.

The low, flat roof iris (*I. tectorum*) is a crested iris and is actually grown on the thatched roofs of Japanese houses. It is a charmer whose deep, powder blue to lavender-blue flowers, with delicately frilled edges, are smaller than those of its bearded kin. Its foot-high stalks grow in what looks like a nest form; that is, they curve upward and outward from the center of their cluster, as if an elf had rested there in the middle of the night.

The white form, 'Alba', which I recently discovered has been growing at my Grandmother's farm for generations, is particularly appealing and, like all white flowers, simply glows in the garden in the evening. My dear gardening friend, Corrinne Osley, has planted an evening "moon garden" in Narragansett, Rhode Island. This stone-edged circle is filled with white flowers that offer continuous bloom throughout the season. And about that name, "moon garden." Is it for the shape of the moon or the glow of the flowers? Who knows. When queried, Miss Corrinne is as enigmatic as the Sphinx or the Mona Lisa. "Secrets," says she, "are a special part of gardening."

Iris pseudacorus, a water iris, brings to mind a favorite phrase of an old country gardener I know who says of an invasive plant, "It'll get away from you." Several years ago my friend Fred Brooks planted a few pieces of this old yellow iris in a small goldfish pool in the middle of a city park near his house. The following year the irises bloomed spectacularly with two- to three-foot-high stalks carrying rich, butter-yellow flowers with faint brown veining radiating from the center of the falls. The next year the clump of dark green, sword-like leaves enlarged, the number of flowers increased, and the plant left its pool boundaries to fill adjacent sidewalk cracks. Each year the clump grows larger still and, like the seductive danger of the Sirens, all concern for potential disaster is lulled away by beauty. But what a perfect choice along with Siberian iris and Japanese iris for natural plantings along streams and ponds.

The Siberian iris (*I. sibirica*) is a beardless type whose tall hollow stems rise from heavy, grass-like clumps of foliage. A rapid grower, it has a profusion of blossoms even on plants that have not been divided for years, a great feature to the lazy gardener or in the large flowering border where getting in or out to divide plants may prove difficult. Appearing primarily in many shades of blue, the Siberians are available in white as well. Its flowers bloom before and slightly overlap those of Japanese iris.

Another beardless type, the Japanese iris (*I. ensata*) has large, flat saucer-like blooms with short standards and great, arching falls that seem to be made of crepe paper, like an origami flower. Their forms, varying from the simple singles, which I prefer, to doubles that resemble peonies, offer a bewildering assortment of colorings from solids to variegations. This iris proves its worth in those low, moist spots in the garden that are not tolerated by other plants. Its fibrous root system must be kept constantly wet, or, as some say, "it likes to have its feet wet and its face in the sun."

Let me tell you about a particular iris that is having its day in the sun. Because so many plants in the garden come from other parts of the world, it is a source of great regional pride when a remarkable plant is native to one's own area. The Louisiana Iris grows naturally in the Mississippi Delta, though it will grow as far north as New England and will grow on drier soil as well as in boggy areas. When you create garden scenes with this rampant grower, expect sweeping iris panoramas in practically every color of the rainbow (except green).

There are other irises such as the small, crested woodland iris (*I. cristata*) that find special places in our hearts and in our gardens. I remember they used to grow under the sweet bay tree in our lightly shaded front yard in Stokes Bridge, South Carolina. They were Lilliputian compared to the bearded Gullivers and great excitement stirred when they bloomed together. We dared not pick those small blue treasures because they were few in number and highly regarded by visitors and by my mother, who cared for and nurtured them.

SPECIALISTS

The sequence of iris bloom for us in Atlanta, with a good deal of overlapping, is:

I. cristata - crested iris

I. germanica - German bearded iris

I. tectorum - Japanese roof iris

I. pseudacorus - yellow water iris

I. sibirica - Siberian iris

The Louisiana Iris group

I. ensata (syn. *I. kaempferi*) - Japanese iris

For fun, one may wish to grow only a particular type of iris in a variety of colors or to use only a certain color found in a number of different iris types. However they are arranged and planted, irises lend perennial elegance and beauty.

SOURCES & ORGANIZATIONS
(See "Sources & Resources" appendix for complete addresses.)

The American Iris Society
Brown's Sunnyhill Gardens
Cooley's Garden
Maryott's Gardens
Roderick Iris Garden
Schreiner's Iris Gardens

Part 5: HERITAGE, NOSTALGIA & DREAMS

The plants and gardens of the past have a tremendous attraction, and most of us find our way into the garden because of their gentle pull. For some, ancient herbs lure us from the comfortable armchair into an actual garden of the present. The visionary may find that some haunting garden of an inner dream shapes all the gardens of his future. Some look to the recent past, remaking cheerful gardens recalled from childhood, or re-creating elegant gardens from England's golden thirties, that peaceful period between world wars. A few strive to recapture a lost garden glimpsed from a train on a summer afternoon, book gardens, or the ghostly garden made when an aging house was new. Heritage, nostalgia, and dreams all play a significant role in garden making, encouraging us to look back through time to better understand the source of inspiration, and leading us onward as we progress in knowledge and ability to interpret that inspiration.

Heritage plants make prized connections with the gardeners of another day. There is great delight in growing the traditional herbs of healing and herbs of grace that filled many a monastic garden. There is enormous pleasure to be derived from growing Jane Austin's favorite flower, the pinks favored by Mary, Queen of Scots, or fruits extolled in Vergil's *Georgics*. Peonies that crossed the plains in our great-grandmother's covered wagon, powdery auriculas raised on the narrow windowsills of Scottish weavers two centuries ago, a silver-speckled white lungwort selected by Vita Sackville-West, all bridge the years that lie between those long-ago gardens and our own. With named plants multiplied only through division, there is a distinct thrill in realizing that these are indeed the very same plants chosen by Vita Sackville-West or Gertrude Jekyll, the same rose that was slipped through the barricades of war to captivate a French empress, the same golden carex that caught E. A. Bowles' attention one soft summer day. Even passing beyond sentiment, heritage plants are invaluable for those who seek to re-create appropriate period gardens to surround a colonial house, a southern mansion, or an early California mission. Every age has

182

its favored flowers and plants, and in them, we see the face of history.

Nostalgia is personal history, the celebration of people, places, and impressions that shaped our taste and directed our lives. Nostalgia often prompts the placement of the plants we knew in childhood. For me, single hollyhocks, snapdragons, and globe thistles instantly conjure up the droning of bees and a persistent impression of warmth and comfort. When I show my children how to make dolls from the full-skirted hollyhocks, snap their small fingers in the velvet mouths of tiny dragons, or grudgingly allow them to wage thistle-ball wars (which my brothers always did, to the disapproval of my mother), I draw them into a link of memory that stretches back through me to generations of mothers and children long gone. When we make gardens that are havens of peace, filled with sweet scents and muted bird song, we offer sanctuary to the inner child, our own and those of our visitors. Nostalgia further teaches us that history need not be ancient to be dear. Some of the most treasured plants in any garden were the gifts from other gardeners. In and out of bloom, they evoke the faces and voices of our friends, memories that increase our enjoyment of the plants themselves many fold.

Dreams lead us onward when frost or cat fights destroy our fond hopes. They ease our way when the garden path grows rough, and encourage us when our splendid hopes are greater than our budding skill. When the garden is very young, and other people see only mud and sticks, the gardener finds nourishment and renewed strength in dreams. When we are bewildered by changes and choices, when our preferences are overshadowed by fashion or fad, we do well to consult our dreams. The wise retreat from the persuasive words and images proffered by experts and rely on inner vision to guide the making of the garden of our hearts.

SCOTT KUNST is a landscape historian and preservation planner, a college instructor and a writer who has published a number of articles relating to garden and plant history. His garden in Ann Arbor, Michigan (USDA zone 5), holds a lifetime's collection of antique ornamental plants, mainly shrubs, perennials, and bulbs, which he loves as much for their tenacious nature as for their historical associations.

Antique Perennials for Every Garden
Scott G. Kunst

I nterest in antique plants is on the rise — with good reason. Gardeners in search of the unusual will find sizes, shapes, colors, and fragrances in antique plants that are unavailable in modern cultivars. The eighteenth-century 'C. T. Musgrave' pink (*Dianthus plumarius*), for example, features a broad green eye, while the darkest peony yet to be developed is a nineteenth-century introduction, 'Mons. Martin Cahuzac'. This distinctive antique cultivar is aptly described by the American Peony Society as "maroon-crimson with a silky black luster."

Gardeners enamored of wildflowers will find that antique flowers offer a kindred grace and subtlety. Indeed, many antiques — such as dame's rocket (*Hesperis matronalis*) and Madonna lily (*Lilium candidum*) — are simply wild varieties brought into gardens centuries ago and developed little if any since then.

And gardeners looking for low-maintenance plants will find that many antiques are sturdy, vigorous, and undemanding. Though some require cossetting, most antiques have survived in part because they can take care of themselves. Old shrub roses, as many gardeners are rediscovering, need far less attention than do modern hybrid teas, while historic irises have survived in sunbaked and overgrown cemeteries through decades of neglect.

The unique pleasure of antique plants, however, is the connection they offer us with the past. As with any antique, age gives an added dimension to these plants which generations of gardeners have loved. The scent of the rose my grandmother grew by her front porch can return me for an instant to the happy summer days I spent with her. So, too, the humble plants of the colonists and pioneers recall their simple lives, and when we grow a plant that delighted Thomas Jefferson, we share something of him that history books cannot convey.

This is not to say that everyone should collect Victorian furniture or that all old plants are wonderful. But some antique plants *are* superb, and I believe more gardeners would grow these plants if they only knew them. To tempt you, here are a few of my favorites, almost two dozen antique perennials that will shine in even the most modern garden. (All are available from sources noted in this article's appendix.)

> . . . **when we grow a plant that delighted Thomas Jefferson, we share something of him that history books cannot convey.**

Among the world's oldest cultivated plants, irises have decorated Cretan palaces and medieval chapels. Numerous historic cultivars survive, though only a handful are available commercially. You can see many at the Presby Memorial Iris Gardens in Montclair, New Jersey, and enthusiasts will want to join the new Historic Iris Preservation Society, a sub-section of the American Iris Society (see Sources, below).

Iris germanica 'Florentina' is one of the oldest iris, cultivated as early as the twelfth century. Fragrant and among the first tall bearded iris to bloom each year, 'Florentina' has long, narrow, pale gray blossoms that seem to shine like silver. Also very old is *I. pallida*, which the great herbalist Gerard grew by 1597. Pallida cultivars are generally pale blue-purple irises that are taller and larger than their antique cousins. I especially like the 1859 'Queen of May' with its pink undertones, eye-catching white blaze at the beard, and characteristic pallida fragrance of Concord grapes.

Another striking antique iris is the bearded hybrid 'Victorine' (1840). Here the standards are bright white (marked with odd dribblings of purple) while the falls are an intense violet (marked by bits of white). Though the contrast might be too much on huge, modern blossoms, on 'Victorine' it just looks crisp and strong.

'Plumeri' (introduced in 1830) may be my favorite iris. Growing about two feet tall, it sports trim, compact flowers in colors an earlier generation would have called "art shades." Its standards are an exotic bronze suffused with rose while its falls are a clear, rosy purple. (A similar but more muted combination is available in the larger 'Sambucina' of 1759.) Though it looks rare, 'Plumeri'—like most antique iris—is easy to grow, generally untroubled by borers and blights.

Peonies are a frequent companion of iris in old gardens. The vibrant ruby-red *Paeonia officinalis* was brought to English gardens from the Mediterranean by 1548. Its double form, 'Rubra Plena', was the old red "piney" of American colonists and pioneers, and it is still widely available today.

Most garden peonies, however, derive from the Oriental *Paeonia lactiflora*, cultivated in China for at least a thousand years. Soon after its arrival in Europe about 1800, hundreds of new cultivars were developed. One enduring classic is 'Festiva Maxima'. This sturdy double form, white flecked with crimson, was introduced in 1851 and is still a top-selling variety. Other long-standing favorites include the early, white 'Duchesse de Nemours' (1856), often described as the finest-scented peony; 'Mons. Jules Elie' (1888) with its huge, dark pink flowers marked with a silvery sheen; and the floriferous, rose-scented, deep crimson 'Philippe Rivoire' (1911).

Pinks are another classic perennial, and are more at home in most gardens than their even older relative, the carnation. By 1629, the renowned plantsman John Parkinson was growing seventeen varieties of *Dianthus plumarius*, while Victorian "florist societies"—much like today's hosta and daylily fans—developed hundreds of cultivars.

Probably the best-known nineteenth-century pink is 'Mrs. Sinkins' (1868), a pure white double with a robust constitution and rich clove fragrance. No one seems to mind that it consistently splits its calyx. Smaller and more fringed but just as white and fragrant is 'Her Majesty' (1891).

'Gloriosa' (late 1700s) is a clear pink double with a bit of a crimson eye and wonderfully blue foliage, while 'Rose de Mai' (1820) is a large double of a lovely lilac-pink. Similar in color but half the flower size is another of my favorite pinks, a nameless antique that I discovered in a nearby country cemetery. There, despite no watering and constant mowing, it had grown to cover an area six feet in diameter.

Daylilies are exceedingly popular today, but even the most modern plant has a history as well as surviving antique varieties. Though the common orange daylily (*Hemerocallis fulva*) and the lemon lily (*H. lilioasphodelus*, formerly *H. flava*) were both introduced to Europe in the 1570s, others were unknown until the nineteenth century or later. One Oriental daylily that reached the West in 1864 was the double-orange 'Kwanso Variegata' with its unusual white-striped foliage. In 1892, the first hybrid daylily, 'Apricot', was exhibited in London. Rather short in stature, its early, clear orange-yellow flowers are delicately proportioned. In 1925, what is probably the best known antique daylily was introduced — 'Hyperion', a vigorous, lemon-yellow variety that is still considered a standard. Daylily breeding gained enormous impetus from the work of A. B. Stout in the 1920s and 1930s. Some of his best introductions are still available, including 'Mikado' (1928) with a red eye, and golden 'Wau-Bun' (1929) with an interesting twist to its petals.

Two good places to see antique daylilies are the Missouri Botanical Garden and the New York Botanical Garden where they grow alongside some of today's spectacular cultivars. With a little luck and care, the best of today's lavender giants and frilly near-whites will still be growing in American gardens a hundred years from now — right next to my current antique favorites.

SOURCES & ORGANIZATIONS
(See "Sources & Resources" appendix for complete addresses.)

Adamgrove (Iris.)
Brand Peony Farm
Lee Bristol Nursery (Daylilies; a few antiques, many new varieties.)
Canyon Creek Nursery (Antique pinks and more.)
Historic Iris Preservation Society
Thomas Jefferson Center for Historic Plants Monticello (Antique pinks and other Jeffersonian plants.)
New Peony Farm
Saxton Gardens (Daylilies.)
Sunnyridge Gardens (Daylilies; antique and new. Dates of introduction.)

AMBER KARR is a Physician's Assistant at an inner-city neighborhood health clinic in Seattle, Washington. Her tiny urban garden (USDA zone 8) holds hundreds of minor bulbs, rock plants, perennials, and vines as well as several fruit trees, a small terrace, and a play area for her daughter, Alena. The lawn gets smaller every year. She and her husband have recently purchased several wooded acres on the Kitsap Penninsula, and even before the house plans are completed, the garden is beginning to take shape.

A Letter
Amber Karr

Dear Gail,

Your latest letter asking how I became so passionately involved in gardening intrigued me. Like a good fat vacation novel, gardening offers birth, death, loss, surprise, intrigue, competition, murder (of snails and other pests), smells, tastes, experiments, successes, jealousy, and even sex. As a bonus, if you fall in love with gardening, it's your vacation all year round, even though at all times of the year there are jobs to be done in the garden. Hard work has its rewards. What better way to allay stress than with a vigorous hauling of manure and compost! Healthier and happier plants AND a stronger back! On a cold and dark winter day when I gently lay out my seed packets and dream of color and texture combinations, I feel like a miser counting out his gold. I am forever eagerly waiting for the mailman. He might be carrying not only a long-awaited letter but also the avenues to newer and greater treasures — the latest seed catalogs!

Lately, I have been increasing my wealth by dividing some vigorously spreading plants. These free plants have been added to the new parts of my garden. Yes, I've once again dug up more grass! Won't the heath aster [*Aster ericoides*] be perfect in front of the gooseneck loosestrife [*Lysimachia clethroides*]? If you position yourself between them and the sun, the lysimachia looks like a gaggle of geese. A friend of mine always read her poetry to attentive cows; these flowers are more available to us urban folks.

But before I get totally sidetracked and tell you all about the new areas of the garden, let me return to gardening's greatest treasures: sharing and memories. Gardening is a life-long adventure that touches my life at many points. A week after the birth of my sweet daughter, a large bulb order arrived; she slept in the sun while I bent over my still large belly and chest to plant. Most of these plants have been divided and shared several times and their blooms remind me of that unique time.

Any gardener worth her secateurs always carries a small supply of envelopes and a pencil to gather seed from her favorite plants. These are easy to mail to friends to try. The gardener is then in a position to accept the generosity of fellow gardeners.

And all of this we can share with our children.

Like the sourdough starter Grampa Rakonovich brought back from his gold rush days, which we've so carefully nurtured and fed through the generations, my garden has produced descendants that populate the yard of friends in North Carolina. Another distant friend sent me a Florida gardening calendar so I will know when she's watching the blooming of her guavas, and avocados, as we clear out the last of the Christmas decorations! At least they're plagued with slugs while there's frost on the ground here in the Northwest.

We've gotten to know the neighbors as we share the bounty. A few of the errant unnamed old-fashioned pale pink columbine, which had seeded in all kinds of impossible places, were warmly received for their as-yet empty shade garden. Other seedlings will join with some 'Birch Double' geraniums [*Geranium himalayense*], Bethlehem sage [*Pulmonaria saccharata*] and that friendly white with lavender 'Freckles' violet [*Viola cucullata*] to begin a small shade garden at the community medical clinic.

For, after all, the more plants you share, the more places you will have to turn to if your stock dies out or if for some reason you lose your old favorites. Generosity is returned tenfold; it's like a certificate of deposit with high interest and security. For us sentimental fools, it's our journal and memory bank of friends and times and places.

For example, my path with the gentle pink stonecress [*Aethionema schistosum*] and pale blue ground cover, [*Isotoma axillaris*], will forever remind me of a charming 80-year-old woman whose garden held a view of Mt. Rainier. In my mind's eye, I see her bending to carefully dig me some starts, sharing this good combination she had discovered.

Memories are strong in my garden. Along the east-facing wall of Gramma's house was an expanse of "Pheasant's Eye" narcissus [*N. poeticus* var. *recurvus*]. Mine have never naturalized like hers although I treat them kindly. I willingly replant them every year or so just for the joy of those memories. The starts of ever-so-sweet-smelling lilies of the valley [*Convallaria majalis*] and the snowdrops [*Galanthus nivalis*] she gave me are spreading and have been divided and shared many times. The start of a French pussy willow my aunt gave me thrives in my neighbor's yard where she has room for it, since I don't.

Gail, do you remember nasturtium-sucking when we were kids? That sweet nectar was a secret treat. This summer will be remembered not by a taste but by a smell, that of night-scented stock [*Matthiola longipetala*]. As yet another unusually hot and dry summer begins, the family is spending more late evenings in the cool backyard. I had started seeds of this quite small and unremarkable-appearing plant and placed the seedlings throughout the garden. I'd quite forgotten them until late one night when we tracked down the strong sweet fragrance.

Gardening can be that solitary venture that soothes and nurtures the soul and restores our strength. It can also be the basis for comradeship that is otherwise not available. How else would I find myself with a previously-unknown group of people on a field trip of exploration? How delightful to see others crouched over an exquisite gentian or holding magnifying glasses over an unidentified wildflower on a mountain trail.

Say hello to Theron. The enclosed envelope of seeds is for him, purple-podded stringless snap beans that are vigorous, tasty and beautiful. I know you join me in hoping to show our children the joys of gardening. Theron has a natural interest; my daughter Alena shows typical noninterest. "Oh, Mom, how long will you be at the garden center? Do you have to go?" So, to my great surprise last night, when we were playing a word game naming flowers beginning with each letter of the alphabet, I found that she was a whiz! (Granted, we did have trouble with U and X.) When turned loose with flower shears she's made some smashing bouquets.

So, you can see why I'm so in love with gardening: it is physical (digging and hauling compost to improve the garden or hiking in the mountains and woods to see plants in their environment); it is mental (studying books, experimenting, learning new skills); it is also spiritual (an art form, a meditation). And all of this we can share with our children.

Love,

Amber

7-14-89

RYAN GAINEY is the co-owner of the Potted Plant, The Cottage Garden and The Connoisseur's Garden in Atlanta, Georgia. He is an active garden designer, a passionate plant collector, and a firm believer in the potent role memory plays in imaginative garden making. His garden in Decatur, Georgia (USDA zone 7), has been featured in many articles and books, and he often lectures on his garden plants and plantings. His special interest is in garden refinement, particularly as it applies to gardening in the South.

Path Into The Visitors' Garden
Ryan Gainey

How long did it take God
to create the earth
and find a way to let humanity
make a path on which to walk?

How many words would it take
to write about my garden
in its totality?
Words would be like leaves,
all might fall from the trees
before
I had time
to fully express my thoughts.
The truth is,
there are no words —
for so many aspects of the garden are
new,
gradually being
filled with their own truths.

My garden efforts
are just now in their eighth year;
they began
with the creation
of my first garden room.

Now
the total garden picture has
evolved
into
a series of rooms,
each with its own
horticultural qualities,
architectural elements,
and garden accessories.
All
filled with delight—
a series of captured thoughts and
sought-after dreams.

The Visitors' Garden,
about which I write,
is intended to be
a quiet place.
In a verdant surround
and slightly enclosed,
it is
visible from the sidewalk
of a quiet street.
This small enclave
invites you
to come in
and visit
without intruding.

Nostalgia
has already found
its place
here
for I can easily remember
so many lovely settings
and permeating scents.
Two dear friends were wed here,
when there was only a row of standard tree roses on the street;
the roses are gone

now,
but that memory
is a part of the garden
only time can cultivate
in our hearts.

The esoteric qualities
of Nature
have become a living dream
filled with subtleties
that only She
can
provide, a lesson
so long in the learning,
a vision just now being seen.
When I look
into this setting,
I see the realization
of nature and humanity
becoming
one.
Here the colors in spring are
a blending of
greens,
gray-greens,
chartreuses,
golds,
russets,
browns,
and ambers.
Soft sunny colors,
both cool and warm
(like the memories
time cultivates).
Even the rains are
like a drizzle of dew
that
falls
from heaven.
I have taken
my palette from the colors that

come from nature
Herself.
We
cannot be taught
but we can be
instilled
with the pleasures of learning
and therefore
seeing.

Even in the hottest summer
these same soothing colors
give us the essence
of spring,
but without so many flowers.
In the Fall,
the leaves drained
of their green
dreams cover the ground
with the same color scheme;
one walks
on a carpet
made for a king.

In winter,
bare branches,
exfoliated trunks,
inner structure,
and seeds
decorate
the garden with subtlety,
and suddenly
on a warm winter day
a fragrance comes
from a flower just then
seen. The light
changes through every season
and we must find another way of
seeing.
Vision and ideas
have become
an everlasting reality.

HERITAGE, NOSTALGIA & DREAMS

I have not named
the trees,
or leaves,
or flowers.
The bulbs
are not called by name.
Nothing has been said
of the effort
or all the labor therein.
I have given
and I have taken
and I have received
a dream.

MARGARET WARD has lived and gardened on Bainbridge Island (USDA zone 8), in Washington's Puget Sound, for many years. Her first garden, long neglected, is now being restored and renovated by an island neighbor. Though well into her eighties, Ward is an active gardener whose present beachfront garden is an island landmark. Small and sunny, it remains colorful with flowers, berries, and foliage all through the year.

Cottage Garden Perennials By The Sea
Margaret Ward

Today, both the flowers and I are happy to be alive and thriving in our waterfront garden on the shores of Bainbridge Island, looking across Puget Sound to Seattle. It is mid-July, and we have just survived being part of a garden tour which brought seven hundred pairs of feet tramping over the paths of crushed shells and beach sand. Not one plant was disturbed, not one edging brick knocked out of place! Gardeners and garden appreciators are the world's finest people.

July can be a difficult time for this dry garden, and preparation for the tour called for much dead-heading, watering, and weeding, and sometimes the moving of full-grown plants into more suitable locations. Since this is a completely organic garden, fish emulsion was used liberally to water in transplants and boost some lazy growers. Helpful friends brought extra plants to fill in any gaps, and finally the garden was ready for other eyes.

The first day, a Saturday, dawned cool and overcast. This was a desirable condition, since my garden can seem too hot and bright in harsh midday light. The first visitors began to arrive, passing between the retired row-boats which now serve as planters at the entrance to the garden. A wide row of the old tawny double daylily, *Hemerocallis fulva* 'Kwanso Variegata', edges the low white front fence, and many people admired the contrast, as well as the huge golden flowers of another daylily, 'Bengaleer', which also performs well in the sandy soil. A large clump of the Matilija poppy, *Romneya coulteri*, in full bloom captured a lot of attention. The huge white flowers with golden centers top stems five to six feet high. The Matilija poppy is slow to get started, but is very tough and cold hardy once established, and in good soil will spread all too fast. It stays put nicely here, because the soil is sandy, and the plant is never watered or fed. Opposite the poppy, a tall 'Golden Showers' rose sits next to the lamp post. This bushy Floribunda rose seems to bloom for most of the summer, producing hundreds of big yellow roses.

People seem to enjoy seeing all the color in my garden, and I try to keep it colorful and bright all year round. Since the garden is so small, this means looking for plants that stay in bloom a long time. Experience has taught me that many colors will blend together attractively so long as most shades of red and pink are avoided. I don't like bright orange, which eliminates orange marigolds, but many beautiful lilies in shades of peach and apricot bloom in midsummer, and they blend well with another rose, 'Just Joey', a Hybrid Tea that has huge apricot flowers and reddish new leaves. The tiger lilies, *Lilium lancifolium*, so easy to reproduce from the little bulblets formed above each leaf, come in many colors now, including cream and peach, and they stay in bloom for a long time. My only dahlias, long time favorites called, 'Andre's Orange' or 'Andrie's Orange', a good dark apricot, are now in bloom; such early flowering comes from leaving the tubers in the ground all winter. They have survived below freezing temperatures many times. Nearby is a large clump of dark *Ligularia dentata* 'Desdemona' with black· stems and blackish red leaves, a background which really makes the dahlias stand out.

Even though the garden is small, I like to use a few taller plants. The plume poppy, *Macleaya microcarpa*, gets over eight feet high, and caused quite a stir on the tour. Everybody wanted to know what that plant was, with its interesting cut-out leaves that look so silvery in the wind, and big coral plumes. The globe thistle (*Echinops ritro*), with round blue flowers on four-foot stems, is not quite so tall, but this also got a lot of comments. Once so common that it was in almost every garden, today nobody knows what it is. My Maltese cross (*Lychnis chalcedonica*) makes a big bush, at least four feet high and as much across, that is covered with dark red flowers for more than a month. This is another big, old-fashioned plant that seems rare these days, and attracts a lot of interest.

Many visitors confused the lavender daisy bush, an *Erigeron speciosus* hybrid, with *Aster* x *frikartii*, a much later bloomer. It does look similar, though the flowers are not so dark, and it blooms almost all summer. I grow mine near a refined *Solidago*, a hybrid of the wild goldenrod, which is so old I have lost the name. It gets to be more than four feet tall, and blooms for many weeks with old gold plumes, starting now in midsummer.

Hollyhocks (*Alcea rosea*) are such nostalgic, sentimental flowers, and a clump of single cream and pink ones looks pretty beside my gray and white gazebo. They are so often plagued by ugly rust, and must be dusted with sulphur, but I am convinced that providing the right conditions is the best cure for all ills. I don't seem to get around to dusting them anymore, but I take a chance, and sometimes win. So far, they have stayed healthy, so they must like their home by the sea.

Don't be afraid to be different, to make a garden that is like nobody else's.

The second day of the tour was cool and rainy, but still the visitors came, with colorful umbrellas, raincoats, and rubber boots. They were a fine cheerful group despite the weather, for gardeners aren't discouraged by a little rain. All my cream-colored California poppies (*Eschscholzia californica*) were closed for lack of sun, but many people asked about them anyway. My daughter loved these best, and for many years she pulled all the bright orange ones, leaving just these cream ones to set seed. Now, they are everywhere and bloom all summer long and well into fall.

Even on a rainy day, there was plenty of color in the garden. Blue pansies and white roses bloom together with *Rosa rugosa* hybrid 'Blanc Double de Coubert', the coneflower *Rudbeckia triloba* 'Nutmeg' in shades of copper, brown, and gold, and the tall red and gold sneezeweed, *Helenium autumnale* 'Moerheim Beauty'. White Japanese anemones (*A. x hybrida* 'Alba') and the *Echinacea purpurea* 'White Lustre' grow and look just lovely in front of a woven straw bee skep that is surrounded by *Lavandula angustifolia* 'Munstead Dwarf' as well as a big old clump of pineapple sage, *Salvia elegans*, that comes back every year, though supposed to be so tender.

Now the tour is over and the visitors are all gone. Sitting in the gazebo listening to the red-winged blackbirds in the salt marsh next door, I remember my long-ago dream of a garden full of country flowers that would seem to have wandered up from the beach. This small lot was my artist's canvas, to plant as I wished with the plants of my choice. Looking back over the many years spent making this garden, I think the principal lessons to be learned here are that poor soil can be made to support many and various plants using only organic additives and with surprisingly little water. Seaweed hauled from the beach, leaves and grass clippings from the neighbors—I never wanted any grass myself—all go into compost, which is the most helpful additive of all. Rocks and sand and shells used for paths and edging came from the beach, and the bricks that edge the beds were gathered from an old shipyard sawmill, bringing a bit of history into the garden.

Every garden needs an enclosure. Mine came about when I answered an ad for cedar rail fencing years ago. That call resulted in the appearance of a very young man who arrived on the job early in the morning, completely equipped and ready to go to work. He had an even younger helper with him, all the fencing already cut to size, and a little tin sign with his name and phone number to hang on the finished fence. At the end of the day, he presented me with an extremely modest bill, which I paid enthusiastically. He explained that his father owned a sawmill, which the son used to furnish and cut his materials; it wouldn't surprise me to hear that the fence builder now owns and operates an even bigger mill. The gazebo, topped with cedar shakes, was also the work of a clever local man with a sense of style, and looks right with the gray shingled Cape Cod house.

Well-worn pots and planters fit perfectly into the cottage garden, and it all adds up to an atmosphere that gives visitors great pleasure, and makes them think, "I could do that too." Summing up after 50 and more years of gardening, I would say, plan your garden to make yourself happy. Do it slowly, starting with what's achievable, for failure does not make for happiness. Don't be afraid to be different, to make a garden that is like nobody else's. Finally, I would say, the garden should never be finished; there should always be room for that new perennial to surprise you with its wonderful bloom next year.

Here is a list of seaside cottage garden favorites, in order of bloom and with maximum heights:

Doronicum caucasicum (Caucasian leopard's bane). Yellow daisies in earliest spring; two-three feet.

Trollius europaeus (common globeflower). Like giant early butter-cups; two feet.

Aubrieta deltoidea (rock cress). Low edging plant in mauve and pur-ple; two inches.

Iris sibirica (Siberian iris). Bright blues and pure whites are the love-liest; three feet.

Campanula (bellflower). White and blue peach-leafed; two and a half feet.

Achillea (yarrow). Especially *A.* x 'Coronation Gold' and *A. tomen-tosa* 'Moonlight'; three and a half feet.

Hemerocallis (daylily). Especially *H. fulva* 'Kwanso Variegata' and the hybrid 'Bengaleer'; three feet.

Anemone x *hybrida* (Japanese anemone). Pure white 'Alba' blooms all late summer and fall; three feet.

Echinops ritro (globe thistle). Steel blue balls, long lasting; five feet.

Helenium autumnale (common sneezeweed). 'Moerheim Beauty' blooms and blooms; three and a half feet.

Solidago (goldenrod, the improved varieties). Tall, golden and late; four feet.

Aster novi-belgii (Michaelmas daisies). Late-blooming asters in lavenders and blues; some short edging plants, others to four feet.

DAPHNE STEWART awoke to gardening when she moved into an old farm on Bainbridge Island, Washington (USDA zone 8). As she cleared out the overgrown beds, she wondered about the long-ago gardener who had planted the resilient survivors, for flowers and shrubs abounded. Through the kind offices of a mutual friend, she was introduced to that original gardener, Margaret Ward, who now watches over Stewart's garden progress with delight.

The Evolution Of A Gardener
Daphne Stewart

In late 1986, my family and I moved from the East Coast to the Pacific Northwest. There, on a small island near Seattle, we had found our dream home—or what we had fondly imagined our dream home to be. The rambling house, shipboarded and shake roofed, originally may have been a barn. It had undergone numerous makeovers over the years, and was charming, if not quite as structurally sound as it first appeared. It was set in the middle of five acres, about half of which was fenced pasture land. A small fir wood filled one corner, and the rest was divided between lawn and garden. The lawn was made up of closely cropped weeds, turf, meadow grasses, and moss, in about equal proportions. The garden beds that framed the house and surrounded the lawns consisted chiefly of perennial garden weeds, as we were to learn, but at first sight, we found them delightful.

Everything was slightly unkempt, but there were some good trees, particularly a beautiful old Belcher crab, and several fine shrubs, including a handsome if overgrown *Osmanthus delavayi*. At some point in the past, the shrubs had been well pruned, but all were now shaggy and overgrown. Although clearly in need of work, the garden beds were basically good shapes that suited the setting. I had always pictured myself as having a garden someday, and here at last was, if not a garden, at least the remains of one. However, its restoration was obviously going to take some doing, and not only did I know next to nothing about gardens and gardening, I didn't even own a shovel.

I did, however, own a diary and I began to record garden observations. My earliest garden diary entries read hopefully:

August 20 I've been here a week, and I mostly wander around wondering what things are and feeling overwhelmed at the amount there is to do. How do you go about identifying anything? There are soft purple flowers that look like oversized crocuses coming up around the huge old vine maple tree, and around the edges of the front beds, they are growing in thick bunches. No leaves; they can't really be crocuses in August!?

August 29 Here I am in the Pacific Northwest, where it is supposed to rain constantly; after only a few dry weeks, I have begun to water the garden. It is strange to feel that these plants are counting on me now. I am surprised to learn that, even in this part of the country, there are often droughts in the summer and fall. Some things seem to be dying back because it is time for them to do so, but surely the leaves of the wisteria draped over the chicken coop door should not feel like crackling old paper? The lavender bushes are in bloom, and yesterday I found a white bellflower that I thought might be a campanula. Today, I found a plastic label lying in the dirt nearby which read, "*Campanula persicifolia* 'Alba' " — hooray, an identified plant!

> **Would I have been a gardener and had a garden if there had not been plants already here?**

September 1 The *Sunset Western Garden Book* says that *Deutzia* grows to six feet. Mine must be a rare breed, or a grandmother plant, as it's at least double that in height and girth. The little metal tag on the trunk insists it's a deutzia, though; bless whoever put all those label tags on the plants! The huge bush by the chicken coop is identified as a flowering quince (*Chaenomeles japonica*), and I found another tag for Mexican orange (*Choisya ternata*); now, if I can only just find the matching plant! The garden is overrun with the following: white field daisies, small orange poppies, mints, and two kinds of yellow-orange somethings. They are all nice, but they are all everywhere.

September 4 Hey! Japanese anemones! At least, that's what I think they are; lovely, tall things with white flowers, growing in front of the gray garage walls. Some silvery pink ones are coming up through the ferns by the patio, too. Where can I find a really useful book to help with the identification of these things? I have taken to prowling the local nurseries for plants that look similar to mine, then making notes from the labels. Today I resorted to taking the tag from a six-pack of *Doronicum*; I forgot my pad and pen, and knew I would never remember the name. There are lots of them growing under the big fir tree to the east of the house. I am starting to give the different beds names like "fir bed" and "east bed" and "quince bed" to keep areas straight in my mind; it helps a little.

September 12 Our first garden project is to build three large compost bins behind the chicken coop. This place is going to need lots of compost; just making enough to cover each bed thinly could turn into a full-time job. I am also going to need a few tools, like a shovel, a rake, pruners, and maybe a trowel.

September 14 One of the yellow and orange things is *Crocosmia masonorum*. I wonder whether these plants are ultrahardy and have been multiplying for years, or whether the last owners had a thing for them? There are lots now, everywhere. The holly tree has greenish powdery mildew and aphids all over it. Next to it are two shrubs that I think are viburnums; one is not terribly attractive, and the other looks dead. The *Sunset Western Garden Book* says they are showy and have good fall color; they definitely weren't looking at mine! I also have two *Viburnum davidii*—at least identified, from plants at the nursery, of course. I found a reference to them once in George Schenk's *The Complete Shade Gardener*, which Cathy gave me, but I'll be damned if I can find it now.

September 20 The plants with popping pods that shoot seeds about five feet are *Alstroemeria aurantiaca*. Someone liked this plant, too. I got a new book, *The Color Dictionary of Flowers and Plants* by Hay and Synge . . . it just may save my gardening life.

September 21 The maples are turning. Everything looks unpruned and untidy and I am too largely pregnant to do much about it, so I am making plans on graph paper of the existing yard and beds, penciling in some things, but inking in little features like 70-foot-tall fir trees. Some plants are likely to be here awhile . . .

February, 1989, some two and a half rather fuzzy, new baby and house-remodeling years later. Looking over this year's journal, I am amazed at my progress and how much I have learned, despite having significant claims on my time and attention, notably Patrick, now a two-year-old toddler. Much of this new knowledge has come from doing, from clearing and reshaping the old beds and borders. Much more has come from avid reading, often while the baby nursed and napped. More still has come from spending time with people who love plants and gardens; I follow them through their gardens and my own, notebook in hand, writing hieroglyphic Latin bits like "cary-op-teris(?)," which I then look up patiently, learning plant after plant. It is not always so easy, and sometimes can be horribly frustrating, reminding me of my childhood, when I spent hours trying to look up words in the family's fat dictionary without the foggiest notion of how to spell them. Anyway, I think my garden is becoming a real garden again, and better yet, it is becoming MY garden.

> **February 6**   There is a huge sheet of small lavender crocuses in the lawn surrounding the biggest maple. Thank you to whomever planted the originals; I look forward to this sight all winter. Our three boys and the dog wipe out the fairyland effect rather quickly, but I love the way the crocuses look when they first open. I have finally learned that these are *Crocus tommasinianus*, a species crocus that spreads nicely in grass. Like so many plants in this garden, they deserve preservation, and we let the grass get long here in order to be sure the bulb foliage is well ripened. I haven't yet figured out how to handle the sprawling old flowering quince by the chicken coop; this is another treasured plant, for it was Margaret's birthday present long ago, which earns it a special place both in my heart and in the garden.

[Margaret Ward is the woman who created this garden originally, starting in the 1930's, and it is to her that I owe a great deal of what remains wonderful here. She still lives on the island, and is now my dear friend; meeting her, learning of her connection with this garden, seeing her old photographs and hearing her stories has added immeasurably to the joy of living here and resurrecting the old garden.]

> **February 9**   Margaret called today to say I could stop photocopying pages out of her copy of Josephine Nuese's *The Country Garden*; it has been reissued in paperback, and she ordered me a copy — how very nice of her! I must have some *Iris cristata*, the darkest blue ones, and certainly a Daphne lilac, *Syringa microphylla* 'Superba'. I've gone from not knowing the names of anything to having a specific want list several pages long. Now I need to know how to get hold of these plants I can no longer live without having!

> **February 13**   Prune and weed, weed and prune. I have all the really good weeds, those hardy gems that would make even the her-

bicide Roundup shake in its boots. *Campanula rapunculoides* — you have to have a little respect for a plant with survivalist roots like these. *Alstroemeria aurantiaca*, with roots that go down to China. The variegated bishop's weed, *Aegopodium podagraria*, really gets around, as does the equally running snow-in-summer (*Cerastium tomentosum*). Field daisies and dandelions, all manner of invasive grasses, and the stoutest blackberries I've ever seen, are all here in abundance. Perhaps I am a fool, rushing in where angels fear to tread, but I still believe that I can control these things without resorting to strong poison. If I pull them out, over and over, year after year, surely the roots will starve sooner or later? They do seem smaller, and are certainly less rampant than they were when I first arrived.

There are also some nice garden weeds here; incredibly persistent scillas (*Hyacinthoides non-scripta*), mostly blue, but a few pinks and whites, wash every border blue each spring, and even appear in the lawn. *Crocosmia masonorum* is also all too plentiful, though the hot-orange flower spikes bring a welcome glow to the late summer border. Lettuce-leaved opium poppies (*Papaver somniferum*) come in force, some single, in soft lavender, the rest ruffly doubles of warm rosy pink. The soft orange poppies with sage gray leaves turn out to be *Papaver atlanticum*; mine are double, which is uncommon (I am told), but apparently when they are kept isolated from the usual single form, the doubles will come true from seed. This seems to be so, for I've got them in spades! Although they all appear in excessive quantities, I don't consider any of them true weeds, for they all can be pulled or dug up easily; running roots are what makes a weed of a garden plant.

I have now enlarged all the beds and borders, giving them more pleasing proportions — or at least, more to my taste. I am finally learning to plant roses exactly where I want them, and not allowing an existing path of scilla to displace them, as I used to do. Respect for old plants is all very well, but it can be taken too far. Where I used to buy one or two of a plant that I liked, I now purchase plants by the boxcar load, and still they shrink to tiny specks in the large expanses of bare dirt. This is a BIG garden. I have planted plants and moved them, made new plans and moved the same plants again, and yet again. I remain amazed at their resilience and perseverance. A small patch of pink and mauve New England asters (*Aster novae-angliae*) has been divided again and again, and now it makes a large and impenetrable aster forest. The Chinese dwarf astilbe (*Astilbe chinensis* 'Pumila') blooms in the same blend of pink and mauve, and although these astilbes can be hard to place, I am hoping they will look spectacular at the asters' feet. They have been moved six times in the two years I've owned them but they seem none the worse for all their wanderings and have never looked better than in what I trust will be their permanent home.

June 2   Rain again today; it has been very wet, and I haven't been able to do much. I wish patience were available by mail order. I'd order a six-pack of patience from Canyon Creek Nursery along with lavender 'Hidcote' and a rare lobelia. I try to remember that I have all the time there is in the world, to stop and enjoy the process of gardening. I keep trying to skip parts to get to the "end" more quickly, when there really isn't one.

June 6   No one mentions what colchicums look like in June, great masses of dying brown leaves that smother smaller plants. Why is there no picture in the *Smith & Hawken Bulb Book* catalog of this disaster?

August 3   The 'Yellow Magic' petunias that Patrick (now a sturdy two and a half, and a fine garden helper) picked out have been truly spectacular for weeks. Pale golden yellow, slightly ruffled and always full of bloom, they tower over the tiny new shrub starts nearby. I would never have chosen petunias myself, yet they are perfect in my front bed, now the "gold garden". *Sambucus racemosa* 'Plumosa Aurea', the lacy golden cut leaf elder, is dwarfed by those petunias now, but next year, when it reaches five or more feet high, they may reappear, but properly humbly, at its feet. Actually, I probably would go out of my way to find those particular petunias again, they have been that good, to my great surprise.

The diary will go on, I'm sure, for many years to come. I will continue to experiment, to read and dream, to plan and order plants by what feels like the gross. I will probably always wander through the yard holding a pot of some plant too wonderful not to try, wondering just where to put it when, after all, it isn't in The Plan that is intended to reduce all to order and harmony. But I am learning something about The Plan itself, that it must often give way to reality. *Rodgersia tabularis* (shieldleaf rodgersia) will not grow well in the dry shade under the fir, even though I wanted it to succeed there. It needs to be moved to damper soil. I keep reading that plants thrive when matched to climate and soil (mine is very sandy). But I think all of us, once or twice, must fall into the trap of trying unsuitable plants, hoping that love will conquer all. Well, it doesn't work in gardens, either.

I am not sure, looking back, when these plantings became a garden, and whether it has shaped me or I it. Would I have been a gardener and had a garden if there had not been plants already here? I am sure I would have started something — but what would I have had the courage to do? It is, as I search for campanula roots under the deep bark mulch and a layer of prickly holly leaves, intriguing to ponder.

And yet, I find that most of my musings look ahead. I have a wistful desire for more than The Plan, a desire for a Master Plan. This Master Plan would not only knit together all the beds and spaces but it would also establish priorities: what has to be done now and what can possibly be put off until March, when I am SURE I will have more time.

We are both, the garden and I, going somewhere, as we continue to evolve and grow together, just like the holly and the ivy.

SOURCE
(See "Sources & Resources" appendix for complete address.)

Canyon Creek Nursery

Part 6. PUSHING THE LIMITS

T hese are the plant hunters among us, gardeners whose drive to broaden their horizons enrich us all. Some are travelers who return from the gardens of England and Germany laden with dozens of divisions. Some trek into remote parts of China and Japan, bringing back packages of fresh seed labeled with names to conjure with in elevated horticultural circles. Some are armchair travelers who forge international friendships with paper, pen, and seed packet. Others are ardent swappers, now networking locally, now part of a worldwide federation of plant traders. Through the good offices of plantspeople like these, hundreds of perennials have entered the American nursery trade, while thousands more are represented in the gardens of fellow plant lovers across the country.

These advanced gardeners are driven to push the limits, always testing the envelope of hardiness. They experiment with microclimate and technique, selecting plants with superior survival skills by seeking out seed from the extreme limits of a favored species' provenance. They constantly grow plants new to them, learning the conditions under which these little-known creatures might thrive. They have in common the insatiable curiosity of the plant addict, yet they lack the hoarding instinct that marks the selfish acquisitor who values a plant most when it is the only one around. These ardent gardeners share a sense of responsibility that accompanies their unusual abilities and opportunities. Having both in plenty, they take the time and trouble to disseminate their hard-won knowledge as widely as they share their plants and seeds. While few would knowingly toss pearls indiscriminately, all have sent countless excited beginners home with higher goals, glowing eyes, and arms full of divisions and cuttings. This sets an invaluable lesson for us all, to share our skill and vision as well as our plants, in the open-handed spirit of the true plantsperson.

WAYNE WINTERROWD is a garden designer and a frequent contributor to *Horticulture* magazine. At North Hill, his chilly Vermont garden (USDA zone 4), he and his partner, Joe Eck, push the climatic limits to the maximum. The garden is irresistible to plantsman and aesthete alike, rich in variety, yet restrained and harmonious in design. Visitors to North Hill usually come away with gifts of seeds and plants, and always receive renewed vision.

New Perennials
Wayne Winterrowd

G ardeners are people who are not easily satisfied, and they are notoriously unable to let well enough alone. With almost all serious gardeners, the time comes, sooner or later, when they are no longer content to grow the range of plants offered by the local garden center or passed over the back fence.

The first stage of this malaise usually expresses itself in a vague discontent with one's finest effects, especially when they have reached perfection. The phlox are lovely this year, hardly blemished by mildew, and the asters, for once, are not too leggy, due to careful staking and pinching. The daylilies were never finer, and the fat healthy bushes of chrysanthemums give promise of a long season of autumn luxuriance. But the garden has a sameness from last year or the year before, and even the cruel eye of perfection cannot lay the blame on poor culture or neglected care. It all looks distressingly like Mrs. Smith's garden, from which many of the plants came, and who has had similarly good luck this season. The terrible thought slowly creeps into one's mind: "Isn't there anything else I can grow? Something Mrs. Smith doesn't have?"

Once the critical spirit sets in, it spreads through the garden like a noxious weed. All the odd corners come under scrutiny: the bed at the top of the wall, which is too dry for most things and which one clothed, rather desperately, with annuals from the local garden center; that dark damp corner next to the garage, where even the sturdiest hosta looks depressed and depressing. Somehow the whole effect lacks spice. It just won't do.

The second stage of this discontent is to turn to the picture books and catalogs, thinking that if one just has some new names in one's head the plants will turn up, sooner or later. If the books are English, so much the better and worse, for one may quickly find the plant needed to leaven the mess or bring interest to that hopeless corner, and just the plant that will knock Mrs. Smith out of her garden clogs. But where to get these treasures? Can one order from England by mail? Perhaps a trip over there? Can one safely bring back plants without getting clapped into jail, or worse, introducing a pest more virulent than Dutch elm disease into this country? Will the garden become a sort of vegetable Typhoid Mary?

It is possible to order from Europe by mail, though the plants, once they have been bare-rooted, washed with strong fungicides and insecticides, held in quarantine and delayed in the mail, may have the greatest difficulty settling into the garden. The problems any new plant faces in adapting seem always in direct proportion to its desirability and the trouble one went to in securing it. A fair proportion may be "D.O.D.," which is the gardener's acronym for "dead on delivery." Unless the plants are rampant weeds, they may languish and finally expire from homesickness, leaving one, after all one's efforts, with the sour comfort of saying to unimpressed visitors, "That *was* my . . . "

Some of these troubles can be avoided by bringing plants back from overseas holidays oneself, if one secures a plant permit, avoids species that are forbidden (including some of the nicest, such as dianthus), and meets with a customs inspector who knows his business and is enthusiastic about the venture. I once dealt with an inspector who passed through everything I had while I nervously waited, and then looking me straight in the eye, unexpectedly said, "I think you are doing noble work. I am a gardener." One does not meet with such camaraderie normally, however, and most inspectors will treat you with the sullen suspicion reserved for those who smuggle drugs.

Since I am among those unfortunate souls who always feel guilty when going through customs, I have always avoided attempting to smuggle in plants in the dirty laundry. It has, however, been done, with success. I once saw a thriving plantation of hardy cyclamen the start of which had been smuggled in in the toe of a boot, and I knew, briefly, an avid young gardener who claimed that her best things had come in wrapped in the baby's dirty diapers. Gardeners, in pursuit of their passion, are not known for their moral scruples, as any arboretum director familiar with "finger-blight" will tell you. But most of us, either because we are pure gold or because we are pure coward, prefer the legal path. [See appendix for information on plant importation.]

American gardeners are fortunate these days, as a renaissance is taking place in our garden scene. Many small nurseries have sprung up, dedicated to propagating the new and the unusual. There are a number of plants just appearing in commerce that will be new to many American gardens, and that should, for a brief time, quell the nervous quest for the rare and unique. I am offering a short select list of plants that are new at least to me. (If they are old hat in your garden, please, please don't tell me.) All of them are possible, though not necessarily easy, to come by, and all are surprisingly easy to grow. Several, such as *Begonia grandis*, will surprise you also by their hardiness. All of the plants that I mention have proved their mettle by surviving at least three winters at North Hill, in southern Vermont (USDA zone 4), where winter temperatures routinely dip to minus 20 degrees Fahrenheit. This is not to say that they will not expect a little extra protection from winter's cold, in the form of evergreen boughs or loose straw mulch. (Such precautions are always a good idea when a plant is new or cannot be replaced easily.) None of them are the kind of backbone plants that phlox or asters are, but these plants do provide pleasant and sometimes startling accents in the perennial border.

Once the critical spirit sets in, it spreads through the garden like a noxious weed.

First on the list would have to be *Crambe cordifolia* (colewort), a fine bold plant that can provide an unforgettable accent at the back of a perennial border and that is also capable of holding its own in shrubbery. The plant will be familiar to browsers of English garden books. It is that airy gypsophila-looking thing that is a feature of the White Garden at Sissinghurst and that appears in pictures of the borders at Great Dixter. (Those are what one calls garden credentials!) Crambe is a perennial cousin to cabbage, and is about as easy to grow, though its bold three-foot leaves are more suggestive of a lusty horseradish than of any other kitchen relative. In June *Crambe cordifolia* sprouts many-branching stems that produce thousands of tiny white flowers in early July. After the flowers pass, the architecture of the stems still produces an impressive effect, and seed-set is abundant. I have not grown crambe from seed, though it is offered this year by Park's Seed Company, and should be easy. The usual propagation method for crambe is to take root cuttings, and a plant that has been moved or even disturbed by a trowel is quick to sprout several lusty plants from its severed roots. Crambe, when it is new in the garden, takes two or three years to settle down to the business it has in mind. After that, it can remain in place for many years, becoming steadily more impressive with each season. The only pests to which it seems prone are slugs, which disfigure the handsome leaves. Since crambe should be planted at the back of the border and as the flower scapes are never harmed, a few holes can be tolerated.

Another crambe, *C. maritima*, is very garden-worthy, though its flowers are not so magnificent. *C. maritima* is grown for its leaves, which look like kale, but which are gray suffused with purple and are beautifully curled at the edges. Known as sea kale, it is grown in European vegetable gardens and eaten when blanched as cooked greens. *C. maritima* is probably the plant seen under the splendid antique terra-cotta blanching pots in pictures of classic European vegetable gardens. Unlike its above-mentioned cousin, it does not seem as troubled with slugs, which is a good thing, whether its destiny is the table or the perennial garden.

A fine white accent plant for the garden, again about four feet tall at maturity, is *Artemisia lactiflora*. When I first saw photographs of this plant, I assumed it was a tall astilbe or possibly an unusually graceful goatsbeard (*Aruncus dioicus*). It is unlike all other members of its genus in that it is valuable for its flowers and also that it is not gray in foliage. The leaves are a tidy, ferny dark green, and the white flowers, borne in graceful panicles, last a surprisingly long time, from mid-July to late August. It prefers good soil, but is, like all artemisias, untroubled by pests.

Boltonia asteroides is a native plant that used to be grown a good bit in gardens of the last century, until our own native asters, which it somewhat resembles, crossed the seas again from England as "Michaelmas daisies" to crowd boltonia out of favor. *Boltonia asteroides* has lately made an impressive reappearance of its own in the cultivar 'Snowbank', and it is becoming widely available again. The flowers are small white aster-like daisies, and in the form of

'Snowbank' they appear very abundantly on three-foot branching stems. It will be worth the gardener's trouble, however, to locate the unimproved species, a noble thing that grows to six feet, but that is free of the floppy untidiness of the asters. Boltonia has a cool gray-green foliage, handsome in itself, but its real advantage in gardens is that it blooms late in September, among the last perennials to flower. It adds to this virtue the fact that it is immune to damage from all but the heaviest of frosts.

Patrinia scabiosaefolia is a plant that took me completely by surprise the first year it flowered. I had ordered it with a lot of other things, and in the desperate carelessness I always fall into when the spring orders arrive, I poked it into the only available spot I could find, which was in the front of the perennial border. The first year it merely settled in, and did not flower. I managed somehow to avoid yanking out the tidy eight-inch mat of wild-looking foliage it produced. The second season, *P. scabiosaefolia* shot up several four-foot stems that were later packed with hundreds of tiny yellow flowers of the true daffodil color not often encountered in the garden after the great spring flush. Had I paid more attention to the treasure I had, I would probably have placed it mid-border. As it happened, nothing could have been lovelier than the way it broke rank, reminding me once again that the "short-medium-and-tall" rule, though in the main the right design idea for a perennial border, profits enormously by being broken now and again with a tall forward-placed accent. Patrinia is very easy to grow, and may be divided for increase in early spring.

The genus *Phlomis* includes many sub-shrubs, mostly Mediterranean in origin, which are familiar to gardeners in climates more gentle than mine. One of its members, however, is a wonderful and very hardy perennial that is just beginning to appear in American catalogs. *P. russeliana* forms a mound of very handsome rough wedge-shaped leaves of sage green, about a foot high and neatly arranged as if it were a pulmonaria or lungwort. If it did nothing else this would be enough, but in midsummer it sends up four-foot rods along which, at six-inch intervals, are puffs of tightly packed green flower bracts. The butter-yellow flowers, half-inch tubes shaped rather like those of a penstemon, appear for the rest of the summer, and gain from the fine architecture of the plant what they lose in individual showiness. Though *Phlomis russeliana* might serve as a border plant, it is so interesting in all its parts that I have preferred to use it as an accent among evergreens, where its fineness of form can be appreciated without other floral distractions.

I have always envied English gardeners their successes with *Nepeta*, at least judging from the photographs in British books. *Nepeta cataria* is an erect perennial more familiar to most gardeners from the pet supply shelf of the supermarket, where it is labeled catnip, than in the garden. It loves dry soil and produces lovely small violet-mauve flowers on three-foot bushes in late June, if the cats let it. I love cats, though I would encourage their presence even if I didn't, because I love gardens even more; I would not have a single crocus without the cats' help in exterminating mice, moles, and voles that would otherwise decimate the garden. But the cats in turn have decimated my catnip, which grew lustily at first, but which was quickly reduced to a pulpy mattress when the cats finally discovered it. I have had no better success with *N. mussinii*, which though clearly second best in their eyes, was better than nothing (once they had reduced *N. cataria* to nothing). My only surviving plant, the choice hybrid form 'Six Hills Giant', must live under a dome of chicken wire and sharp bamboo stakes. It appears to know that if it were to venture beyond its palisade and fortress it would be squashed, like its predecessors, by feline admirers.

I feel lucky, therefore, to have discovered a member of the *Nepeta* clan that so far has proved unattractive to cats and very attractive to me. It is *N. govaniana*, hardly second best in anyone's eyes, though it lacks the misty mauve flowers one so admires in all the English garden pictures. It is a strong-growing perennial to three feet, bushy, with abundant pale yellow flowers borne throughout July. This species originates in Kashmir, and is extremely hardy. Thriving in a moist soil, it will not put up with the parched and baked spots to which the catnips or cat mints add garden glory. *N. govaniana* comes extremely easily from seed, and flowers even the first year after sowing. It can be found in the lists of several perennial nurseries.

Centaurea, both the annual and perennial members of the Composite Family (or Asteraceae) always find a ready sucker in me. In its annual form, *Centaurea cyanus*, it was one of the first flowers I grew as a child. The popular names it bears—knapweed, ragged robin, bachelor's buttons—attest to its homely charm. A perennial sort that greatly resembles the annual, at least in flower, is *C. montana* (mountain bluet or perennial cornflower), grown apparently forever in American gardens as an old-fashioned perennial. Like many another old-fashioned plant, it is both lax and invasive. Still it is a lovely thing, blooming before most perennials have gotten well started, and it comes in lavender, pale yellow, rose, and white forms, as well as the more familiar blue. The blue is best.

Within the genus *Centaurea*, however, are several other fine perennial garden plants that are not seen often enough in gardens. *C. macrocephala* (yellow hardhead) is a very good one-of-a-kind plant. One would not want a drift of it, but its three-inch leaves and large ragged yellow flowers borne on four-foot stems produce what might be called a "full stop" in the perennial border. *C. macrocephala* seems as long-lived as a peony, providing the soil is well drained; this plant is capable of enduring a surprising amount of drought.

Centaurea dealbata (Persian cornflower) has fine silvery green leaves that somewhat resemble the stylized acanthus leaf of Corinthian columns. It produces rosy to red thistle-like flowers on two-foot branched stems throughout the summer. Indeed, this centaurea seems never to be out of bloom, and may even be coaxed into a late autumn crop of flowers by judiciously cutting back the plant in late summer.

Best of the centaureas, however, or at least best to me, is the newest one in my garden, *C. ruthenica*. It produces pale yellow thistles on three-foot branching stems from a mass of finely-cut leaves. This species has more delicacy of form than any other members of its family in commerce. All centaureas have the added charm of throwing their ragged petals from an amazingly finely-crafted bract like a diminutive artichoke, as if in an attempt to make up in the beginning for their lack of floral discipline in the end. All are lovely in bud.

Strobilanthes atropurpureus bears the unpleasant popular name "stinking nettle," and given such a name, one wonders how popular it could ever be. I should have been warned. This plant first came to me after it had been placed high on my list of desirables due to a conversation I overheard among horticultural authorities about its name. It seems that the plant's identification is uncertain at best; it is sometimes offered as *Caryopteris divaricata*. Whatever its true name, I planted it as a thing rare and to be treasured, at the edge of a small terrace where the family dog passes regularly. She is not often washed. The smell emitted from the plant as the dog brushed by was ranker than any canine, bathed or unbathed! I have since moved the plant, and now that I can keep my distance, I revel in the splendid effect it produces. The early frosts reduce it to the ground but it makes a fine five-foot bush with surprising swiftness by early summer, many-branched, and covered with the sort of soft clear green leaves one would want to crush unless one knew better. From late July until frost the whole plant is covered with small purple tubular flowers, which though in themselves modest, are borne in such abundance that the whole plant appears a hazy violet. Stinking nettle is a fine thing, entirely nice in its out-of-the-way place. *S. atropurpureus* loves shade, and thrives in soils that remain permanently moist.

The last on the list of perennials new to me is the so-called hardy begonia, the proper name for which we are now told is *Begonia grandis*. (It often shows up in catalogs, when it is listed at all, as *Evansiana* or *B. evansiana*.) It is by anyone's measure a curious thing to find hardy in a garden. Its leaves look exactly like the old-fashioned angel's wing begonia (*B. coccinea* or *B. rubra*) treasured for so many years in New England parlor windows. The leaves are splendid, especially in deep dappled shade where the late afternoon sun can shine through to reveal their rich red undersides. At the very end of the season, just before the frosts, the two-foot canes sport pink flowers that look exactly like . . . angel's wing begonias. Each spring, just when one expects they won't, new canes emerge from the underground tubers. *Begonia grandis* also comes in a rare white form, and is a wonderful thing to grow if one is not shy of having visitors suppose that houseplants have been bedded out for the summer.

One of the greatest pleasures for the serious gardener is searching through catalogs for new and unusual plants. All of the catalogs listed below should have one or more—heaven forbid *all*—of the plants I have mentioned. They will also list other rarities for which you may have been searching, and to which, if you hurry, you may even beat Mrs. Smith.

SOURCES
(See "Sources & Resources" appendix for complete addresses.)

Canyon Creek Nursery
Carroll Gardens
Lamb Nursery
Montrose Nursery
We-Du Nurseries

PAT BENDER's humor and modest disclaimers can't disguise her plant expertise. Bender grows hundreds of uncommon plants from seed each year, distributing them with unrivaled generosity. Visitors rarely leave her garden without a few pots of seedlings, and any new gardener is sent staggering home under a bundle of plump divisions. An active member of more than twenty plant societies and international seed exchanges, she has served on many national and regional boards.

The Evolution Of A Gardener
Pat Bender

To paraphrase Stephen Sondheim, how did I get there from here? From a window box filled with seed-grown petunias to a patio filled with 1100 pots of seed and countless cuttings, it is just a few years, much labor and many dollars. An indulgent husband helps—a *strong* indulgent husband.

Before the green fingers of this enveloping hobby closed around my throat and checkbook, I was told that no one grows petunias from seed. "You must buy plants from a nursery." When I ventured to ask how nurseries fashioned these plants without seed, and why Mr. Burpee hadn't been told of the "petunia seed caper," my friends laughed at my naiveté. With nothing to lose and flowers to gain I tossed a package of petunia seed outdoors in a west-facing window box, watered them well and covered the box with plastic. This was in March. By June the same friends who laughed were lining up for seedlings.

The first success with petunias challenged me to find greener fields, preferably evergreen fields since it looked so bare when the annuals died down. In the Pacific Northwest, rhododendrons are almost a cliché because of the ease of culture. So, off to join the American Rhododendron Society. And what did I find? Seed, and more seed—hundreds of kinds, in what is called a "seed exchange." Members save their seed, or collect it in the wild, and donate it to the Society. It is then listed and sold at a dollar a packet. What a bargain! But—and here is the quicksand—you cannot grow rhododendron seed readily by tossing it in a window box. Much better to grow it under mist in a greenhouse. I had no greenhouse, so the aforementioned indulgent husband placed fluorescent lights under the upper kitchen cabinets, and beneath them I placed cottage cheese cartons planted with seed and enveloped in plastic sandwich bags. A few weeks in these ersatz greenhouses and the little seedlings surfaced, and grew, and grew, and grew. Now here was a problem: prolific germination, more plants than I had room for, and the wait of several years to see if the blooms were worthwhile. Further, many rhododendrons grow so large that moving them supports the many orthopedic surgeons who belong to the Rhododendron Society.

On to dwarf conifers. I joined the American Conifer Society, and started visiting nurseries in search of little "buns." When I visited a friend's former nursery and was informed that the conifer we were standing under was a dwarf I realized that the term "dwarf" was a relative one.

When . . . informed that the conifer we were standing under was a dwarf I realized that the term "dwarf" was a relative one.

Frustrations of plant size continued until my friend Alice suggested that we join the American Rock Garden Society. Most of the plants they specialize in are small and easy to move, and, wonder of wonders, they have a seed exchange (5,813 kinds in the 1988 seed list). Now that should take me through my golden years and then some. Best of all, the seed can be germinated outside over the winter. (There is a limit to kitchen counter space.) The Society meetings are inspiring, with slide programs of wonderful plants in beautiful places. Summer brings field trips to see these tiny rubies in the wild. There are study weekends in the early spring that offer concentrated study of alpine plants, plus—and this is a big, expensive plus—nursery booths that sell beautiful, rare items that you simply must have to be an authentic plantsperson. The same events are repeated at the annual meetings, together with field trips and visits to perfect gems of gardens. These visits are a mixed blessing; they provide inspiration at seeing such gardening skill, and a desire to return home and ravage one's own turf and start over.

By this time I had discovered other alpine garden societies in England, Scotland, New Zealand, and Canada. They all had seed exchanges! What exhilaration when I heard the news! Each society publishes a journal, usually quarterly, with inspiring articles and beautiful pictures. But wait — here is the best part — the journals announce an international meeting of rock garden societies to be held in England, the nirvana of gardeners. My husband observes that gardening has become an expensive hobby.

On our first trip to England we note that alpine plants are being grown in old cattle drinking troughs. Now there is an idea! Troughs are hard to come by in the U.S., but plans are offered to make one's own out of peat, sand, and cement. Sounds like heavy work, so we purchase an old cement mixer to make our own mix. I have fashioned other troughs from the huge pots used to cook soup on ships, from whiskey barrels, and from foam shipping crates disguised with a sand coating. The great advantage of container growing, aside from keeping our wrestling dogs off the rarities, is that small treasures are less likely to be overwhelmed by their more assertive brethren.

Many of our new gardening friends have become interested in perennial plants. These are much like alpines, but larger. Often much larger. My husband announces that he likes the big stuff. I am glad he does because another trip to England is in the works, this time for "hardy plants," a British term for perennials. This time I am smart enough (?) to get an import permit from the U.S. Department of Agriculture before we leave so that I can bring home the plants I have bought overseas. This proves to be not exactly a mistake, but a great drain on the budget. But how could I resist buying from the likes of Alan Bloom and Christopher Lloyd? And didn't John say he liked the "big stuff"?

We join the British Hardy Plant Society, and, lo and behold, they have a seed list. Stateside, the American members of the Society are busy putting on yearly study weekends for perennials. The English are coming this direction for a change and are telling us how to grow these wonderful glories. This is fine for the Pacific Northwest, but Eastern gardeners have a hard time with some English plants. So enter the Dutch and Germans with their hardier plants, and enter those who are doing what we should all be doing — growing our native species.

On the study-weekend display tables are fliers for individual plant societies, British and American. There are groups for primulas, clematis, and penstemons. Will we join these? You bet we will.

They, too, have seed lists, journals, and meetings. Who could ask for anything more?

By now, the proliferation of seed pots at home has become a problem. The lower patio has been completely taken over by flats, and the refrigerator is so full of seed being cold stratified that a brunch must be postponed until the peony seed is done. (This is a vast improvement over storing ladybugs in the fridge. They become restless if the door is opened too often. And why did we have the ladybugs? Because we had read that they were an environmentally safe method of aphid control. "Store in the refrigerator to keep the ladybugs dormant until a suitable time to release them." What was not mentioned was that they knew no property boundaries, so on the day of release those that did not go up my husband's pant legs headed for the neighbors. Months later a neighbor mentioned the ladybug scourge she had suffered. I looked suitably blank.)

As you can tell, my kitchen is garden headquarters. I sterilize soil in cottage cheese cartons in the microwave. When the carton changes shape, the soil is done. The microwave is also used for heat stratification of selected seeds. The seeds, placed on a paper plate, are zapped for ten seconds, then the plate is given a quarter turn and zapped again. When you do this four times you have come full circle. This has proved to be much safer than my playing Mother Nature with burning pine needles.

Although we have visited as many nurseries as possible to obtain selected forms of perennial plants, I still prefer to raise them from seed for several reasons. Most of all, it is fun. What a thrill when some difficult plant germinates; there's old Mother Nature again. Secondly, there is the matter of economy. For the price of a packet of seeds you can carpet an area with choice beauties. And if some of the seedlings die, you do not shed the bitter tears you would over a one-of-a-kind rarity. Thirdly, many unusual plants are only available from seed.

This leads us to a sticky wicket. Where do these seeds come from? Most are commercially raised, and sold by catalogs and in garden stores. Many of the seed exchange items are garden raised. Others are collected in the wild, sometimes by individuals, and often by seed expeditions. Sometimes these expeditions are led by botanical gardens, while others are privately subscribed. Several notable individuals make their livings collecting seed in the wild and offering it for sale. While it is wonderful to have the seed, when is collecting overcollecting? There has been some criticism of such expeditions recently, and perhaps we should consider whether harm is being done to our environment. Many times the seed does not germinate under our local conditions, or the plant is lost to unsuitable conditions or neglect. Certainly some plants have been saved by means of collected seed, but this is the exception, not the rule.

Growing plants from cuttings is also a thrill, and it is the only way to perpetuate selected forms of plants. I have found fellow gardeners to be extremely generous and I try to do the same. One of the finest plantsmen I know says that he doesn't want to have a one-of-a-kind plant; if a plant is worth having it is worth distributing widely. What price glory if the only plant in existence turns up its toes and heads for the compost pile? If you have shared the plant you can ask for a piece back again. This has happened to me more often than I would like known.

My evolution as a gardener is so complete that all of our vacations are planned well in advance around plant meetings and study weekends, both here and abroad. All tours are garden tours or are turned into such. On our tour of Italy last fall we were the only tourists at Hadrian's Villa and Pompeii on our hands and knees looking for seed. And you should see what grows on the walls of the hill towns in Tuscany! Actually, you can see it here now in my garden.

The love of gardening has extended to our book collection. I was a book collector before becoming a plantsperson, but my collecting turned to plant books early on, and led my husband into bookshelf carpentry. Soon we will run out of walls, but never out of books.

What aspect of gardening has meant the most to me? The friends we have made are the most important dividend. Gardeners are generous, intelligent, interesting, funny, and so extraordinarily healthy and long-lived. My dear friend and garden mentor, Frances Roberson, is 86 and runs rings around me. My ambition is to emulate Frances and run rings around someone else when I am 86. If anything will do it for me, gardening will.

I have included a list of plant societies for those who are interested, and I hope this includes every reader of this book.

ORGANIZATIONS
(Societies marked by (*) have seed exchanges. See "Sources & Resources" appendix for complete addresses.)

*Alpine Garden Club of British Columbia
*Alpine Garden Society
American Conifer Society
American Hosta Society
*American Penstemon Society
*American Primrose Society
*American Rhododendron Society
*American Rock Garden Society
*Hardy Plant Society
*International Clematis Society
*New Zealand Alpine Garden Society Inc.
*Royal Horticultural Society
*Scottish Rock Garden Club
*Species Iris Group of North America (SIGNA)

ELAINE CANTWELL is an ardent plantswoman and a free-lance garden writer who has published numerous articles in America and England. Her waterfront garden, on the south shore of Long Island, New York (USDA zone 7), holds considerable collections of ornamental shrubs and clematis as well as alpines and rock plants, hardy geraniums, and a few hundred other things. Cantwell is always on the lookout for a good plant.

Little-Known Perennial Treasures
Elaine Baxter Cantwell

A gardener rarely reads a new book, thumbs through a nursery catalog or visits a garden without being keenly on the lookout for "something different." I'm certainly no exception, and my never-ending search for new and unusual plants has often led to the acquisition of choice specimens. Some of these have turned out to be disappointments in the garden, some are indeed useful, and others proved to be real treasures deserving of much wider popularity than they currently enjoy. The following is a selection of "gems" that has proved its worth over the past several years in my USDA zone 7 garden; why these plants are virtually unknown in the domestic nursery trade is a mystery.

Coreopsis rosea Everyone is familiar with such garden cultivars as 'Moonbeam' (*C. verticillata*) and 'Goldfink' (*C. grandiflora*, sometimes listed under *C. lanceolata*). They all provide a billowing cloud of yellow through most of the summer. But if you would, for a moment, imagine the flowers of 'Moonbeam' not as butter yellow but instead as a bright lilac pink; you are imagining *Coreopsis rosea*. Foliage is identical in form to *C. verticillata* although slightly darker green (which makes me wonder if this is actually a pink form of that species), and this plant shares its relatives' adaptability to a range of conditions from normal to light and sandy soils. It is hardy to at least the warmer areas of zone 4, and will presumably thrive anywhere that *C. verticillata* would; it is easily propagated by division.

Trilisa odoratissima Here is a wonderful perennial for those constantly wet or boggy spots in a garden, even more so because, unlike traditional bog bloomers such as *Astilbe* and *Trollius* (globeflower), *Trilisa odoratissima* flowers in the autumn. The best description of this plant is that it resembles a branched gayfeather

(*Liatris*). The flowering stem rises from the center of a six-inch rosette of leaves, and may reach four to five feet in height; it bears several spikes, composed of many small deep rose-magenta flowers with conspicuous stamens. Curiously, its name refers not to the fragrance of the flowers but to the dried leaves. However, it does contribute striking color and form during the time of year that is often dominated by yellow, orange, and russet tones in the garden. In my own bog corner, it keeps company with the double white *Anemone* x *hybrida* 'Whirlwind' that flowers at the same time. *Trilisa odoratissima* has been offered as *Carphephorus odoratissimus*; zone 7 seems to be the northernmost limit of its hardiness range. Propagation is best done by division; seed germination is unpredictable.

> **Someone recently described my garden as a "plantswoman's garden" rather than a designer's garden. . . . .**

Erodium chrysanthum   This plant is related to the hardy geraniums, and is one of the very few evergreen perennials with year-round decorative foliage. Truly, it is worth growing for its foliage alone, which resembles froths of lush, silvery blue-green curly parsley that is velvety soft to the touch. A single plant will easily cover a square foot of garden space. As if this were not enough, *Erodium chrysanthum* flowers almost non-stop from late April through September. Since this species is dioecious (having both male and female forms), the flowers differ slightly in color; male flowers are sulphur-yellow while female plants bear softer, butter-yellow blooms. They are about three-quarters of an inch in diameter, borne in sprays on ten-inch spikes. So long as it receives at least a half day of sun, *E. chrysanthum* will flourish in light to ordinary garden soils. I have never had a single pest or disease problem with my plants, even though our recent summers have been hot and humid. It is hardy to zone 7, possibly even in southern parts of zone 6 with winter protection.

Daphne x mantensiana   Here is a marvelous little shrub that blooms non-stop and combines well with perennials. Despite many daphnes' reputation for fickleness, this evergreen is a notable exception. A hybrid of *D. retusa* and *D. burkwoodii*, it bears small neat oval leaves reminiscent of boxwood and keeps its classic shape without requiring a bit of pruning. Flowers are deep rose pink and incredibly fragrant. My three-year-old shrub begins blooming in late April; there are always flowers appearing throughout the year until the really vicious weather arrives in January. Ultimate height seems to be about two feet with an 18-inch spread, on a single trunk. My plant is situated on a slope that receives full sun in winter and light shade in summer, near rock garden plants such as *Potentilla nitida* (snowline cinquefoil) and various encrusted saxifrages (it is in perfect scale with such companions). *Daphne* x *mantensiana* prefers good drainage. It grows beautifully in zone 7, though in zone 6 it might require protection to avoid winter kill of younger growth. I intend to try an additional pair in stone containers near our door, so that the lovely fragrance can be enjoyed each time we go in or out.

Sabatia kennedyana As long as we are in the rock garden, another unique plant deserves a closer look. At first glance the neat rosettes appear to be some sort of saxifrage, or perhaps a tiny lewisia. This evergreen perennial does enjoy similar conditions of light soil and excellent drainage, but when the flowers appear in July *Sabatia kennedyana* looks just like a miniature cosmos! The petals are clear silvery pink, surrounding a chartreuse sunburst-shaped center; the flowers are carried singly and gracefully on 12-inch stems. In fact, this rare plant belongs to the gentian family (Gentianaceae) and is native to Cape Cod, which should give a clue as to its hardiness range (zone 7). The basal rosettes produce offsets which can be detached for propagation.

Platycodon grandiflorus 'Double Pink' I will admit to an inordinate fondness for the campanula family (Campanulaceae), and I try to obtain as many different species and hybrids as I can possibly fit into my limited space. But if I had to choose just one member of that vast alliance to keep in my garden, this hybrid balloon flower would be it. The color is delightful, about midway between baby pink and lavender-pink; but it is the fully double form of the flower that stops people in their tracks to ask what it is. The overall effect is of an 18-inch spike of miniaturized double pink clematis. I grow it next to various other *Platycodon* cultivars in blue, pink, and white, which in turn are neighbors of several tall campanulas enjoying a well-drained slope. If faded flowers are removed, this remarkable perennial will flower all summer in either sun or light shade and ordinary garden loam. Though late to break ground in spring, it is dependably hardy to zone 3. This plant is sometimes offered as *Platycodon grandiflorum roseum 'Flore Pleno'*.

Viola 'Magic'   Several years ago I learned the hard way about the difference between types of violets — by planting too many *V. odorata* in my shade garden! Those are now gone (I hope) but this well-behaved English pansy-flowered hybrid viola is the one I would never chose to remove. Through some peculiar genetic twist, the color of the flowers changes along with the progress of the year. The first blooms, appearing in late March, are rich violet with a white rayed eye. As the weather warms by early May, the flowers appear in shades of lavender, with the eyes now darkening to lilac. As I write this at the beginning of July, the plant is covered with pure white flowers veined in purple! Stems are nice and long for cutting, which I can usually do right through until Labor Day; it shares a shady area with other flower-arrangers' delights such as *Astrantia major* (great masterwort), *Helleborus orientalis* (lenten rose) and the Pacific bleeding heart, *Dicentra formosa* 'Stuart Boothman'. The plant is happy in sun (if kept moist) or shade up to zone 5 and does not share the invasive habits of its' cousins, although I wouldn't mind if it did — one can never have too much magic in the garden!

Someone recently described my garden as a "plantswoman's garden" rather than a designer's garden, and that is a perfect epithet! So, *Coreopsis verticillata* 'Moonbeam' rubs elbows with the hybrid broom *Cytisus* x 'Lucky' not because they look good together (I don't think they particularly do!) but because both are admirably suited to the location, a sunny, well-drained slope. Thriving on the slope's dry top is the cytisus while the coreopsis holds the midway point and keeps the light sandy soil from washing downward. *Coreopsis rosea* is in a different sunny area where its pink flowers look handsome just behind low-growing lavender cotton (*Santolina chamaecyparissus* 'Nana'). My primary criteria of placement is to meet the plants' requirements and if an attractive juxtaposition of color or design occurs — a bonus. What works in my garden conditions might be a disaster in someone else's. All magic is mysterious! What is certain is that the search for little-known perennial treasures is never-ending.

PUSHING THE LIMITS

SOURCES
(See "Sources & Resources" appendix for complete addresses.)

Busse Gardens (*Coreopsis rosea*)

Canyon Creek Nursery (*Coreopsis rosea, Erodium chrysanthum* and *Viola* 'Magic')

Carroll Gardens (*Coreopsis rosea*)

Lamb Nurseries (*Platycodon grandiflorum roseum* 'Flore Pleno')

Milaeger's Gardens (*Coreopsis rosea*)

Montrose Nursery (*Coreopsis rosea*)

Siskiyou Rare Plant Nursery (*Daphne* x *mantensiana*)

Andre Viette Farm & Nursery (*Coreopsis rosea*)

We-Du Nurseries (*Trilisa odoratissima* and *Sabatia kennedyana*)

ALLAN ARMITAGE, previously seen as a regionalist, reveals unsuspected depths as he emerges in a new persona: plantsman and poet. His heartfelt outburst reflects the feelings of all plant lovers when pushed past their personal limits.

They Shout "You're in Hort; Why Don't You Know"
Allan Armitage

Dear Abby, dear Abby, my tale must be told,
For right about now, I'm feeling so old.
I said I was a Horticulturist, you see,
And I went to a meeting for pastries and tea.

Some gardeners started asking questions of me
That started me choking on my cookies and tea.
One that was asked by a particularly devious sort;
With a smirk and smile, he asked "Just what is Hort?"

I suddenly knew this was not to be fun.
I said, "Hort is extremely important to some;
It's a rather large field, much like a zoo,
But I'll try to relate my subject to you."

"We learn about fruits, veggies, and pathology,
Greenhouses, nurseries, and mycology,
Soils and storage, plants large and small,
Genetics and physics, we cover them all."

I said I specialize in ornamental crops;
Then someone asked about green turnip tops.
"That's not really my field, turnips I don't grow."
They say "You're in Hort; why don't you know?"

They shout "You're in Hort; why don't you know?"
I said I wasn't in greens; that just didn't go!
So just when I learn about those God-awful tops,
They ask me about the problem of cranberry spots.

Their cranberry fruits had this brown looking spot;
I've never seen cranberry, I've no idea what it's got.

PUSHING THE LIMITS

These friends of mine quickly turn into foe;
They shout "You're in Hort; why don't you know?"

I check all my books about cranberry spots,
And I begin to discourse on just what it's got,
And just as I feel I can converse with ease,
Someone wants to know about the PAN disease.

I say all I know about any pans
Is how my wife uses them to back her demands.
I see them all look both to and fro;
They shout "You're in Hort; why don't you know?"

They shout "You're in Hort; why aren't you sure?"
I reply that Hort is all of Agriculture.
But excuses that night just wouldn't go;
They shout "You're in Hort; why don't you know?"

Questions of fungi and soils come flying at me,
And some fellow wants to know about phyllotaxy.
Questions of tissue culture, life cycles, and rust,
And corollas, coronas, and strobili dust.

I shout "What is Hort? It seems plain to me;
Your varied questions have provided the key.
We specialize, yes, I think that can be seen
But we also must know how to keep your lawn green.

"Would you ask a doctor about the pain in your knee
If you knew he was a specialist in Gynecology?"
That stopped them right then, the silence did grow;
They could see that in Hort, there's a great deal to know.

So Abby, oh Abby, I'm losing my mind,
Seems I run out of answers all of the time;
How can I field all the questions that come to and fro?
When I'm a hundred, then maybe I'll know.

KEVIN NICOLAY was among America's outstanding plantsmen, growing an astonishing range and variety of rare plants in his miniscule urban garden. He introduced hundreds of plants to America, including antique flowers, rare species, and uncommon border perennials, all of which increased in his capable hands. The best were passed on to specialty nursery growers, for Nicolay hoped both to preserve little-known plants and to broaden the American garden palette. Teacher and mentor, artist and botanical illustrator, plantsman and superb colorist, Kevin Nicolay was a man of enormous talent who will be sorely missed. Nicolay, who had just turned 33, died as this book was going to press.

There Must Be More To Life Than This
Kevin Nicolay

Every gardener goes through a giddy phase, when first he or she sets out to grow things, in which all plants are Gorgeous and all seedlings Worth Saving. Like wondering-eyed kindergartners, drunk on the fairy tales in glossy English garden books, it never occurs to us to take our discriminating adult opinions out into the garden. It is all heady and splendid and isn't gardening grand. We enter every plant nursery like toddlers in toyland, checkbooks barely under control. Instead of bringing home every stray puppy, we rescue a wide and catholic assortment of supermarket foundlings and Woolworth rejects, and then line up at the garden fences of new friends, waiting for the latest vegetable wonder to be passed over on a spade. Never mind that what we grow is as common as spuds. The world is our salsify, horticulturally speaking, and it is impossible to keep from walking around open-mouthed and amazed at any little green thing that makes an appearance.

Fortunately, this state passes. The Age of Innocence evaporates and our critical faculties return to pinch us. Kindergarten snacks of hot dogs and Twinkies lose their appeal; we have developed an unfortunate taste for fois gras and 30-year-old Scotch. Casting a hardened eye over Eden, prickled by the faint unease of dissatisfaction, the blush has gone off the apple. A favorite clematis now looks hopelessly washy. Those hardy geraniums are dreadful floppers, and they only flower for about 15 minutes, usually when your back is turned. The phlox you got from the neighbor is a really nasty

233

shade of magenta and it is screaming, not flowering, from amidst Aunt Mae's tired orange daylilies and Granny's pushy red lychnis. Our adult tastes have followed us out of doors, and we are left thinking, "There must be more to life than this."

And there is. One of the wonderful things about gardening is that, just when you think you've seen it all, some further surprise turns up to delight and amaze. There are always double forms, ones with white flowers or variegated leaves or bigger blossoms. You know this is all true because you've seen them in the cool and inviting gardens of older and wiser plantspersons. You've also noticed these unusual forms winking at you in a meretricious way from those slick British books, and worse, seductive catalogs. There they are, the phlox with variegated leaves, a geranium with double flowers that last, clematis so red they open black, daylilies like sublimely frosted sugar cookies. Just when you thought your love affair with cosmos was getting a little stale, some know-it-all shows you one that is *perennial, Cosmos atrosanguineus*, with flowers as dark as garnets and smelling of chocolate.

How lovely, how enticing, how frustrating. Having expanded your horizons and arrived at an advanced and discriminating taste, how are you supposed to get your hands on these plants? They certainly don't show up at the local nursery! Too often, the staff doesn't even know what you're talking about when you ask for some of the things you've seen. So where are these surprises supposed to come from? After finding the banquet of Flora chock-a-block with goodies beyond all imagining, where does the desperate gardener obtain them?

Let me assure you that the plants you are after are out there, but you have to be resourceful and patient. You don't go out to the 7-Eleven to pick up a bottle of Tattingers champagne or a Hepplewhite sideboard, so don't expect to just stumble on *Cosmos atrosanguineus* at Kmart. These items have to be run to earth and savored.

The thrill is in the chase and I have some helpful suggestions for the wiley hunters, gathered together for you from my long years of greed. The first and easiest way to bring unusual plants to your garden is to spend money. If you and your checkbook are willing, you can either allow the mail to bring plants and seeds to your doorstep, or you can get out of your gazebo, go to the plants, and bring them back alive. A second way is more demanding. It does not require tracking, trailing, buying, or acquiring. It requires not the jingle of loose coins but instead a change of heart—it demands giving.

But first, the path of the pocketbook—discover mail order. The United States is thick with specialist nurseries all delighted to send you their catalogs for free or for a few dollars. Their owners are honest and generous (for the most part) and are only too pleased to provide a well-wrapped, well-stocked parcel of heavenly plants, all for an impulsive little signature. Catalog shopping is the best way to put an ear to the ground as far as plants are concerned, and a friend of mine has said, "Anything you want is out there; you just have to be persistent and send for lots of different plant lists."

My garden is like a photo album, and as I go over the fresh new greenery, I see plants but remember people. . . .

To that end, make it your job to become a catalog connoisseur. Even if you never order a plant, the catalogs can be useful learning aids for familiarizing yourself with the likes, dislikes, and general profiles of many plants rich and strange. There are other benefits to sitting down with a massive pile of catalogs. For those who live to comparison shop, this is the perfect opportunity to check out the competition. Very often you can find a horrendously expensive offering in one of the glossy high-profile catalogs for much less at a smaller nursery. For those who thrive on rationalism, you can justify your expenditures as beneficial to the economy, since you are helping to support the little firms that usually offer the rare stuff. It is certainly true that the more of these we keep in business, the more plants; and the more plants, the greater our palette and sophistication as gardeners.

There is even a book to help you in this plunder. *Gardening by Mail* by Barbara Barton (Houghton Mifflin Co., 1990) is a Thanksgiving table of names and addresses for an immense range of nurseries. Listed here are places that stock everything from *Acacia* to *Yucca*, as well as seed houses and garden suppliers. The book is organized up, down, and sideways, so it is very easy to use. Among the information she gives is whether the catalog costs money, what is the nursery's specialty, and whether one is able to visit. It can be a pleasing winter pastime, stuffing envelopes full of requests for every plant list under the sun.

Some people balk at mail order as too much of a gamble, but considering that the gardener's art is one lifelong bet on climate, soil, weather, bugs, and the state of our backs, it seems silly to be intimidated by a little catalog risk-taking. Some good advice for the wary is to send small orders first, as a way of the testing the waters. Once you see what the plants look like, how they are packed, and what is the best shipping method for your area, you can act accordingly and not face the horror of three hundred dollars' worth of plants arriving in a crushed shoebox. Another thing to remember when shopping by mail for rare or unusual plants is that it is like looking for antiques: If a choice plant shows up in one of the catalogs, snap it up and go without lunch. Very often a small nursery will be able to offer only a limited stock of some rarity, advertise it, and then quickly sell out of all stock. Years or decades may pass before they can replenish their supply. Remember, when faced with a decision whether to buy some choice item for which you have been searching or to pass, remember that those who hesitate may lose their plants.

After conquering plants that travel by domestic air, you might then feel ready for a foreign order. Several British nurseries will export and, as you would expect, they offer a range of plants so exciting that you may feel feverish when looking through their catalogs. The best way to find the nurseries that export is to go through copies of the Royal Horticultural Society's bulletins and the various journals from English plant societies.

Placing overseas mail orders is not a process for the fainthearted, however. In the first place, some of the nurseries have very steep minimum orders. These can be overcome by pooling an order with friends or by going through a local horticultural organization. You will need to be very organized and on top of each stage of the process to avoid foul-ups, and you will have had to form a pleasant relationship with your local inspector, known officially as an employee of the Plant Protection and Quarantine Programs, Animal and Plant Health Inspection Service, U.S. Department of Agriculture. According to some stories I've heard, you need to have an actual affair with someone at the office to really expedite matters, but on the whole, I've had no problems so long as I was prepared and had communicated well with the nursery and the local office of the USDA.

Apply for a plant import permit. An application for a written permit should be submitted at least 30 days prior to the arrival of imported plants at the port of entry. Apply to Plant Protection and Quarantine Programs, Permit Unit, Animal and Plant Health Inspection Service, U.S. Department of Agriculture, Federal Building, Hyattsville, MD 20782. The application should include your name, address and telephone number; the approximate quantity and kinds (botanical designations) of plants intended to be imported; intended United States port of entry; means of transportation, such as mail, airmail, air freight, or baggage; and expected date of arrival. Application forms are available without charge from the above noted address or from local offices that are listed in telephone directories. I don't mean to put you off from this avenue of attack, as it certainly beats the expense of actually going abroad, but in matters concerning plant importation, it is best to have one's eyes wide open. [See Appendix for additional information on plant importation.]

The final money-spending method, rather than bringing the plants to you, demands that you go to them. Travel is one of the most direct, pleasant, and expensive ways to accomplish your education as a gardener. Visiting nurseries and gardens removed from home ground is a great way to see what's going on in the world, and to take advantage of the fact that each distant nursery seems to have its own plant specialties, distinctive as the regions in which they are located. Interstate nursery-hopping is relatively easy; all you need to do is get where you want to be, having first provided yourself with maps, made sure the nursery of choice is open to visitors, and that you are going at a time of year when they have something to sell you. Meeting the people behind the operation is one of the pleasures too since it puts a face on order blanks and correspondence and can lead to lovely friendships.

The real reason for exercising the travel option is to get to England, Mother of Gardens and Cornucopia of Horticulture. Depending on whether you choose to go the bed and breakfast or Grand Tour routes, it can be either reasonably or horrendously expensive, but the outlay is worth every penny. What I said in the previous paragraph goes double for Great Britain. The amount, variety, and diversity of specialist nurseries offering everything under the sun made me break out in hives, and the English gardeners and nursery proprietors were delightfully hospitable, ready to answer intelligent questions, and often making me welcome to their homes as well as their nurseries.

If you are going after plants, I would recommend taking advantage of the cheapest winter fares and visiting in February or March when all plants are dormant and are resilient enough to withstand the sort of handling necessary to appease the import folks. Granted that you will miss out on castles swathed in roses, but bringing plants home in high June is risky and it can be brain-taxing in the extreme to be suffering from garden overload and then have to face the details of preparing plants for importation. Cutting the roots and tops from growing plants is traumatic and makes your purchases very cross. While it is astonishing how many plants do survive a summer trip, remember that you will need to run interference with the authorities and that the weather at home may impair plant vigor. Go down to Kew at lilac time, but pay your money and take your chances.

As with the mail order acquisition of plants, you must familiarize yourself with the import and export regulations attendant on your permit. There are some plants that are denied entry and it can be very dispiriting to pay money for some rare willow or dianthus only to have it chucked upon arrival in the U.S. The other point of great importance is that no plants are allowed into this country with soil on their roots. Along with maps and reservations, make plans to be in a place with good drains towards the end of your sojourn. If you have friends in the country this process is much easier, although bed and breakfast proprietors can be sympathetic as are some nursery owners. On the Grand Tour, you are on your own; the toilet is the best bet in this situation, since the last thing you want to do is to clog the plumbing at Claridges.

Going to the nurseries and motoring around the English countryside is the fun part. Getting the plants through customs can be traumatic. Make sure you declare your plants and have the necessary paperwork ready when you are herded through the gate. Again, a few bits of timely advice will help. Make sure that all your goodies are properly labeled. Schedule your return arrival time during business hours. If not, your precious haul may have to languish overnight or longer because plant inspectors, like other bureaucrats, go home promptly at five o'clock.

One other thing will be valuable to you: Make a respectable appearance. If you are a little gray-haired old lady, a mother (preferably expectant), or a well-dressed scholar complete with horn-rims and Brooks Brother blazer, you will be treated with the utmost civility. Hirsute men with knapsacks, on the other hand, inflame the suspicions of the authorities. Your fate in these situations frequently depends on the side of bed the official sprang from on that particular morning.

Perhaps the preceding approaches strike you as a little extreme, and even as a little too Las Vegas. For the nervous, the budget-minded, the non-traveler, and the home-rooted gardener, there is another, more satisfactory way to obtain elusive plants. It is not nearly as easy as spending money and requires that you be earnest, thoughtful, polite, intelligent, and keen, as well as resourceful, patient, brave, clever, faithful, and true. It wouldn't hurt to be well-read, either. Most important is that you conquer the mysteries of propagation or the art of making something out of next to nothing.

The reason for all this virtue and handiness is that, in order to really pursue the good plants, you'll need to plug into the Freemasonry of Gardening. This sounds like a secret society, but it isn't. You can join up by becoming a member of the Hardy Plant Society or any good horticultural organization; asking intelligent questions of your elders and betters; solving problems posed by your own garden with brains and aplomb; and taking delight in every facet of the gardener's art. This freemasonry is probably one of the most democratic on the face of the earth, and carries the motto "Good Plants for All," rewarding diligence and a sharp eye with a passkey into the floral kingdom. It is characterized by an embarrassing generosity that sees to it that good plants get around to those who crave them.

You have seen freemasonry in action by now, I'm sure. On a visit to some experienced and friendly local plantsperson, you stumble around the garden in a state of euphoria, open-mouthed. "Oh God," you say to yourself, "look at all these amazing plants." There are so many, and so many about which you have only read. Politeness quells wishful thinking, as you desperately want to ask for a division of that, and a cutting of this. Then the pregnant question from your host, "That's a very good form, would you like some of that?" Before you have time to catch your breath, your benefactor comes flying out of the garage or potting shed with great fistfuls of assorted plastic bags, spades, trowels, secateurs, labels, and pots. You end up staying past the time you intended, and go away with the car stuffed with bags of cuttings, pots of delights. It is heavenly.

Now many people are made uncomfortable by this sort of generosity, saying things like, "But I haven't anything to give you." It seems hard to believe that someone would want to give you all this for nothing, and harder to keep from thinking about ways to repay. You needn't worry, though; the orgy of swapping is just as heady for the benefactor and makes him or her feel quite smug. Giving plants to those who care about them passionately is the mark of a freemason.

There is an etiquette that goes with the generosity, though. Remember your politeness, and don't start taking advantage of the situation, becoming one of those crude, demanding sorts who bluster through a garden pointing and begging. Remember your resourcefulness, too. If you haven't any rare plants (yet), use your imagination. Offer an elderly benefactor one or two days' weeding time; volunteer to help stake the garden during the helter-skelter days of early spring; hire yourself out as a spadeperson or a pruner. If you have any sort of skill like carpentry or household repair, trade plants for a pergola or install garden lighting for bulbs. You might keep an eye out for those once-in-a-lifetime offerings from a faraway nursery, ones for which your plant-giving friend might be longing but can't afford. No gardener, as anyone knows, can ever have enough plants. And come to think of it, no gardener can ever have enough manure. Manure and compost are irresistible, and the way to your benefactor's heart may very well be through a surprise truckload of Bossy's finest. Give advance warning if the gift is to be fresh rather than aged!

The most effective way to give as good as you get, and keep

your freemason's account current, is to become a propagator. Nothing is so flattering or so generous as keeping a flat of some rare seedlings or choice cuttings for garden gate give-aways, and nothing is as satisfying as being able to surprise a friend with something he or she has been coveting. Become an expert at germinating difficult seeds, or at increasing slow plants from root, tip, or half-hard cuttings. The Freemasonry will thank you.

For many people propagation is a closed rite, and I have even heard some remark, in a self-congratulatory tone, that they never propagate anything. Well, so far as I'm concerned, you aren't a gardener if you don't undertake to conquer some aspect of plant reproduction. From a very practical standpoint it's the heart and soul of the freemason's art, and without it, scarce and unusual plants would remain so forever. It is your duty and privilege to divide and multiply.

I am not alone in this opinion. As a matter of fact, I have some august bodies to support my view. Edward A. Bowles, for instance, who had an uncanny eye for a fine plant (think of all the plants with 'Bowles Form' or 'Bowles Variety' tacked onto their names) is one. He, along with many others, looked on himself as a plant steward, charged with the responsibility to make plants available to those with a taste for them. Margery Fish, Gertrude Jekyll, and E. B. Anderson all kept the post busy by sending out parcels of generosity. Canon Ellacombe furnished many of the great Victorian and Edwardian gardeners with their rarest plants, believing that it was his solemn calling to increase and multiply the bounty God provided. One Victorian writer went so far as to say that the three key principles of gardening are "Propagate, Propagate, Propagate!"

I know that propagation, sharing, mail order plant shopping, domestic and international nursery hopping, and the other suggestions I have made do work because that is how I made my own garden. May these ideas serve you in your search for that phlox with variegated leaves or a rare double-flowering white form of a favorite plant. One method of plant hunting is no better than another. Actually, these means work best when taken in conjunction rather than singly; they work because they open a new world. I've been able to satisfy my taste for the exotic by buying some plants, going after others, and starting some from scratch, from seeds or cuttings.

PUSHING THE LIMITS

But the plants I love best are the ones that came from some member of the fellowship. In the spring, when I can barely bring myself to come indoors, I stand and take stock of all the treasures winter made me forget. My garden is like a photo album, and as I go over the fresh new greenery, I see plants but remember people: the *Roscoea* from an English friend, the black columbine from Ann, the *Adonis* from another friend. Spending money is fun but the garden is always best where you can detect the hand of a freemason.

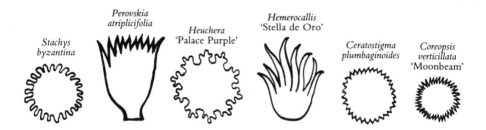

Stachys byzantina   *Perovskia atriplicifolia*   *Heuchera 'Palace Purple'*   *Hemerocallis 'Stella de Oro'*   *Ceratostigma plumbaginoides*   *Coreopsis verticillata 'Moonbeam'*

FINALE

We American gardeners are working our way toward something new. We are in an exciting position, able to draw upon past and present for plants and planting ideas, with ready access to the lessons and techniques prized by gardeners in other cultures. Futuristic technology (antitranspirants, hydrogel crystals and other modern marvels), now widely available, replaces in part the once ubiquitous garden help that built the great gardens of the past. With every material at hand, there is nowhere to go but further up the garden path. Some people find the ceaseless flow of garden books from other shores to be a sign of our own poor horticultural health. It might equally be interpreted as a sign that American gardeners are educating themselves avidly.

This hunger for knowledge is indeed a sign of health, for solid, comprehensive education is the one element we lack. Until we know what the possibilities may be, our own choices — whether of design, plants, or techniques — must remain haphazard and impoverished. This is not to say we are hopelessly ignorant; many of us are good gardeners, who only need introduction to the wider range of plants in order to employ them artfully. Education does not imply the wholesale adoption of accepted guidelines laid down in other countries and other times. It does not mean we should copy plant combinations or garden designs created for other climates and other lifestyles. However, only when we know of them can we adapt the given rules to suite our circumstances. Education does not mean that our intuitive knowledge is worthless, but it can save us a good deal of time and unnecessary sorrow. Only when our knowledge is greater than our immediate experience can we make an educated evaluation about what advice to follow and what to ignore, which traditions to keep and which to discard. It behooves us, then, to learn all we can from each other, sharing experience, plants, and information freely, pooling them into national assets.

American gardeners are entering a new era, an age in which ornamental gardening is valued as it has not been valued for many years. These will be good times for garden makers. From the crossroads, the garden path extends in all sorts of directions. With all of them open, where are we bound? In the last essay, Henry Ross makes a heartfelt plea for real gardens and real gardening.

HENRY ROSS, founder and director of Gardenview Horticultural Park, recipient of countless horticultural awards, honors, and distinctions, affiliated with a staggering number of plant societies, hybridizer of hostas, hellebores, sweet violets and ornamental crab apples, might reasonably be considered the standard bearer of American ornamental gardeners. In 1987, his article was presented as a lecture to the Garden Club of Ohio. His willingness to question conventional wisdom is salutary, if sometimes a bit startling, but Mr. Ross makes a terrific omelet with all these broken eggs.

A Plea For Real Gardens And Real Gardening

Henry A. Ross

During my lifetime, it has become clear to me that Americans have not yet even begun to scratch the surface of ornamental gardening. I have been increasingly aware of this during recent years. Many Americans do not even understand what the terms "gardening" and "gardener" mean.

Compared with England and other European countries, this country is centuries behind. In England, ornamental gardening has always been a way of life that provides immense pleasure and personal satisfaction to those who engage in it. The people are born with a love of gardening, and they garden because they love to do it and they love the results. They spend countless hours working in their gardens, visiting other gardens and searching out choice selections to add to their gardens. European flower and garden exhibits and shows are the most magnificent in the world.

In England, many boys are eager to become gardeners because they have gotten the love of gardening from their fathers, who got it from their fathers and on down the line. In this country, people can hardly expect youngsters to have any such interest, since parents have no interest in gardening. In America, people look at gardening as sissy. Too many parents would react to a teenage boy's statement that he would like to become a gardener with the same horror that they would to a teenage girl telling them she was pregnant.

In this country—for the most part, at least—there has hardly been any understanding of, or interest in, creating beautiful gardens. People have little desire to spend any time working in a garden.

Mention the word "garden," and most Americans immediately think of a vegetable patch or a landscaped area, which are not gardens at all. Mention the word "gardener," and most people immediately think of a person who comes in once a week to mow the grass or to rake the leaves. That is not a gardener; that is a handyman.

These terms have been so corrupted and distorted in this country that they no longer mean what they say. If America is ever to become a nation of beautiful gardens and knowledgeable gardeners, people must begin to use these terms properly. If they do not understand the problem, or are unwilling to accept the fact that something is wrong, it will never be corrected.

By the time she was finished, the only materials left to use were plastic plants. . . .

It is time people recognize that gardening is a very special art form and that those who have the knowledge, talent and skill to practice it are truly artists and professionals. They are not menial laborers, as many people perceive them to be.

Gardening versus Landscaping

In most instances, what are referred to as gardens in this country are not gardens. They are, in fact, landscaped areas made up of green lumps of specific shapes and sizes that are intended to fill space, to look the same year-round and, above all, to require a minimum of, or preferably no, care.

The difference between a landscaped area and a garden is that, in a landscaped area, the entire emphasis is upon architectural features and effect — not upon plants. The plants used in a landscaped area are looked upon only as architectural components, green lumps of specific sizes and shapes that remain the same all season and require little, if any, care. In a garden, the primary emphasis is upon each plant as such, upon what a plant does and how it changes from season to season, day to day, and hour to hour.

In a garden, change is desirable and is considered an asset rather

247

than a liability. Gardeners take for granted that a garden requires a substantial amount of effort and care to maintain. They see their efforts as part of the cost of having a beautiful garden and do not consider the necessary care to be undesirable or an unacceptable liability.

For that reason, a garden is dynamic, ever-changing, and extremely beautiful, while a landscaped area might just as well be made up of plastic plants that remain the same all year, require no care, and fulfill the designer's goal perfectly.

Unfortunately, what is taught in American schools is almost entirely landscaping, not gardening. I vividly recall that while I was a student at Ohio State University, Columbus, in the late 1940s, the landscaping curriculum was moved from the horticulture department into the school of engineering. I believe this is how the curriculum is viewed by most colleges and universities in this country.

Horticultural practices promoted in newspapers, magazines, and books are landscaping, not gardening. And most people in America landscape; they don't garden.

Instead of staying at home and creating, maintaining, and enjoying beautiful gardens, Americans prefer to spend their time on the golf course, at a football or baseball game, or jogging around the block to work off their potbellies and dissipate pent-up energy.

Materials

Choice and desirable plants are available in this country, for those who search them out and are willing to pay the price. But for the most part, sources only offer the same rubbish that they have always grown because it propagates easily, grows rapidly, looks the same from spring to fall and, above all, requires minimal care.

Books and articles written in this country invariably stress only common and ordinary schemes and the desirability of low-maintenance or, preferably, no-maintenance areas.

The author of an article in a national garden magazine repeatedly suggested that plants requiring staking, dividing, spraying, pruning, or any care at all, be left out of American gardens. By the time she was finished, the only materials left to use were plastic plants, since they are the only ones that do not require any care.

There is a world of plant treasures for gardeners to use. With them, Americans could create such gardens as the world has never seen. If the English have been able to create magnificent gardens using primarily old and obsolete plant varieties, just think of the kind of gardens Americans could create with the vastly superior hybrids available in this country.

If American gardens are ever to not only begin to catch up with English gardens, but to surpass them in magnificence, it is essential that we begin to educate Americans about how much pleasure they can gain from creating beautiful ornamental gardens and from getting out and working in them. We should encourage them to garden, not only to gain pleasure, but to compete with one another — to create a garden more beautiful than the one next door.

We must search out and use choice and uncommon plants, and discourage the use of weedy and invasive ones like vinca, pachysandra, and common ivy. With the proper approach, and some effort on our part, America can become a country of beautiful gardens and avid gardeners.

I have spent my entire life creating 16 acres of the kind of gorgeous gardens that anyone in the world would be proud of, hoping that they might start the ball rolling and that others would follow. But, although beautiful gardens and knowledgeable gardeners can be found on both the West Coast and the East Coast, things are different in the Midwest.

For some mysterious reason, most people in the Midwest would love to have a gorgeous garden only if it costs them nothing to create or to maintain and does not require any physical exertion on their part.

Inspiring Change

If we work together, we can make a change. We should increase our emphasis on practical, down-to-earth gardening, to encourage people to take an increased interest in creating real gardens so that entire states can become massive and gorgeous gardens.

Perhaps the single most potent way of doing this is to sponsor local and statewide ornamental garden contests that are highly publicized and thereby both prestigious and fashionable. I am sure that you are aware of the enormous popularity of the vegetable garden contest conducted each year on television's "The Victory Garden." The same thing could be done with an "Ornamental Garden Contest."

I also urge you to demand that newspapers and magazines broaden their scope to emphasize advanced gardening, rather than continue to publish only articles for beginners. Demand that they publish articles written by real gardeners instead of journalists.

Perhaps the most important thing you can do is to insist that schools initiate real honest-to-God, practical gardening courses designed to train individuals who are interested in real, practical gardening instead of individuals who are only interested in sitting behind desks, designing plastic landscaped areas. People falling into the latter group know nothing about real gardening and could not do it if their lives depended on it.

By myself, I have not been able to get the ball rolling—in spite of 40 years of effort. But with your help, we sure can.

The results will be breathtaking.

APPENDIXES

Bringing In The Leaves
IMPORTING GARDEN PLANTS

W hen vacation time rolls around, Americans abandon their native shores in droves. Gardeners are no exception, and if they plan ahead a bit, they can fill the garden rather than the photo album upon their return. How many of us have moaned about this or that plant we admired in English or German gardens, but couldn't find at home? How few of us realize that, most of the time, there is no reason why we can't bring the newly beloved plant home with us, provided we have done our homework first. Traveler or stay-at-home, anybody who wishes may import garden plants, so long as USDA quarantine rules are observed.

The first step in the process if very simple; call the nearest regional USDA (United States Department of Agriculture) office to request an application for an import permit. If there isn't a USDA office nearby, write to:

United States Department of Agriculture
Animal and Plant Health Inspection Service
Federal Center Building
Hyattsville, MD 20782

The application form is short and simple, and mostly quite obvious. You are asked what plants you intend to bring into the country, and how many of them. If you aren't sure, put down "ornamental border perennials" and state approximate quantities. It's best to start small for a variety of reasons. One is that people bringing fewer than twenty plants are viewed as home gardeners, and while their inspection will be as rigorous as the law requires, it is not usually a time-consuming or uncomfortable process. Also, armchair importers who do not live near an international port of entry where U.S. customs officers can clear plants may not receive their order as quickly as those who do. Even in port entry cities, the process can go awry, and losses or disappointments are better tolerated on a modest rather than a mammoth scale. Plants that can travel by airmail fare best, for they will be forwarded on to you from the nearest entry port. However, heavier packages must go as air cargo which means that you must travel to the nearest airport to pick up the shipment. In the Dakotas, for instance, this could involve quite a journey. Even if you are accompanying your new treasures home, it pays to remember that plants are fragile and don't mingle well with other trophies of travel. The fewer you bring, the better their survival chances, so greed does not pay.

Anyway, once you decide to file a permit, you can expect to get a response to your application within a month or so. You will receive a packet containing your import permit number (which has an expiration date, you might note, but which is usually good for a number of years). There will also be some green and yellow labels that state, "This package contains plant quarantine material— Deliver to USDA . . . " and gives the appropriate address for the closest inspection office. These must appear on all incoming boxes of plants, whether carried with your luggage or arriving from overseas nurseries. Non-travelers send the labels abroad with their order, while the peripatetic gardener takes a few along on every international vacation. Identified by such a label, plants sent by air or sea go straight to the customs at the nearest port of entry. When they clear customs, they will be forwarded to you, except in the above-mentioned case of an air cargo box; for these, the importer is informed upon their arrival. Usually. With airports unaccustomed to such happenings, it doesn't hurt to call every day and ask if the box has come as soon as you have reason to think it might be arriving. Keep the conversation light, but get on a first name basis with the airport personnel; when it finally arrives, everyone will know all about it, and your precious box is unlikely to be shuffled off to a corner until somebody has time to figure out what to do with it.

Be aware that any prohibited plants, any deliberately mislabeled plants, any improperly cleaned plants, or any plants that look infected by insects or disease may well be confiscated. If you long for European willows or citrus relatives, this may seem absurd, and it might be tempting to try to circumvent the long arm of the law. However, it really isn't worth the risk, neither the personal one of losing import privileges and having to stump up a hefty fine, nor the far worse one of unleashing another Dutch elm disease or an new Japanese beetle or tent caterpillar. Nobody means to do such a thing, but it can happen just the same. The laws are not made for the annoyance of gardeners, nor for the amusement of the USDA, and those who disregard USDA prohibitions will find the reaction far from amusing.

Another thing you will find in your import permit packet is a lengthy and daunting list of forbidden plants. Some are blanket prohibitions, as with terrestrial or ground orchids, none of which are permissible to import. Others, like gladiolus corms, are conditional, for they may be currently brought in if they come from England, Germany, or Holland, but not from Spain, Italy, or Portugal. Since the rules change often, it is always worth calling ahead, explaining your interests to the plant inspector, and asking which plants to avoid. Presently, one may not bring any willows or citrus fruit relatives, but most border perennials are permissible.

Shrubs and edible plants have many importation restrictions, all of which are detailed at length in the USDA bulletins. Foreign roses, for instance are not generally allowed into the United States. If you have Canadian friends, you can arrange to ship roses to them, but they must then be grown for a full year in Canadian soil, and their health status documented by a Canadian plant inspector, before they are permitted into the States. It usually proves simpler to find Canadian nurseries that sell the roses in question, and to order the plants directly from them. So long as your order is not too large, it can come by airmail straight to your door in a matter of days.

In many respects, shopping from Canadian nurseries is a good idea. Hundreds of English border plants seldom seen in America are available in Canada, partly because of the close cultural ties but also thanks to trade and importation agreements, for the Canadians don't need to request the soil washing that the USDA requires. This is the worst aspect of the importing process for Americans, since many perennials resent the washing—plants must be completely free of soil—and are apt to die in a huff when so rudely treated. One way to minimize this is to avoid plants with fragile or brittle root systems. Stick with plants that have fat storage roots or sturdy networks of feeder roots. Many perennials travel best when dormant, so if you can request shipping in February, do so.

When cruising those overseas nurseries, choose healthy plants that look like survivors, for they are going to suffer for you. Even legal plants must be washed clean of every scrap of soil for importation, but you can pack them tenderly in damp peat, vermiculite, or moss. Washing should be put off until the last possible minute, but allow plenty of time, because it is a lengthy job. English hotels have come to view American plant importers with deep suspicion, for they already have problems with the plumbing, and endless quantities of grit and soil don't assist troubled toilets one bit.

If you want to reduce the horrors of this job, borrow or buy two buckets, and find a place to work outside. If this is impossible, hotels will often let you work in a covered garage, where water is usually available. Use one bucket for soaking the unpotted plants, the other for rinsing. Pack each newly cleaned plant immediately in a plastic zip-closure bag with some damp peat. Fasten on the green and yellow labels with scotch tape, and tuck the packets in your handbag or luggage, preferably where they won't get crushed. A shoe box makes a good stash, and is easy to produce for customs.

Before you get on the plane, write up a clear and accurate list of what you have; most of the inspectors are quite aware of what a given plant should look like, and will be quick to confiscate pretenders, slapping the errant importer with a fat fine. Again, if this seems petty, those who know their horticultural history will recall any number of cases in which a smuggled plant or unseen soil-borne pest caused enormous and usually incredibly expensive havoc in its new country, sometime irreversibly.

When your plane is circling the home field, you are given a customs declaration form, where you must check the box marked "plants." You will be sent straight to the inspection office, where you must present your written list and the plants. Your booty will be cleared and you are home free. Rush home, plant those poor things immediately, and set them in the shade to recover. Keep them cool, moist, and calm; they will probably look worse before they look better, but with any luck at all, they should pull through and reward you—and all the folks with whom you share them—for your adventurous persistence for many years to come.

SOURCES & RESOURCES

SOURCES

ADAMGROVE
Route 1 Box 246
California, MO 65018
Catalog: $ 2.00

ANTIQUE ROSE EMPORIUM
Route 5 Box 143
Brenham, TX 77833
Catalog: $ 1.00

C.H. BACCUS
900 Boynton Avenue
San Jose, CA 95117
S.A.S.E. for a list sent in July

BAY VIEW GARDEN
1201 Bay Street
Santa Cruz, CA 95060
Catalog: $ 1.50

KURT BLUEMEL INC.
2740 Greene Lane
Baldwin, MD 21013
Catalog: $ 2.00

BRAND PEONY FARM
P.O. Box 842
St. Cloud, MN 56302
Catalog: $ 1.00

LEE BRISTOL NURSERY
Bloomingfields Farm
Gaylordsville, CT 06755
Free Catalog

BROWN'S SUNNYHILL
    GARDENS
Route 3 Box 102
Milton-Freewater, OR 97862
Free Catalog

BURPEE
300 Park Avenue
Warminster, PA 18974
Free Catalog

BUSSE GARDENS
Route 2 Box 238
Cokato, MN 55321
Catalog: $ 2.00

CALIFORNIA FLORA NURSERY
P.O. Box 3
Fulton, CA 95439
Free List

CALLAHAN SEEDS
6045 Foley Lane
Central Point, OR 97502
Free Catalog

CANYON CREEK NURSERY
3527 Dry Creek Road
Oroville, CA 95965
Catalog: $ 1.00

CARROLL GARDENS
P.O. Box 310
444 E. Main Street
Westminster, MD 21157
Catalog: $ 2.00

COOLEY'S GARDEN
11553 Silverton Road NE
P.O. Box 126
Silverton, OR 97381
Catalog: $ 2.00 (deductible)

THE COUNTRY GARDEN
Route 2 Box 455A
Crivitz, WI 54114
Catalog: $ 1.00

CROWNSVILLE NURSERY
P.O. Box 797
Crownsville, MD 21032
Catalog: $ 2.00

FANCY FRONDS
1911 4th Avenue West
Seattle, WA 98119
Catalog: $1.00

FORESTFARM
990 Tetherow Road
Williams, OR 97544
Catalog: $ 2.00

SOURCES & RESOURCES

THE FRAGRANT PATH
P.O. Box 328
Fort Calhoun, NE 68023
Catalog: $1.00

GILBERG PERENNIAL FARMS
2906 Ossenfort Road
Glencoe, MD 63038
Catalog: $ 2.00

GREER GARDENS
1280 Goodpasture Island Road
Eugene, OR 97401
Catalog: $3.00

HASTINGS
1036 White Street SW
P.O. Box 115535
Atlanta, GA 30310–8535
Free Catalog

HERITAGE ROSE GARDENS
16831 Mitchell Creek Drive
Fort Bragg, CA 95437
Catalog: $ 1.00

HISTORICAL ROSES
1657 West Jackson Street
Painsville, OH 44077
Free Catalog (#10 envelope)

HOLBROOK FARM AND
  NURSERY
Route 2 Box 223B
Fletcher, NC 28732
Catalog: $ 1.00

THOMAS JEFFERSON CENTER
  FOR HISTORIC PLANTS
  MONTICELLO
C/O P.O. Box 316
Charlottesville, VA 22981
Free Catalog

KLEHM NURSERY
Route 5 Box 197
Penny Road
South Barrington, IL 60010–9555
Catalog: $4.00

LAMB NURSERIES
East 101 Sharp Avenue
Spokane, WA 99202
Free Catalog

LARNER SEEDS
P.O. Box 407
Bolinas, CA 94924
Catalog: $ 1.50

LAS PILITAS NURSERY
Star Route Box 23X
Santa Margarita, CA 93423
Catalog: $ 4.00

LIMEROCK ORNAMENTAL
  GRASSES INC.
Road 1 Box 111-C
Port Matilda, PA 16870
Catalog: $ 1.00

MARYOTT'S GARDENS
1073 Bird Avenue
San Jose, CA 95125
Catalog: $ 1.00

MELLINGER'S INC.
2310 West South Range
North Lima, OH 44452–9731
Free Catalog

MILAEGER'S GARDENS
4838 Douglas Avenue
Racine, WI 53402–2498
Catalog: $ 1.00

MONTROSE NURSERY
P.O. Box 957
Hillsborough, NC 27278
Catalog: $1.50

MOON MOUNTAIN
  WILDFLOWERS
P.O. Box 34
Morro Bay, CA 93443
Catalog: $ 2.00

NATIVE GARDENS
Route #1 Box 494
Greenback, TN 37742
Catalog: $ 1.00

NATIVE SONS WHOLESALE
  NURSERY
379 West El Campo Road
Arroyo Grande, CA 93420
Free Catalog

NEW PEONY FARM
P.O. Box 18235
St. Paul, MN 55118
Free Catalog

OLD FARM NURSERY
5550 Indiana Street
Golden, CO 80403
Free Catalog

PARK SEEDS
Cokesbury Road
Greenwood, SC 29647–0001
Free Catalog

THEODORE PAYNE
  FOUNDATION
10459 Tuxford Street
Sun Valley, CA 91352
Catalog: $ 2.00

PICKERING NURSERIES INC.
670 Kingston Road Highway 2
Pickering, Ontario
Canada L1V 1A6
Catalog: $2.00

PLANTS OF THE SOUTHWEST
930 Baca Street
Santa Fe, NM 87501
Catalog: $ 1.50

CLYDE ROBIN SEED CO. INC.
P.O. Box 2366
Castro Valley, CA 94546
Free catalog

ROBINETT BULB FARM
P.O. Box 1306
Sebastopol, CA 95473–1306
List Only (Stamped #10 envelope)

RODERICK IRIS GARDEN
Route 2 Box 2199
Farmington, MO 63640
Free List

ROSES OF YESTERDAY AND
  TODAY
802 Brown's Valley Road
Watsonville, CA 95076
Catalog: $ 3.00

RUSSELL GRAHAM
4030 Eagle Crest Road NW
Salem, OR 97304
Catalog: $ 2.00 (Refundable on 1st
  purchase)

SAN SIMEON NURSERY
Villa Creek Road
Cayucos, CA 93430
Free Price List

SAXTON GARDENS
1 First Street
Saratoga Springs, NY 12866
Catalog: $ .50

SCHREINER'S IRIS GARDENS
3625 Quinaby Road NE
Salem, OR 97303
Catalog: $ 2.00

SISKIYOU RARE PLANT
  NURSERY
2825 Cummings Road
Medford, OR 97501
Catalog: $ 2.00 (Refundable)

SMITH AND HAWKEN
25 Corte Madera
Mill Valley, CA 94941
Free Catalog

SUNNYRIDGE GARDENS
1724 Drinnen Road
Knoxville, TN 37914
Stamped Envelope

THOMPSON AND MORGAN
P.O. Box 1308
Jackson, NJ 08527
Free Catalog ($ 2.00 for first class
  requested)

TREE OF LIFE NURSERY
  (WHOLESALE)
P.O. Box 736
San Juan Capistrano, CA 92675
Free Catalog Listing

TYTY PLANTATION BULB CO.
Box 159
TyTy, GA 31795
Free Catalog

SOURCES & RESOURCES

VAN BOURGONDIEN
  BROTHERS
Box A Route 109
Babylon, NY 11702
Free Catalog

ANDRE VIETTE FARM &
  NURSERY
Route 1 Box 16
Fisherville, VA 22939
Catalog: $ 2.00

WE-DU NURSERIES
Route 5 Box 724
Marion, NC 28752
Catalog: $ 1.00

GILBERT H. WILD AND SON
P.O. Box 338
1112 Joplin Street
Sarcoxie, MO 64862–0338
Catalog: $2.00

WILDWOOD NURSERY
3975 Emerald Avenue
La Verne, CA 91750
Catalog: $1.00

YERBA BUENA NURSERY
19500 Skyline Boulevard
Woodside, CA 94062
Free Catalog (Legal size S.A.S.w/$.45
  postage)

RESOURCES

ALPINE GARDEN CLUB OF
  BRITISH COLUMBIA
Denys Lloyd, Membership Chairman
3281 West 35th Avenue
Vancouver, British Columbia
Canada V6N 2M9

ALPINE GARDEN SOCIETY
Secretary
Lye End Link, St. John's
Woking, Surrey
England GU21 1SW

AMERICAN CONIFER SOCIETY
Secretary, Mrs. Maxine Schwarz
Box 242
Severna Park, MD 21146

AMERICAN HOSTA SOCIETY
Jack Freedman, Secretary
3103 Heather Hill S.E.
Huntsville, AL 35802

AMERICAN IRIS SOCIETY
Membership Secretary
c/o Marilyn Harlow
P.O. Box 8455
San Jose, CA 95155

AMERICAN PENSTEMON
  SOCIETY
Ann Bartlett, Membership Secretary
1569 South Holland Court
Lakewood, CO 80226

AMERICAN PRIMROSE SOCIETY
Brian Skidmore
6730 West Mercer Way
Mercer Island, WA 98040

AMERICAN RHODODENDRON
  SOCIETY
Executive Secretary
P.O. Box 1380
Gloucester, VA 23601

AMERICAN ROCK GARDEN
  SOCIETY
Buffy Parker, Secretary
15 Fairmead Road
Darien, CT 06820

BROOKLYN BOTANIC GARDEN
Order Department
1000 Washington Avenue
Brooklyn, NY 11225

CALIFORNIA NATIVE PLANT
  SOCIETY
909 12th Street Suite 116
Sacramento, CA 95814

HARDY PLANT SOCIETY
Membership Secretary Simon Wills
The Manor House
Walton-in-Gordano
Clevedon, Avon
England BS21 7AN

HISTORIC IRIS PRESERVATION
  SOCIETY
Route 3 Box 135
Blackstone, VA 23824

INTERNATIONAL CLEMATIS
  SOCIETY
3 La Route du Coudre
Rocquaine, St. Pierre du Bois
Guernsey, Channel Islands
Great Britain

LOUISIANA MARKET BULLETIN
P.O. Box 44365
Baton Rouge, LA 70804

NEW ZEALAND ALPINE GAR-
  DEN SOCIETY INC.
Hon. Treasurer: A.T. Mahan
238 Greers Road
Christchurch, 5
New Zealand

NORTHWEST PERENNIAL
  ALLIANCE
P.O. Box 45574 University Station
Seattle, WA 98145

OREGON HARDY PLANT
  SOCIETY
33530 SE Bluff Road
Boring, OR 97009

ROYAL HORTICULTURAL
  SOCIETY
Membership Chairman
80 Vincent Square
London
England SW1P 2PE

SCOTTISH ROCK GARDEN CLUB
Subscription Secretary Miss K.M.
  Gibb
21 Merchiston Park
Edinburgh
Scotland EH10 4PW

SPECIES IRIS GROUP OF NORTH
  AMERICA (SIGNA)
Florence Stout
150 North Marie Street
Lombard, IL 60148

USDA Plant Hardiness Zone Map

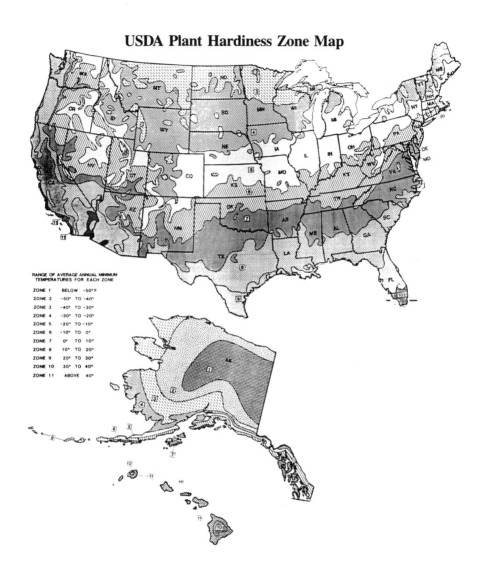

RANGE OF AVERAGE ANNUAL MINIMUM
TEMPERATURES FOR EACH ZONE

ZONE 1	BELOW	-50°F
ZONE 2	-50°	TO -40°
ZONE 3	-40°	TO -30°
ZONE 4	-30°	TO -20°
ZONE 5	-20°	TO -10°
ZONE 6	-10°	TO 0°
ZONE 7	0°	TO 10°
ZONE 8	10°	TO 20°
ZONE 9	20°	TO 30°
ZONE 10	30°	TO 40°
ZONE 11	ABOVE	40°

260

Index to Common Names

Aaron's beard: *Hypericum calycinum*
Acidsoil lithodora: *Lithodora diffusa*
Adam's-needle: *Yucca filamentosa*
African daisy: *Gerbera jamesonii*
African iris: *Dietes vegeta*
African-lily: *Agapanthus*
Alkanet: *Anchusa*
Allegheny foamflower: *Tiarella cordifolia*
Alpine erysimum: *Erysimum linifolium*
Alumroot: *Heuchera*
American alumroot: *Heuchera americana*
Amur Adonis: *Adonis amurensis*
Antelope bush: *Purshia*
Arkwright's campion: *Lychnis x arkwrightii*
Armenian grape hyacinth: *Muscari armeniacum*
Asiatic poppy: *Meconopsis*
Auriculate lady fern: *Athyrium otophorum*
Autumn fern: *Dryopteris erythrosora*
Autumn sage: *Salvia greggii*
Avens: *Geum*
Azure monkshood: *Aconitum carmichaelii*
Azure penstemon: *Penstemon azureus*

Baby's-breath: *Gypsophila elegans, Gypsophila paniculata*
Bachelor's-button: *Centaurea cyanus*
Balloon flower: *Platycodon grandiflorus*
Barneby's columbine: *Aquilegia barnebyi*
Basket-of-gold: *Aurinia saxatilis*
Beach wormwood: *Artemisia stellerana*
Beard-tongue: *Penstemon*
Bear's breeches: *Acanthus*
Bearsfoot hellebore: *Helleborus foetidus*
Bee balm: *Monarda didyma*
Bellflower: *Campanula*
Bells-of-Ireland: *Moluccella laevis*
Bethlehem sage: *Pulmonaria saccharata*
Betony: *Stachys*
Bigleaf hydrangea: *Hydrangea macrophylla*
Bigleaf ligularia: *Ligularia dentata*
Bird-of-paradise: *Strelitzia reginae*

Blackberry lily: *Belamcanda chinensis*
Black-eyed Susan: *Rudbeckia hirta*
Blackfoot daisy: *Melampodium leucanthum*
Black snakeroot: *Cimicifuga racemosa*
Blanket flower: *Gaillardia x grandiflora*
Blazing star: *Liatris*
Bleeding heart: *Dicentra*
Bloodroot: *Sanguinaria, Sanguinaria canadensis*
Bloody cranesbill: *Geranium sanguineum*
Blue African lily: *Agapanthus africanus*
Blue Cupid's dart: *Catananche caerulea*
Bluebells: *Mertensia*
Blue false indigo: *Baptisia australis*
Blue Felicia: *Felicia amelloides*
Blue flax: *Linum perenne*
Blue mist: *Caryopteris x clandonensis*
Blue oat grass: *Heliotrotrichon sempervirens*
Blue sheep's fescue: *Festuca amethystina superba*
Blue star flower: *Amsonia*
Blue wild indigo: *Baptisia australis*
Boneset: *Eupatorium*
Bonytip fleabane: *Erigeron karvinskianus*
Bouncing bet: *Saponaria officinalis*
Bowles golden grass: *Carex stricta* 'Bowles Golden'
Brazilian verbena: *Verbena bonariensis*
Broad buckler fern: *Dryopteris dilatata*
Bugbane: *Cimicifuga*
Bulbous oat grass: *Arrhenatherum elatius, bulbosum variegatum*
Bush cinquefoil: *Potentilla fruticosa*
Butterbur: *Petasites*
Butterfly ginger lily: *Hedychium coronarium*
Butterfly weed: *Asclepias tuberosa*

California fescue: *Festuca californica*
California poppy: *Eschscholzia californica*
California redbud: *Cercis occidentalis*
Campion: *Lychnis*

INDEX TO COMMON NAMES

INDEX TO COMMON NAMES

Index

To assist gardeners, this index supplies information on plant type, average height, and hardiness as well as page number(s). Hardiness zones are based on the USDA system. Height is given in inches unless otherwise specified. These are general guidelines. Garden microclimates, cultural practices and anomalies of local weather affect plant growth.

INDEX

PLANT NAME	ZONE	HEIGHT	TYPE	PAGE
tanguticum 'Pink Feathers'	4–9	16	Bulb	18
Alstroemeria aurantiaca	7–	36–48	Bulb	204, 206
Althaea officinalis	5–	36–72	Per.	81
Amaryllis			Bulb	122
Amsonia tabernaemontana	3–9	12–36	Per.	11
var. *montana*	3–9	12–15	Per.	37
Anchusa				66
azurea	3–8	36–60	Per.	57
Anemone				
blanda	4–8	6–8	Bulb	21
x *hybrida*	4–8	30–48	Per.	70, 137, 147
'Alba'	4–8	36	Per.	199, 201
'Honorine Jobert'	4–8	36–48	Per.	168
'Whirlwind'	4–8	48–60	Per.	70, 227
tomentosa	5–8	18–36	Per.	71, 72
'Robustissima'	3–8	18–36	Per.	137
Anemonella thalictroides	4–	4–10	Per.	22
Anthemis tinctoria	3–8	24–36	Per.	23
'Pale Moon'	3–8	24–30	Per.	11
Aquilegia				65, 66, 121
barnebyi	4–	14	Per.	93
caerulea	3–8	12–24	Per.	93, 136
canadensis	3–8	24–36	Per.	81, 122, 135
'Corbett'	3–8	24–36	Per.	37
chrysantha	3–9	30–42	Per.	22
flabellata	3–9	8–18	Per.	22
hinckleyana	5–10	18–24	Per.	81
Arabis caucasica 'Snow Cap'	4–7	8–10	Per.	169
Armeria maritima	4–8	6–12	Per.	17
Arrhenatherum elatius bulbosum				
variegatum	4–9	12–24	Grass	154, 172
Artemisia				
abrotanum	3–9	24–36	Per.	81
absinthium	3–9	24–36	Per.	81
'Lambrook Silver'	3–9	30	Per.	70
'Canyon Gray'	10	6–12	Per.	98
lactiflora	4–8	48–72	Per.	214
ludoviciana	4–9	24–48	Per.	81
'Silver King'	3–9	24–36	Per.	30, 35

INDEX

INDEX

INDEX

PLANT NAME	ZONE	HEIGHT	TYPE	PAGE
Gunnera manicata	7–10	6–8 ft.	Per.	157
Gypsophila				
elegans		10–18	Annual	66
paniculata	3–9	24–36	Per.	102
'Pink Fairy'	3–9	18	Per.	71

H

Hamelia patens	10	to 25 ft.	Shrub	82
Hedychium coronarium	9–10	48–72	Per.	124
Helenium				66
autumnale 'Moerheim Beauty'	3–8	36–48	Per.	199, 201
Helianthemum				
nummularium	5–7	12–24	Subshrub	52, 58
scoparium	10	36	Per.	98
Helianthus				
angustifolius	6–9	5–7 ft.	Per.	34, 35
x *multiflorus*				
'Flore Pleno'	3–8	48–72	Per.	17
'Loddon Gold'	3–8	54–72	Per.	17
Helichrysum bracteatum		24–36	Annual	66
Helictotrichon sempervirens	4–	12–36	Grass	11
Helleborus				
foetidus	5–9	18–24	Per.	21, 135
niger	3–8	12–18	Per.	21, 135, 168
orientalis	4–9	15–18	Per.	12, 21, 135, 229
Hemerocallis				124
'Apricot'	3–10	30–34	Per.	187
'Bengaleer'	3–10	36	Per.	197, 201
'Bitsy'	3–10	24–36	Per.	16
'Daily Bread'	3–10	24–48	Per.	16
fulva	3–10	36–72	Per.	82, 186
'Kwanso Variegata'	3–10	40	Per.	82, 187, 197
'Fuzz Bunny'	3–10	18–36	Per.	16
'Hyperion'	3–10	36–40	Per.	187
lilioasphodelus	3–9	30–36	Per.	82, 187
'Mikado'	3–10	30–36	Per.	187
'Stella de Oro'	3–10	12–36	Per.	15–16, 47
'Wau-Bun'	3–10	34–36	Per.	187

INDEX

INDEX

PLANT NAME	ZONE	HEIGHT	TYPE	PAGE
Stachys byzantina	4–8	12–15	Per.	11, 37, 70, 163, 168
'Shelia McQueen'	4–8	12	Per.	163
Sternbergia lutea	7–	12	Bulb	24
Stipa				
arundinacea	8–10	4–5 ft.	Grass	11
gigantea	7–	36–72	Grass	159
Stokesia laevis	5–9	12–24	Per.	29
'Blue Danube'	5–9	12–24	Per.	55
'Wyoming'	5–9	12–24	Per.	55
Strelitzia reginae	10	36–60	Per.	125
Strobilanthes atropurpureus	4–	60	Per.	217

T

Tagetes lucida	9–10	18	Per.	85
Thalictrum				
aquilegifolium	5–8	24–36	Per.	13
delavayi 'Hewitts' Double'	4–7	36–48	Per.	17
Tiarella cordifolia	3–8	6–12	Per.	135
Thymus				
x *citriodorus*	5–9	4–12	Per.	109
praecox ssp. *arcticus*	5–9	4	Per.	108
pseudolanuginosus	5–9	24	Per.	109
serpyllum	3–	4	Per.	108
Tradescantia				
x *andersoniana*	4–9	12–24	Per.	55, 170
Trichostema lanatum	9–10	18–40	Shrub	99
Trilisa odoratissima	7–	36	Per.	226
Trollius				
x *cultorum* 'Empire Day'	3–6	24–36	Per.	170
'Prichard's Giant'	3–6	36	Per.	12
europaeus	4–8	20–24	Per.	201
ledebourii 'Golden Queen'	3–8	48	Per.	58

V

Verbascum bombyciferum				
'Arctic Summer'	6–10	to 5 ft.	Biennial	45
Verbena				
bonariensis	7–9	36–48	Per.	137, 160
canadensis	6–10	8–18	Per.	137
x *hybrida*		6–18	Annual	137
rigida	8–10	12–24	Per.	137

Ann Lovejoy gardens on an old farm on an island near Seattle, Washington (USDA zone 8), with her husband, Mark, and their two young sons, as well as a large number of cats, rabbits, chickens, and a circus dog. She is a contributing editor to *Horticulture* magazine and a frequent contributor to other national gardening publications. Her most recent book is *The Border in Bloom* (Sasquatch Books, 1990). Her garden interests are legion.